Poissons Marins • Pesci Marini • Peces Marinos • Peixes Marinhos

MARINE AQUARIUM COMPANION

SOUTHEAST ASIAN VOLUME

By Pablo Tepoot & Ian M. Tepoot
With a Foreword by
John E. Randall Ph.D.

NEW LIFE
publications

MARINE AQUARIUM COMPANION
(Southeast Asia Volume) European Edition
Copyright © 1996 by New Life Publications,
A Subsidiary of New Life Exotic Fish, Inc.

Published by:
New Life Publications
25855 S.W. 193 Ave.
Homestead, Fl. 33031
Tel: (305)245-2404
Fax: (305) 248-7450

ISBN 0-9645058-3-5

Printed in Hong Kong.

is
Dedicated to
Linda Loreen Tepoot

publications

Fishes of Southeast Asia

Photographs:
Pablo Tepoot
Ian M. Tepoot

Written by:
Pablo Tepoot

Editors (English):
Diane Grindol
Ian M. Tepoot

Translation (French):
Elise Gechon

Editor (French):
Guy Robert
(G.I.E. Zolux of France)

**Translation &
Editing (Spanish):**
Augustine Cerice
(Del Mar International)

**Translation &
Editing (Italian):**
H. de Jong
Andreas de Jong
(Primaris)

Translation (Portuguese):
Regina Da Silva

Editor (Portuguese):
Marco Antonio Augusti
José Manuel Melo

**Book Design &
Organization:**
Ian M. Tepoot

**Translation Agent
(French • Portuguese):**
Seven Languages Translating.

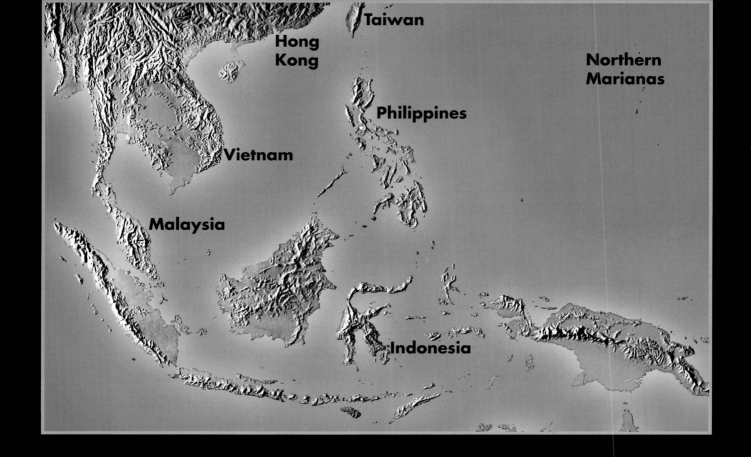

Taiwan

Hong
Kong

Northern
Marianas

Philippines

Vietnam

Malaysia

Indonesia

SOUTHEAST
ASIAN REGION

•

The fish in this book
were collected in the
Asian Pacific Ocean
around the Philippine
and Indonesian Islands.

ACKNOWLEDGEMENTS

We wish to thank Augustine Cerice (Del Mar International Corp.) without whom creating this book would be extremely difficult. He went the extra mile by providing a majority of the marine fish that appear in this book and obtaining specimens for us. Also, he allowed us to use his facilities for our photographic setup. Finally, Augustine spent many hours sharing his knowledge of marine aquarium fishes with us.

In addition, we would like to thank Mario Cerice of Del Mar International Corp. for being generous with his time and effort when helping us setup tanks and catch specimens.

The following people have reviewed our information and have made many helpful suggestions which have contributed to much of the data in the final product:

- Julian Sprung (author of *The Reef Aquarium, Volume 1* and the *Reef Notes* series).

- Martin Moe (author of *The Marine Aquarium Handbook* and *The Marine Aquarium Reference*).

- Robert Fenner (author of *The Conscientious Marine Aquarist* and *A Commonsense Handbook for Successful Saltwater Hobbyists*).

- Barry Wisebram of Marine Life Atlanta, a wholesale marine fish distributor.

We would also like to thank Richard Pyle and John E. Randall, Ph.D. of the Bishop Museum (Honolulu, Hawaii) for reviewing and providing many of the scientific names/classifications in this book.

Finally, thanks to Millie Chua of All Seas (Miami), who sold us some of the fish that have appeared in this book.

FOREWORD

This book was written and illustrated by two aquarists for the home marine aquarium enthusiast, and therein lies its special value. The fishes contained in this volume are generally available in the aquarium trade. Most identification books are not written specifically for aquarists. They are often designed primarily for divers, snorkelers, or fishermen (and thus include many species which become too large for the home aquarium); or they may be written by ichthyologists like myself for other scientists and therefore contain technical information such as details of the anatomy of a fish, why it is classified in a particular genus, its relationship to other species of its family, etc. — all things of little interest to the aquarist.

The authors of this book are to be complimented for their effort to educate the consumer to avoid buying species of fishes which are doomed to die in their aquarium. Unfortunately, the aquarium industry is guilty of marketing species which may be beautiful or uniquely appealing in some way, but will either soon grow too large for the aquarium or die because they cannot long survive in the conditions aquarists are able to provide. Many of our most beautiful butterflyfishes of the genus *Chaetodon* feed only on coral polyps. Obviously, the aquarium enthusiast cannot continuously provide live coral for these fishes. The exotic Moorish Idol (*Zanclus cornutus*) likes to nibble on live sponges, tunicates, etc. It needs a very large aquarium with much thriving invertebrate life to do well. The lovely little anthiine fishes (*Pseudanthias* species) — variously called anthias, basslets, or perchlets — feed almost continuously on the small animals of the zooplankton. They are used to a huge area for feeding, with current bringing a continuous supply of plankton, and they are generally found in large aggregations. Few do well in the captivity of a small tank. And then there are fishes like the cute dark-spotted babies of the Humpback Grouper (*Cromileptes altivelis*), which enter the aquarium trade as Panther Groupers. They grow rapidly and soon start eating other residents in the tank. Once I was called to a market in Honolulu to examine a grouper that had never been seen in Hawaii before. It was an adult of the Humpback Grouper, no doubt released in the sea by an aquarist.

The islands of the East Indes — the Philippines, New Guinea, and Indonsesia — have the richest marine life in the world. Over 3,000 species of fishes are known from this insular region. In this area, the cost of labor is very low, so these islands — particularly in the Philippines — have dominated the marine aquarium industry for years. Unfortunately, many of the fishes are being caught with the use of sodium cyanide (which is readily available because of its use in the mining industry). The cyanide makes the capture of small fishes very easy. However, those that survive the initial onslaught of this chemical will often die some weeks later, and the unsuspecting aquarist will think it was his or her fault. A major effort is being made in the Philippines to stop the widespread use of cyanide for fish collecting. One American has a new large facility for marine aquarium fishes in Manila; his divers do not use chemicals to catch fishes. If a collector he does not know brings a fish to him that is in perfect condition, he will not accept it because he knows it was probably taken with cyanide. Fishes caught with nets usually show some damage such as missing scales or torn fins. The authors stress the need for consumers to inquire of the source of the fishes they intend to purchase. Does the supplier know if the fishes he sells have come from a company known for not using cyanide?

Richard L. Pyle and I of the Bishop Museum have assisted the authors in the identification of their impressive photographs of live fishes for this volume. With the same high-quality color reproduction as seen in the "Cichlids: The Pictorial Guide" series, this book can expect to be a best-seller for home aquarists. It is the first of a series of books cataloging marine aquarium fauna from around the world.

Aloha,
John E. Randall, Ph.D. (Zoology/Ichthyology)
Bishop Museum. Honolulu, Hawaii.

NOTES ON NAMES

The scientific names provided in this book were reviewed, corrected (and — in some cases — provided) by Richard Pyle and John E. Randall or the *Bishop Museum of Natural and Cultural History*, Honolulu.

- In some cases, they were unable to confirm species or genus from the photographs. In other cases, the family is under review or a species is undescribed. In these circumstances, the authors have sole responsibility for the names used in this book.

- All names in this book provided *by the authors without confirmation* from either Richard Pyle or John Randall of the Bishop Museum are marked with an asterisk (✻).

- All undescribed species whose genus is known are written using the convention:

    genus (in italics) followed by "sp." and a common name.
    Example: *Amblyeleotris* sp. "Flame-stripe"

- All undescribed species whose genus is under revision or unknown are written using the following convention:

    Family name (not in italics) followed by a common name in parenthesis.
    Example: Batrachoididae (Pacific Toadfish).

- The fish in this book are organized alphabetically by family. This is for the sake of ease-of-use by laymen (such as hobbyists) and does not reflect how scientists organize fishes. A list giving the scientific taxonomy as used by scientists is provided on the following page.

PRÉFACE

Un aquarium marin plein de vie est merveille à admirer, car les poissons marins arborent une éblouissante diversité de couleurs et de formes. Ils présentent une variété surprenante de caractéristiques et de comportements, véritable défi à l'imagination. Les aquariums marins offrent aux passionnés, à la fois la beauté et la fascination d'un travail fondé sur la reconstitution d'un mini-écosystème complexe. Cette complexité est cependant une arme à double tranchant car l'entretien d'un aquarium marin n'est pas chose facile. Ceci était particulièrement vrai à l'époque où j'ai commencé à étudier la faune marine tropicale au début des années 70, à l'époque, le travail était encore plus difficile qu'aujourd'hui; la technologie et les connaissances sur les techniques d'entretien des aquariums marins étaient très limitées. Je ne crois pas me tromper en disant que fort peu de gens osaient installer un aquarium de type « récif corallien », la technologie aquariophile des années 70 ne permettant pas d'obtenir une qualité d'eau suffisante à la maintenance du corail vivant. Le matériel, aujourd'hui standard, tel que: écumeurs de protéines, filtres secs-humides, lampes à ultraviolet et générateurs d'ozone, était soit inexistant soit de conception très sommaire. Avant les filtres secs-humides par exemple, on utilisait des dispositifs relativement inadéquats du type «filtres sous gravier» pour éliminer nitrites et ammoniaque de l'eau de l'aquarium. Aujourd'hui, l'aquariophile marin peut maintenir aisément une eau de bonne qualité si son aquarium est correctement installé.

Au cours des années 70, lorsque l'engouement pour les aquariums marins a commencé à se manifester aux Etats-Unis, on prit l'habitude, pour la capture des animaux, de recourir à des produits chimiques, parmi lesquels la quinaldine mélangée à l'acétone ou, pire encore, le cyanure. On rapporte que certains « récolteurs » répandaient ces substances chimiques, destinées selon eux à paralyser temporairement le poisson, sur les récifs coralliens. Les poissons, tétanisés, flottaient alors à la surface de l'eau, ce qui permettait de les prendre facilement au filet pour les charger ensuite à bord du bateau.

Cet emploi « excessif » de drogues lors de la collecte causait la mort « différée » de la plupart des poissons, mort attribuée à l'époque à un «syndrome mystérieux». En fait, ces drogues, utilisées pour la pêche, endommageaient définitivement les ouïes des poissons et provoquaient bien d'autres traumatismes irrémédiables.

Aujourd'hui encore, la capture d'un grand nombre de poissons se fait à l'aide de substances chimiques, mais certains sont heureusement toujours capturés grâce à des méthodes de « pêche naturelle » en particulier le filet. Les poissons pris au filet coûtent cependant plus cher que les poissons pris à l'aide de ces drogues, ce qui implique que la préférence aille souvent vers ces derniers aux prix plus modestes, et ce malgré un taux de survie très médiocre. Il est possible que le consommateur, mal informé de ces pratiques peu orthodoxes et stressantes, ne comprenne pas toujours la valeur d'un poisson pêché par des méthodes plus naturelles et moins traumatisantes ; notre rôle est de l'en avertir.

Quelle que soit la méthode de collecte, chez certains poissons le taux de mortalité est particulièrement élevé. Certains exportateurs et importateurs les expédient pourtant, en dépit d'un potentiel de survie très faible. Je pense que si l'on indiquait aux consommateurs les types poissons aptes à vivre en aquarium, on pourrait influencer quelque peu la demande en faveur des espèces ayant de plus grandes chances d'acclimatation. Réduire la demande pour ces poissons fragiles au profit de poissons plus robustes, encouragerait à la fois la collecte naturelle et la gestion écologique de l'environnement, tout en donnant satisfaction aux aquariophiles. A quoi bon avoir dans son aquarium un spécimen magnifique si ses chances de survie sont limitées, voire quasiment nulles ?

La motivation principale de cet ouvrage est de traiter les questions évoquées dans cette préface, nous espérons réussir à convaincre et à sensibiliser le lecteur. La description de chaque poisson indique si celui-ci peut être gardé en aquarium, ainsi que son degré de difficulté. Bien qu'il existe un grand nombre aquarium. La vie des poissons est influencée par la manière dont ils sont capturés ainsi que par les exigences spéciales auxquelles il est possible ou impossible de répondre en captivité. En informant le consommateur, nous contribuerons peut-être à réduire quelque peu la demande de poissons capturés à l'aide de drogues, au profit de poissons pris au filet. Ce processus permettrait de réduire la capture inutile d'espèces trop fragiles retirées ainsi de l'écosystème.

Je voudrais indiquer que les informations données dans ce livre ne sont pas infaillibles, si certaines données devenaient obsolètes à la suite d'une meilleure connaissance ou de nouvelles informations, nous ferions les révisions correspondantes dans les éditions futures.

Bien que l'un des buts essentiels de ce livre soit la prise de conscience, de la part des consommateurs, des possibilités d'adaptation de chaque espèce, l'intention de cet ouvrage est de vous fournir un guide illustré des poissons d'aquarium provenant de l'Asie du Sud-Est. Des informations claires et accessibles sur chaque poisson, pouvant être appréhendées de manière pratique et rapide, complètent celui-ci. La conception de ce livre vise à la fois la convivialité et la qualité esthétique. Un autre objectif est d'offrir au lecteur de magnifiques photos de chaque espèce.

Afin de contrôler le plus précisément possible la détermination scientifique de chaque espèce, Richard Pyle, du musée Bishop à Honolulu, et le Docteur John Rendall nous ont fait l'honneur d'examiner tous les poissons répertoriés dans ce livre. Nous espérons que cet ouvrage sera agréable à compulser et vous sera utile lors du choix des espèces qui iront agrémenter votre aquarium d'eau de mer.

PREFÁCIO

Um belo aquário marinho é uma maravilha a ser admirada, uma vez que os peixes marinhos apresentam uma incrível variedade de formas e cores. Eles exibem uma quantidade igualmente incrível de comportamentos e características surpreendentes que desafiam a imaginação. Os aquários marinhos oferecem aos praticantes desse hobby a beleza e a fascinação de trabalhar com um complexo mini-ecossistema. Esta complexidade é uma espada de dois gumes, pois significa também que manter um aquário marinho é um desafio, o que pude constatar especialmente quando comecei a trabalhar com peixes marinhos tropicais no início dos anos 70. Era ainda mais difícil que hoje, uma vez que tanto a tecnologia quanto o conhecimento sobre aquários marinhos eram bastante limitados. Não me recordo de muitos praticantes do hobby ousando montar um aquário de recife de coral. A tecnologia dos aquários nos anos 70 não era capaz de oferecer a água de qualidade particularmente boa necessária para os corais, e equipamentos padrões como separadores de proteínas, filtros wet/dry, lâmpadas ultravioleta e geradores de ozônio apresentavam projetos pouco desenvolvidos ou não existiam. Antes do advento de filtros úmidos/secos, por exemplo, os filtros de saibro, relativamente ineficientes, eram utilizados para eliminar nitrato e amônia da água do aquário. Atualmente, se o aquário for montado de maneira adequada, o aquarista marinho não terá problema em manter uma excelente qualidade da água no aquário.

O método padrão de coleta de peixes marinhos nos anos 70, quando a manutenção de aquários marinhos começou a se estabelecer como um hobby nos E.U.A. era o uso de drogas cáusticas. As drogas utilizadas incluíam quinaldina misturada com acetona, ou ainda pior, cianeto. Foi relatado que alguns pescadores espalhavam cianeto ao redor do recife, de forma que os peixes flutuassem à superfície, onde os pescadores poderiam puxá-los para o barco com uma rede.

Devido ao uso excessivo de drogas no processo da coleta, a maioria dos peixes morriam de uma "misteriosa síndrome". O que acontecia, na verdade, é que as drogas utilizadas para a coleta desses peixes queimavam suas guelras e causavam outros traumas. Para o consumidor, comprar muitos dos peixes marinhos era como comprar flores cortadas. Muitos deles eram bonitos, porém não sobreviviam quase nenhum tempo.

Atualmente, muitos peixes são ainda apanhados com o uso de drogas, mas alguns deles são apanhados utilizando-se métodos aperfeiçoados de coleta, especialmente peixes que são vendidos como "apanhados com rede" (significando que não se utilizam drogas no processo da coleta). Entretanto, os peixes "apanhados com redes" são mais caros que os apanhados com drogas, os quais ainda são preferidos, devido ao seu baixo preço. Isto apesar do fato de que os peixes apanhados com drogas têm uma taxa de sobrevivência muito pequena. Mais uma vez prevalece a "mentalidade para flores cortadas". Os clientes podem não ter consciência do valor de um peixe apanhado através de métodos menos agressivos.

Alguns peixes apresentam uma alta taxa de mortalidade, não importa como sejam apanhados. Apesar disso, alguns exportadores e importadores continuam embarcando esses peixes, embora eles tenham pouca chance de sobrevivência em ambiente de aquário. Creio que se os consumidores fossem informados sobre quais os peixes que se desenvolveriam num ambiente de aquário e quais não, a demanda poderia ser relativamente influenciada a favor dos peixes que podem ser mantidos com êxito. Diminuir a demanda por espécies frágeis a favor das mais resistentes incentivaria a manutenção e a coleta de peixes sem prejudicar o meio ambiente, além de aumentar a satisfação do cliente. Afinal, qual a vantagem de possuir uma bela criatura que tenha pouca chance de sobrevivência em seu aquário doméstico?

Abordar os assuntos discutidos neste prefácio foi a principal motivação para escrever este livro. Espero que possamos aumentar o conhecimento do consumidor. Na descrição de cada peixe informamos se o peixe pode ser mantido em aquário e o nível aproximado de dificuldade. Embora existam vários livros sobre a montagem de aquários e sobre peixes marinhos em geral, poucos deles, de acordo com meu conhecimento, abordaram a sobrevivência dos peixes em aquários. A sobrevivência de um peixe pode ser afetada pela maneira como ele é geralmente apanhado ou por suas exigências especiais que podem ou não ser atendidas no cativeiro. Ao educar os consumidores, podemos ajudar a reduzir a demanda por peixes apanhados utilizando drogas em relação aos peixes apanhados com redes e a remoção desnecessária de espécies frágeis do ecossistema.

Gostaria de ressaltar que as informações reunidas neste livro não são infalíveis. À medida que elas se tornem desatualizadas devido às circunstâncias em mudança ou advento de novos procedimentos ou informações, faremos as revisões correspondentes nas próximas edições.

Embora a conscientização do consumidor e a condição de sobrevivência das espécies sejam os principais objetivos deste livro, não são os únicos. Este livro tem por finalidade oferecer-lhe um extenso guia ilustrado de peixes para aquários do sudeste de Ásia, bem como fornecer informações básicas e de consulta rápida para cada peixe. O livro todo foi organizado tendo em mente o uso fácil e a beleza. Um dos objetivos é oferecer ao leitor fotos perfeitas e inigualáveis de cada espécie. Temos a sorte de contar com Richard Pyle e o Dr. John Rendall, do Bishop Museum, para revisar este livro, a fim de assegurar que o mais preciso nome científico seja usado para cada peixe. Esperamos que este livro lhe seja útil na seleção de espécies para aquários marinhos. Além do mais, esperamos que o considere também agradável e encantador!

INTRODUZIONE

Un acquario marino di successo è una meraviglia, perché la livrea dei pesci marini è generalmente caratterizzata da una gamma di colori spettacolari e le loro forme sono innumerevoli. Offrono inoltre una varietà tanto ampia e sorprendente di comportamenti e caratteristiche da sfidare l'immaginazione di ogni acquariofilo.

Gli acquari marini forniscono ai principianti la splendida e affascinante possibilità di riprodurre un mini ecosistema molto complesso. Occuparsi di un acquario marino è una costante sfida. Quando cominciai a prendermi cura di alcuni pesci marini tropicali, all'inizio degli anni Settanta, il tentativo si rivelò molto più difficile di quanto non sia oggi, perché le risorse tecnologiche e la conoscenza dei sistemi di manutenzione dell'acquario marino erano molto limitate.

Ricordo che pochi acquariofili si azzardavano ad allestire un acquario da barriera. Con gli strumenti allora a disposizione era quasi impossibile fornire ai coralli un'acqua di ottima qualità e le attrezzature ora divenute d'uso comune, come lo schiumatoio, i filtri a percolazione, le lampade UV e i diffusori di ozono, avevano forme rudimentali o neppure esistevano. Oggi, se l'acquario è ben curato, mantenere acqua di eccellente qualità non rappresenta più un problema per l'acquariofilo.

Il metodo più diffuso per pescare i pesci marini negli anni Settanta, quando l'hobby dell'acquariofilia iniziava a diffondersi negli Stati Uniti, era quello di utilizzare potenti prodotti tossici. Le droghe includevano la quinaldina mescolata con acetone o peggio ancora con il cianuro. Alcuni pescatori mettevano il cianuro attorno alla scogliera, in modo che i pesci galleggiassero sulla superficie dell'acqua, potendoli così catturare con le reti direttamente dalle barche.

A causa del dosaggio quasi sempre troppo elevato del veleno durante la pesca, la maggior parte dei pesci moriva per via di una "sindrome da malattia misteriosa." Infatti i prodotti utilizzati per pescare questi pesci danneggiavano irreparabilmente le loro branchie e causavano altri gravi traumi. Per l'acquariofilo spesso l'acquisto di pesci marini era paragonabile all'acquisto di fiori freschi. Molti pesci avevano un bell'aspetto, ma non potevano sopravvivere a lungo.

Oggi la pesca con i veleni è quasi ovunque proibita e per garantire i clienti, molti esportatori indicano espressamente "raccolti con la rete" per sottolineare, che questi pesci non hanno subito i pericolosi danni causati da veleni. Ovviamente, i pesci "raccolti con la rete" sono più costosi di quelli catturati con i veleni, ma solo in questo modo si riesce a debellare il fenomeno della "malattia misteriosa". Alcuni pesci soffrono di un alto tasso di mortalità indipendentemente dal metodo di pesca usato. Nonostante ciò, alcuni esportatori e importatori continuano a commercializzare questi pesci anche se sussiste solo una scarsa possibilità che sopravvivano nell'acquario dell'appassionato. Credo che se i consumatori sapessero quali pesci prosperano in acquario e quali non hanno molte possibilità di sopravvivenza, la domanda si orienterebbe verso le specie che si possono allevare con maggior successo. La diminuzione della richiesta delle specie più fragili e l'aumento di quella relativa a pesci più robusti, incoraggerebbero gli esportatori e gli importatori a un allevamento e a una raccolta più accurati ed "ecologici", aumentando la soddisfazione di quanti si dichiarano veri appassionati acquariofili. Insomma, quale sarebbe il piacere di allevare nell'acquario di casa un pesce bellissimo, ma condannato a morire?

L'analisi dei complessi temi discussi in questa introduzione è stata la principale motivazione che ci ha spinto a pubblicare il presente libro. La nostra speranza è quella di poter contribuire all'acquisizione, da parte degli acquariofili, di importanti nuove cognizioni. Attraverso i dati che accompagnano le immagini relative a ogni pesce, intendiamo fornire al lettore tutti i dati utili a comprendere le possibilità di sopravvivenza del pesce in acquario e, approssimativamente, il livello di difficoltà di allevamento.

Benché esistano molti libri sulla manutenzione degli acquari, pochi hanno preso in considerazione il problema della effettiva sopravvivenza dei pesci in acquario. Il successo dell'allevamento di una specie può essere influenzato sia dal metodo di pesca, sia dalle particolari esigenze che non possono essere soddisfatte in cattività.

Vorrei anche segnalare che le informazioni raccolte in questo libro non sono infallibili. I dati a nostra disposizione vengono superati e modificati rapidamente; a seconda delle circostanze e dell'avvento di nuovi procedimenti o conoscenze, provvederemo quindi ad aggiornare nelle successive edizioni tutti quegli elementi che saranno cambiati.

Ampliare le conoscenze degli appassionati e segnalare le specie per diversi motivi improponibili per la vita in acquario, non sono gli unici due obiettivi che ci siamo posti. Questo libro è stato progettato come guida fotografica ai pesci d'acquario del Sudest asiatico e per fornire indicazioni utili per l'allevamento di ogni specie. Il testo punta a coniugare la facilità d'uso alla bellezza. Uno degli scopi è quello di fornire al lettore accurate fotografie di ognuna delle meravigliose specie trattate.

Ringraziamo per l'aiuto fornitoci Richard Pyle e il dottor John Rendell del Museo Bishop, che hanno compiuto una revisione del testo per verificare la scelta del corretto nome scientifico di ogni pesce. Ci auguriamo che questo volume sia, per l'acquariofilo, utile strumento di scelta delle specie adatte per l'acquario marino. Infine, speriamo che si riveli anche divertente.

This book was designed with an eye toward providing basic information, at-a-glance, about keeping any particular fish. Therefore, we use an easily understood "Information Bar" at the top of each fish's entry. Below is an example of the information bar. The icons and text always appear in the same order.

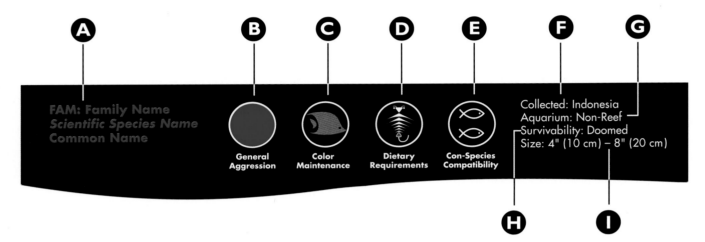

Poisonous Icon.

This icon does not appear in every entry. It is only displayed when the fish shown is poisonous. When it is used, the icon appears *before* the name line, on the far left-hand side of the information bar.

Ⓐ *The Name Line.*

The three name lines located at the far left of the information bar contains the (1) family name, (2) the latin/scientific name of the fish, and (3) a common trade name for that fish. In addition, if two or more distinct forms of a fish (juvenile, male or female) are displayed in the book, the form is noted on a special, fourth line.

Ⓑ *The General Aggressiveness Icon.*

This icon represents the fish's aggressiveness toward fish *other than* those belonging to its own species. This icon serves as a gauge that determines its compatibility with other fish in a mixed-species community tank. Each color disk represents a degree of general aggressiveness. The colors and their meaning are shown below.

Ⓒ *Fading Icon.*

Some fish fade over time when they are kept in an artificial, aquarium environment. They lose the intensity of color they possessed when in the wild. This icon (shown below) informs you of whether the fish will fade when in captivity.

Doesn't Fade   Fades

USER'S GUIDE

D *Diet Icon.*

Each of the symbols (below) represents the diet that will maintain the fish in an aquarium. It does not necessarily represent what they eat in the wild; the diet shown on the icon only represents what they can live on when in captivity. Even if a fish eats fairly exotic foods in the wild, it can frequently be induced to change its diet to a more common food when it is kept in an aquarium.

NOTE: When the diet icon depicts *Coral & Sponges*, this is a sign that the fish is difficult (if not impossible) to keep, since this is hard to provide in an aquarium. If this icon is shown, it means that it will most likely refuse to eat anything else.

| Omnivore | Protein | Plant | Piscivore | Corals & Sponges |

E *Con-Species Aggressiveness/Recommended Aquarium Keeping Conditions.*

This icon informs you of the conditions you need to provide when keeping a fish with its own species. Due to different levels of con-species (within the species) aggression, some fish can not be kept with any fish of its own kind. Others can be kept with fish of its own kind if they are kept in a large group or school. Finally, some are not aggressive toward their own kind and can — therefore — be kept in any arrangement you wish. Each requirement (*Singly Only*, *Singly or In Group* or *Doesn't Matter*) has its own icon (shown below):

| Singly Only | Singly or in a Group Only | Doesn't Matter |

F *Collection Site Information Line.*

This line (marked by the word *Collected*) informs you where they are generally collected for export. It does not necessarily mean that the fish *only* exists in this area.

G *Reef Compatibility Information Line.*

This line (marked by the word *Aquarium*) infoms you whether it is reef compatible when kept in an aquarium. This information line lists compatiblity as *Reef, Non-Reef* or *Reef (Caution)*. *Non-Reef*, means that the fish will tend to eat or damage coral and/or other invertebrates when kept in an aquarium. *Reef (Caution)* indicates that — while most fish in this category are safe in a reef — some individuals may "turn" into coral or other invertebrate eaters. This line does *not* inform you whether — when in the wild — a fish lived in a coral reef or not.

H *Survivability Information Line.*

This line (marked by the word *Survivability*) tells you how difficult (or impossible) it is to maintain a fish in an aquarium. The reasons for its survivability (or lack thereof) can be due to either its unusual diet, delicate nature or the way it is usually collected. The ability to keep the fish alive in a tank is listed as either *Easy, Moderate, Difficult* or *Doomed.*

I *Size Information Line.*

This line is fairly self explanatory. It shows the size range of a fish in an aquarium: *Small* [Less than 4 in. (10 cm.)], *Medium* [4 in. (10 cm.) — 8 in. (20 cm.)] or *Large* [More than 8 in. (20 cm.)].

MANUAL DEL USUARIO

Este libro ha sido diseñado con vistas a proporcionar información básica acerca del mantenimiento de cualquier especie de pez con sólo una ojeada. Por tanto, empleamos una "Barra Informativa" de fácil comprensión en la parte superior de la sección de cada especie. Abajo podrán observar un ejemplo de esta barra informativa. Los iconos y los textos siempre aparecen en el mismo orden.

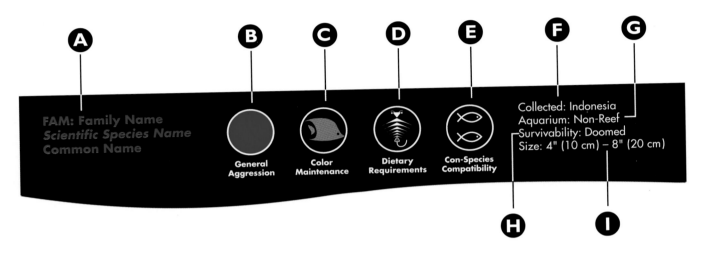

Icono venenoso.

Este icono no aparece en todas las secciones y sólo se incluye cuando el pez que se muestra a continuación es venenoso. Cuando se emplea, el icono aparecerá *antes* del la línea de nombre, al extremo izquierdo de la barra informativa.

A Línea de Nombre.

Las líneas de nombre situadas al extremo izquierdo de la barra informativa contienen el nombre de la familia, el nombre científico o en latín y el nombre más común o comercial de tal pez. Además, si se muestran dos (2) o más formas distintivas del pez en el libro (juvenil, macho o hembra), esta característica se señala en una cuarta línea especial.

B Icono de Agresividad General.

Este icono representa la agresividad del pez hacia otros peces *que no sea* miembros de su propia especie y sirve como una escala para determinar su compatibilidad con otros peces en un tanque comunitario con una variedad de especies. Cada disco de color representa un grado de agresividad general. Los colores y su significado se muestran a continuación.

Pacífico   Moderado   Agresivo

C Pérdida de colores

Algunos peces van perdiendo sus colores con el transcurso del tiempo si se mantienen en un ambiente de acuario artificial y pierden la intensidad de los colores que poseían en estado silvestre. Este icono (que se muestra abajo), le informa si el pez pierde sus colores en cautiverio.

No pierde sus colores   Pierde sus colores

D *Icono de dieta.*

Cada uno de los símbolos que se observan a continuación representa la dieta necesaria para mantener esa especie en un acuario, aunque no necesariamente representa lo que estos peces comen en estado silvestre. La dieta que se muestra en el icono sólo representa lo que deben comer para sobrevivir en cautiverio. Aún en el caso que el pez coma alimentos algo exóticos en estado silvestre, a menudo puede inducirse a cambiar su dieta a alimentos más comunes en una pecera.

NOTA: Cuando el icono de dieta señala *Corales & Esponjas*, esta es señal de que este pez es difícil de mantener, ya que cuesta trabajo proporcionar estos alimentos en una pecera. Si se muestra este icono, significa que esta especie probablemente se negará a comer cualquier otro alimento.

Omnívoro   Proteína   Plantas   Peces   Corales & Esponjas

E *Agresividad hacia su propia especie/Condiciones recomendadas para en el mantenimiento en una pecera.*

Este icono le informa acerca de las condiciones que se deben proporcionar cuando se mantiene a un pez con otros miembros de su propia especie. Debido a diferentes niveles de agresividad hacia otros miembros de su misma especie, algunos peces no pueden mantenerse junto a ningún otro pez de su propia especie. Otros peces pueden mantenerse junto a otros ejemplares de su propia familia si mantienen en un grupo o cardumen grande. Por último, hay peces que no son agresivos hacia su propia especie y, por tanto, pueden mantenerse en cualquier tipo de agrupación que desea. Cada requisito (Sólo unicamente, individualmente o en grupo, o no importa) tiene su propio icono como se muestra a continuación:

Sólo   Sólo Individualmente   No importa
Individualmente   o en grupo

F *Línea de información sobre lugar de recolección.*

Esta línea (marcada por la palabra *Collected*) le informa donde generalmente se capturan estos peces para su exportación, aunque no necesariamente significa que estos peces sólo existen en esa región.

G *Línea Informativa sobre Compatibilidad de Arrecife.*

Esta línea (marcada por la palabra *Compatible*) le informa si el pez es compatible con el arrecife cuando se mantiene en un acuario. Esta línea informativa señala la compatibilidad como *reef, nonreef* o *reef (caution)* [arrecife, no arrecife o arrecife - precaución]. *Non-reef* (no arrecife) significa que los peces tienden a comerse o dañar los corales y/o otros invertebrados cuando se mantienen en un acuario. *Reef (caution)* [Arrecife-precaución] indica que aun cuando la mayoría de los peces en esta categoría son seguros en un arrecife, algunos individuos pueden transformarse en comedores de coral u otros invertebrados. Esta línea *no* le informa si este pez vivía o no en arrecifes coralinos en estado silvestre.

H *Línea informativa sobre resistencia.*

Esta línea (marcada por la palabra *Survivability* - Resistencia) le informa acerca de cuan fácil o posible es mantener un pez en un acuario. En breve, le informa acerca de la *capacidad de supervivencia* de una especie. Las razones de la capacidad de supervivencia (o falta de la misma) pueden relacionarse a su dieta poco usual, su naturaleza delicada o al modo en que usualmente se captura. La capacidad de mantener los peces vivos en un tanque se enumera como *Easy, Moderate, Difficult* o *Doomed* (Fácil, Moderado, Difícil o Caso perdido).

I *Línea informativa de tamaño.*

Esta línea relativamente se explica por sí sola y le muestra la gama de dimensiones de un pez en un acuario: *Small* - Pequeño [menos de 4 pulgadas (10 cm.)]; *Medium* - Mediano [8 pulgadas (20 cm.)] o *Large* -Grande [más de 8 pulgadas (20 cm.)].

GUIDE DE L'UTILISATEUR

Ce livre a été conçu en vue d'offrir la possibilité de trouver très rapidement des informations de base sur la manière de maintenir les poissons d'eau de mer. Sur la partie supérieure de chaque description de poisson vous trouverez donc une «Barre d'icônes» facilement compréhensible. Un exemple de la Barre d'information se trouve ci-dessous. Les icônes et le texte apparaissent toujours dans le même ordre.

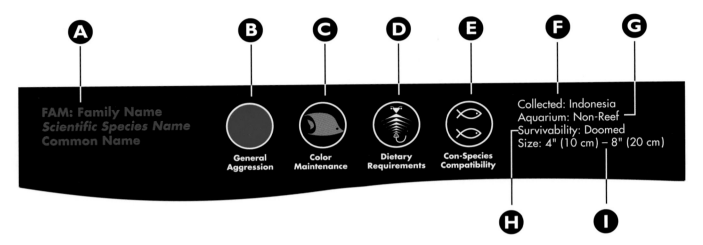

Icône Poison.

Cette icône n'apparaît pas systématiquement, elle est uniquement présente lorsque le poisson illustré sur cette page est venimeux. Lorsqu'elle est utilisée, l'icône figure *avant* la ligne du nom, à l'extrême gauche de la barre d'information.

A La ligne du nom.

Le paragraphe situé à l'extrême gauche de la barre d'information comporte le nom de la famille, le nom scientifique/latin du poisson, ainsi que son nom vernaculaire en Anglais. Dans le cas ou deux (2) formes distinctes d'un même poisson sont illustrées dans le livre (juvénile, mâle ou femelle), la forme exposée est notée sur une quatrième ligne spéciale.

B L'icône d'agressivité générale (relation interspécifique).

Cette icône représente l'agressivité du poisson envers les poissons *autres que* ceux qui appartiennent à sa propre espèce (relation interspécifique). L'icône sert à évaluer la compatibilité de ce poisson vis-à-vis d'autres spécimens dans un aquarium communautaire où les espèces sont mélangées. Chaque disque de couleur représente un degré d'agressivité générale. Les couleurs et leur signification sont illustrées ci-dessous.

Pacifique   Modérément   Très agressif
                   agressif

C Icône d'atténuation.

Les coloris de certains poissons s'atténuent lorsqu'ils sont placés dans un environnement artificiel d'aquarium. Ils perdent l'intensité des couleurs qu'ils possédaient en liberté. Cette icône (illustrée ci-dessous) vous avertit si les couleurs s'atténueront en captivité.

Pas d'atténuation   Atténuation

D *Icône de régime alimentaire.*

Chacun des symboles ci-dessous représente le régime alimentaire souhaitable en aquarium. Ce symbole ne correspond pas forcément la nourriture du poisson en liberté, le régime illustré sur l'icône représentant uniquement ce dont le poisson peut se nourrir pour survivre en captivité. Même si, en liberté, la nourriture d'un poisson est assez spécifique, il peut très souvent être amené sans préjudice, à échanger son régime d'origine pour une nourriture plus commune et plus pratique en aquarium.

N.B. Si l'icône de régime alimentaire spécifie « *Corail et éponges* », ceci veut dire qu'il est probable que le poisson refusera de se nourrir d'autre chose. Ce régime alimentaire étant souvent difficile à se procurer, cette espèce sera très délicate à conserver en aquarium.

Omnivore   Protéine   Plante   Piscivore   Esponges et Corail

E *Agressivité envers sa propre espèce (relation intraspécifique).*

Cette icône vous informe des problèmes de compatibilité entre poissons de même espèce. En raison des différents niveaux d'agressivité au sein d'une même espèce, certains poissons ne peuvent être gardés ensemble sous peine de rixes sanglantes voire mortelles. D'autres, en revanche, n'acceptent de cohabiter avec leurs congénères que s'ils sont en groupe ou en bandes. Enfin, certains ne sont agressifs, ni envers leur propre espèce, ni envers les autres, ils pourront de ce fait être gardés avec les poissons de votre choix. Chaque situation (*Uniquement seul, Seul ou en groupe* ou *Aucune importance*) possède sa propre icône, comme illustré ci-dessous :

Seul ou   Uniquement   Aucune
                seul en groupe   importance

F *Ligne d'information sur le site de collecte.*

Cette ligne (identifiée par le mot *Collected*) vous informe de l'origine du poisson, point de départ des exportations. Ceci ne veut pas nécessairement dire que le poisson n'existe *uniquement* que dans cette zone.

G *Ligne d'information sur la compatibilité aux récifs.*

Cette ligne (identifiée par le mot *Aquarium*) indique la compatibilité de ce poisson avec un Aquarium RECIFAL. Ces informations énumèrent la compatibilité en termes de *Reef* (récifs), *Non-Reef* (non-récifs), ou *Reef Caution* (récifs précautions). *Non-récifs* veut dire que le poisson aura tendance à manger ou endommager le corail et/ou les autres invertébrés lorsqu'il se trouve en aquarium. *Récifs précautions* indique que, bien que la plupart des poissons dans cette catégorie soient sans danger dans un environnement récifal, certains spécimens peuvent, le cas échéant, «se transformer» en mangeurs d'invertébrés ou de corail (ces indications ne sont pas destinées à vous informer si ce poisson, à l'état libre, vivait dans un récif de corail ou non.

H *Ligne d'information sur la robustesse.*

La mention *Robustesse* (identifiée par le mot *Survivability*) vous donne le degré de difficulté pour maintenir un poisson en aquarium. En un mot, cette information vous donne les *chances de survie* du poisson. Les raisons de sa survie (ou de son décès) peuvent provenir d'un régime alimentaire inhabituel, d'une constitution délicate ou de la manière dont il a été capturé. Le degré de difficulté pour garder un poisson en vie dans un aquarium est identifié comme *Easy* (Facile), *Moderate* (Moyen), *Difficult* (Difficile), *Doomed* (Voué à l'échec).

I *Ligne d'information sur la taille.*

Pas besoin d'explication pour cette ligne. Elle montre la fourchette de tailles d'un poisson en aquarium: *Petit* [moins de 10 cm (4 po.)], *Moyen* [10 à 20 cm (4 po. à 8 po.], *grand* [plus de 20 cm (> 8 po.)].

Este livro foi elaborado tendo em vista oferecer informações básicas sobre a manutenção de qualquer tipo de peixe através de uma consulta rápida. Portanto, utilizamos uma "Barra de Informações" de fácil compreensão na parte superior de cada registro de peixe. Segue abaixo um exemplo da barra de informações. Os ícones e o texto aparecem na mesma ordem.

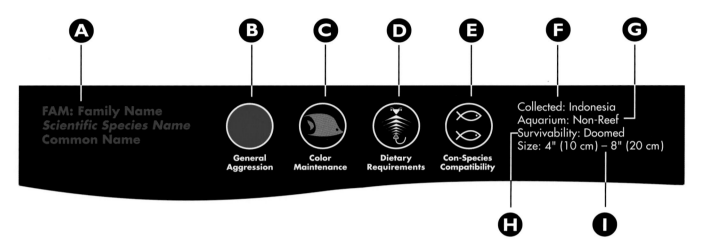

Ícone Venenoso.

Este ícone não aparece em todos os registros. É mostrado somente quando o peixe mostrado a seguir é venenoso. Quando utilizado, o ícone aparece antes da linha do nome, à extrema esquerda da barra de informações.

A *A Linha do Nome.*

As linhas de nomes, que se localizam à extrema esquerda da barra de informações, contêm o nome da família, o nome em latim/científico do peixe e um nome comercial comum para o peixe em questão. Além disso, se forem mostradas duas (2) ou mais formas distintas de um peixe (jovem, macho ou fêmea) no livro, será feita uma observação especial quanto à essa forma na quarta linha.

B *O Ícone de Agressividade Geral.*

Este ícone representa a agressividade do peixe em relação a peixes que não pertençam à sua própria espécie. Este ícone serve como uma espécie de escala que determina sua compatibilidade com outros peixes em um tanque comunitário com espécies variadas. Cada cor de disco representa um grau de agressividade geral. As cores e seus significados são mostrados a seguir.

Pacífico   Moderado   Agressivo

C *Ícone de Descoloração.*

Alguns peixes perdem a cor com o tempo quando são mantidos em um ambiente artificial de aquário. Eles perdem a intensidade da cor que possuíam na vida selvagem. Este ícone (mostrado abaixo) informa se o peixe sofrerá descoloração quando em cativeiro.

Não descolora   Descolora

GUIA DO USUÁRIO

D Ícone da Dieta.

Cada uno de los símbolos que se observan a continuación representa la dieta Cada um dos símbolos abaixo representa a dieta que manterá o peixe num aquário. Não representa, necessariamente, o que o peixe come em seu estado natural. A dieta mostrada no ícone representa apenas o que eles podem comer para sobreviver quando em cativeiro. Mesmo que um peixe coma alimentos bastante exóticos na vida selvagem, geralmente pode ser induzido a mudar a dieta para um tipo de alimento mais comum em um aquário.

OBS.: Quando o ícone da dieta indicar *Coral e Esponjas*, é sinal de que o peixe é de difícil manutenção, uma vez que é difícil fornecer este tipo de alimento num aquário. Se este ícone for mostrado, significa que o peixe provavelmente recusará comer qualquer outra coisa.

Onívoro   Proteína   Plantas   Peixe   Coral e Esponjas

E Agressividade dentro da Mesma Espécie/Condições Recomendadas para Manutenção do Aquário.

Este ícone informa sobre a as condições que você necessita providenciar ao manter um peixe com a sua própria espécie. Devido aos diferentes níveis de agressão dentro da espécie, alguns peixes não podem ser mantidos com nenhum peixe de sua mesma espécie. Outros podem ser mantidos com peixes de sua mesma espécie se forem mantidos em um grupo ou cardume grande. Por último, alguns não são agressivos em relação à sua própria espécie, podendo, portanto, ser mantidos da maneira que você deseja. Cada requisito (*Individualmente Apenas, Individualmente ou Em Grupo* ou *Não Importa*) tem seu próprio ícone mostrado a seguir:

Individualmente   Individualmente   Não importa
Apenas   ou Em Grupo Apenas

F Linha de Informações sobre o Local de Coleta.

Esta linha (marcada pela palavra *Collected*) informa onde os peixes são geralmente coletados para exportação. Não significa, necessariamente, que o peixe existe somente nessa área.

G Linha de Informações sobre a Compatibilidade com Recifes.

Esta linha (marcada pela palavra *Aquarium*), informa se o peixe é compatível com recifes quando colocado em aquário. Esta linha de informações relaciona a compatibilidade como *Reef* (recife), *Non-Reef* (não-recife) ou *Reef-Caution* (recife - cuidado). *Não-recife* significa que o peixe tenderá a comer ou danificar corais e/ou invertebrados quando mantido em aquário. *Recife (cuidado)* indica que - embora a maioria dos peixes desta categoria esteja segura em recifes - alguns indivíduos podem "virar" corais ou outros comedores invertebrados. Esta linha não informa se o peixe vivia ou não num recife de coral na vida selvagem.

H Linha de Informações sobre a Resistência.

Esta linha (marcada pela palavra *Survivability*) informa se é fácil ou possível manter o peixe em um aquário. Em resumo, informa-lhe sobre a capacidade de sobrevivência do peixe. As razões para sua capacidade de sobrevivência (ou falta da mesma) podem ser sua dieta rara, natureza delicada ou a maneira como esses peixes geralmente são coletados. A capacidade de manter o peixe vivo em um tanque é relacionada como *Easy* (Fácil), *Moderate* (Moderada), *Difficult* (Difícil) ou *Doomed* (Impossível).

I Linha de Informações sobre o Tamanho.

Esta linha é auto-explicativa. Mostra a variação de tamanhos de um peixe em aquário: *Pequeno* [Menos de 4 pol. (10 cm)], *Médio* [4 pol. (10 cm)] — 8 pol. (20 cm)] ou *Grande* [Mais de 8 pol. (20 cm)].

Questo libro è stato scritto per fornire uno strumento di facile accesso a informazioni di base sull'allevamento dei pesci marini d'acquario. Per questo motivo, nella parte superiore di ogni scheda descrittiva, si trova una "barra d'informazione" di facile comprensione di cui segue un esempio esplicativo. Simboli e testo avranno, nel libro, sempre lo stesso ordine.

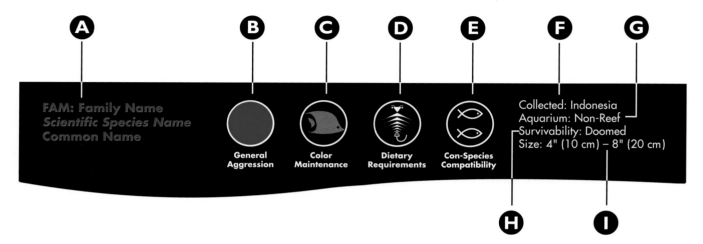

L'icona velenosità

Questa icona non compare in ogni scheda, ma viene utilizzata solo quando il pesce illustrato è velenoso. Quando viene usato, il simbolo appare prima della riga che descrive il nome dell'esemplare, all'estrema sinistra della "barra d'informazione".

A Il nome.

L'indicazione relativa al nome dell'esemplare presentato si trova sulla sinistra della "barra d'informazione" e riporta: il nome della famiglia, il nome scientifico e il nome comune del pesce. Inoltre, se vengono illustrate nel libro due forme differenti del pesce (giovanile, maschile o femminile), la forma viene descritta in una quarta riga speciale.

B L'icona per l'aggressività generale.

Questa icona rappresenta l'aggressività del pesce verso altri pesci che non appartengono alla sua stessa specie. L'informazione è utile per determinare in acquario la compatibilità del pesce in un acquario di comunità. Ogni colore rappresenta un differente grado di aggressività:

Pacifico   Moderato   Aggressivo

C I cambiamenti di colore.

Il colore di alcuni pesci sbiadisce quando vengono mantenuti nell'habitat artificiale dell'acquario. La colorazione della loro livrea perde d'intensità rispetto a quella posseduta in natura. I simboli riportati di seguito indicano se il colore del pesce perderà di intensità in acquario.

Non Sbiadisce   Sbiadisce

GUIDA PER L'UTENTE

D *Mangimi.*

Ogni simbolo riassume il tipo di dieta base che il pesce dovrà seguire in acquario. Le indicazioni fornite non corrispondono necessariamente a ciò di cui il pesce si nutre nell'ambiente naturale, bensì al tipo di nutrizione più indicato per l'acquario. Anche se il pesce nel proprio habitat si alimenta con cibi esotici, potrà spesso essere indotto a modificare la propria dieta, introducendo nella sua alimentazione comuni mangimi utilizzati in acquariofilia.

Nota: il simbolo, che indica "coralli e spugne", vuole significare che il mantenimento del pesce è complesso, perché è difficile provvedere a fornirgli questo tipo di alimento. L'informazione sottintende che sarà molto difficile indurre il pesce a cibarsi, in acquario, di altri alimenti.

| Onnivoro | Proteine | Fitofago | Altri Pesci | Coralli e Spugne |

E *Aggressività verso la medesima specie/condizioni di allevamento raccomandate.*

Questa icona illustra le condizioni di allevamento quando si vogliono tenere più esemplari della stessa specie. A causa dell'intensità differente di aggressività che il pesce esprime nei confronti di conspecifici, alcuni di essi non possono essere allevati in gruppo. Altri, invece, possono spartire la vasca con dei conspecifici solo se associati in branchi numerosi. Infine, alcuni pesci non sono aggressivi verso i conspecifici e possono essere allevati in acquari di qualunque tipo. Ogni esigenza ("soltanto da soli", "da soli o in gruppo", "indifferentemente") è rappresentata da un proprio simbolo.

Soltano da soli   Da soli o in gruppo   Indifferentemente

F *Regioni d'esportazione.*

L'espressione "Collected" ("Pescati") riporta il luogo in cui gli esemplari vengono generalmente pescati per l'esportazione. Non significa necessariamente che la specie viva soltanto nella zona indicata.

G *Compatibilità con l'acquario da barriera.*

La parola "Aquarium" ("Compatibile") fornisce indicazioni sulla possibilità di mantenere il pesce in un acquario da barriera. Le formule usate sono: "reef", "non-reef" o "reef (caution)". "Reef" indica la possibilità di allevare il pesce in un acquario da barriera. "Non-reef" indica l'impossibilità di allevare il pesce in un acquario da barriera perché questi tende a cibarsi o a danneggiare coralli o altri invertebrati. "Reef (caution)" significa che, mentre la maggior parte dei pesci di questa specie trova nella barriera un habitat loro idoneo, alcuni esemplari possono diventare consumatori di coralli o di altri invertebrati. Le informazioni fornite non indicano se l'ambiente naturale del pesce è o non è la barriera corallina.

H *Resistenza.*

Il termine "Survivability" ("Resistenza") indica quanto si rivela facile o difficile (e se è possibile) tenere un determinato pesce in acquario. In breve definisce la possibilità di sopravvivenza del pesce. Le ragioni per cui l'allevamento può avere successo o fallire possono essere individuate nella dieta insolita, nella delicata natura del pesce o negli abituali metodi di pesca. La possibilità di allevamento in acquario viene così riassunta: "easy" ("facile"); "moderate" ("media"); "difficult" ("difficile"); "doomed" ("condannata a fallire").

I *Dimensione del pesce.*

Viene riportata la taglia che il pesce può raggiungere in acquario: "small" ("piccolo"), meno di 10 cm; "medium" ("medio"), 10-20 cm; "large" ("grande"), oltre 20 cm.

COLOFON

The layout and design of this book was created using *Adobe PageMaker 6.0, Adobe Illustrator 6.0* and *Adobe Photoshop 3.0.5* on Apple Power Macintosh 9500 series computers. The initial text was written using *WordPerfect 3.5 for Macintosh*.

Typesetting was likewise performed in both *PageMaker* versions 6.0 and 5.0 Chinese. Typefaces used in the creation of the book are: *Adobe Futura, Adobe Optima, Adobe Gill Sans* and *Fontshop Identification*.

The various icons displayed — as well as the cover logo — were created in *Adobe Illustrator 6.0 for Macintosh*. The images were scanned using a *Linotype-Hell S3800 Scanner*.

The Marine Aquarium Fish of Southeast Asia:

Family: Acanthuridae

(Surgeonfishes & Tangs) Surgeonfishes and Tangs are characterized by deep bodies with a continuous dorsal and anal fin; and their eyes are located high on their heads. Some of the species in this family have venom in their spines, and — therefore — should be handled carefully.

Members of the *Zebrasoma* genus are quarrelsome when there are two fish of the same or similar species in a tank, yet they do well in groups consisting of four or more individuals. Many species belonging to the *Zebrasoma* genus are ideal in a reef tank setup, as they will not harm coral or other invertebrates.

All members of the Acanthuridae family have a spine at the base of the tail; the area surrounding this tail spike is usually brightly colored as a warning (because in a fight they can bend the spike outward so that it sticks out and slashes an opponent).

Larger species in the Acanthuridae family are particularly territorial. This territoriality is mainly — but not soley — directed toward members of its own species. This is especially true of the *Acanthurus* genus. For this reason, it is a good practice when adding new fishes to a tank to watch for aggression. If there *is* a problem, remove the *Acanthurus* species before adding the new fishes and reintroduce it after a few days. The aggressive fishes could also be isolated in a plastic enclosure within the tank. Another option would be to set up all the other fishes that you desire in the aquarium and introduce members of the *Acanthurus* genus last.

Most members of this family are easy to keep in an aquarium setting, though a few of the species are prone to the *Cryptocaryon irritans* parasite that causes Marine White Spot Disease. *Paracanthurus hepatus* (Hepatus Tang) and *Naso lituratus* (Naso Tang) have venom in their dorsal spine, as do all of the members of the Siganidae family (Rabbitfishes). They can inflict
a painful would when handled improperly, although the pain is not as great as a member of the Scorpaenidae family (Scorpionfishes) can inflict.

The juvenile *Acanthurus pyroferus* have the ability to mimic the coloration of the *Centropyge* genus (Dwarf Angelfishes) for protection. This is because members of the *Centropyge* genus are not a favorite target for predators. They tend to be spiny and fast.

Family: Acanthuridae

(Famille: Acanthuridae) La famille des Acanthuridae est caractérisée par des poissons ayant un corps large et plat, portant une nageoire dorsale et anale continue, de plus, leurs yeux sont placés haut sur la tête. Chez certaines de ces espèces, les épines contiennent du venin; elles devraient donc être manipulées avec précaution.

Certains membres de cette famille sont belliqueux lorsqu'il y a deux poissons de la même espèce ou d'espèces similaires dans un aquarium, mais se comportent très bien en groupes de 4 individus ou plus. Tous les membres de la famille des Acanthuridae portent une épine à la base de la queue (scalpel). La zone entourant l'épine est en général vivement colorée et sert d'avertissement. Durant le combat, le poisson peut ériger son épine de manière à la faire ressortir et à blesser son adversaire.

Les membres les plus gros de la famille des Acanthuridae sont particulièrement territoriaux vis-à-vis d'individus de même espèce, voire d'autres espèces. Ceci est particulièrement vrai du genre *Acanthurus*. Pour cette raison il sera conseillé de surveiller l'agressivité lors de l'introduction d'un nouveau poisson dans l'aquarium. S'il y avait un problème, le fait de déplacer certaines pièces du décor peut perturber et limiter l'agressivité territoriale, le poisson agressif pourrait également être isolé dans une enceinte en plastique à l'intérieur de l'aquarium. Une autre option serait de placer d'abord tous les autres poissons désirés dans l'aquarium et d'introduire les membres du genre *Acanthurus* en dernier. La plupart des membres de cette famille sont faciles à garder en aquarium bien que certaines espèces soient plus particulièrement sujettes au parasite *Cryptocaryon irritans* (qui provoque de l'Icktio marin) et au parasite *Amyloodinium* (qui provoque l'*Oodinium*). L'épine dorsale de *Paracanthurus hepatus* et de *Naso lituratus* contient un venin, comme tous les membres de la famille des Siganidae et bien que la blessure soit moins douloureuse que celle infligée par les membres de la famille des Scorpaenidae, ils peuvent véritablement blesser s'ils ne sont pas manipulés correctement.

La forme juvénile d'*Acanthurus pyroferus* a la capacité d'imiter la coloration du genre *Centropyge* par mesure de protection, les membres du genre *Centropyge* n'étant pas la proie favorite des prédateurs.

De nombreuses espèces appartenant au genre *Zebrasoma* constituent un choix idéal pour un environnement d'aquarium récifal puisqu'elles ne s'attaquent ni aux coraux ni aux invertébrés.

Family: Acanthuridae

(Pez Cirujano) La familia Acanthuridae se caracteriza por cuerpos extensos con aletas dorsales y anales continuas. Además, sus ojos se encuentran localizados hacia la parte superior de sus cabezas. Algunas de las especies de esta familia poseen una sustancia venenosa en sus espinas, y por tanto, deben manipularse con cuidado.

Algunos de los miembros de la familia Acanthuridae se tornan belicosos cuando se encuentran dos peces de la misma especie o especies similares en un mismo acuario, aunque se llevan bien cuando andan en grupos de cuatro (4) o más individuos. Todos los miembros de la familia Acanthuridae poseen un aguijón en la base de la cola. El área que rodea este espolón de cola generalmente es de colores brillantes como una señal de advertencia, ya que durante una pelea, estos peces pueden doblar su espolón hacia afuera en forma tal que pueden cortar a su oponente.

Los miembros más grandes de la familia Acanthuridae mantienen una especial territorialidad ante miembros de su misma especie y a veces también con respecto a otras especies. Esto resulta particularmente cierto en el caso del género *Acanthurus*. Por esta razón, al incorporar nuevos ejemplares en un tanque, una buena práctica es mantenerlos bajo observación en caso que se produzcan agresiones. Si se produce un problema, retire los ejemplares de la especie *Acanthurus* e introdúzcalos nuevamente dentro de unos días. Los peces agresivos también pueden aislarse dentro de un recinto plástico perforado dentro del tanque. Otra opción sería la de introducir primero todos los demás peces que desea tener en el acuario y luego introducir como últimos los miembros del género *Acanthurus*. Resulta fácil mantener a la mayoría de los miembros de esta familia en un ambiente de acuario, aunque algunos miembros de esta especie resultan especialmente propensos al parásito *Cryptocaryon irritans* (un parásito que causa manchas blancas en la piel de los peces) y el parásito Amyloodinium (que produce oodinio). El *Paracanthurus hepatus* (Cirujano Azul) y el *Naso lituratus* (Cirujano Naso) tienen veneno en su espinas dorsales, al igual que todos los miembros de la familia Siganidae (pez liebre) y pueden infligir una herida dolorosa cuando se manipulan de forma incorrecta, aunque el dolor no es tan agudo como el que puede infligir un miembro de la familia Scorpaenidae (pez leon).

Los *Acanthurus pyroferus* en su estado juvenil poseen la habilidad de imitar la coloración del género *Centropyge* (pez ángel enano) como mecanismo de defensa. Este mecanismo ha sido desarrollado ya que los miembros de este género no resultan un blanco favorito para los predadores al ser espinosos y moverse muy rápidamente.

Muchas de las especies que pertenecen al género *Zebrasoma* resultan ideales para un tanque de estilo arrecife ya que no causan daño a los corales ni a otros invertebrados.

Estos peces de aguas profundas se encuentran adaptados a condiciones de poca iluminación y poseen órganos productores de luz debajo de su ojos. Estos peces no resultan especialmente atractivos, pero si se mantiene un grupo de ellos en un tanque a oscuras, la muestra asemeja un prado lleno de luciérnagas en una noche de verano.

Family: Acanthuridae

(Família: Acanthuridae) A família *Acanthuridae* caracteriza-se por corpos grandes, com uma barbatana dorsal e anal contínua. Além disso, seus olhos estão localizados no alto da cabeça. Algumas das espécies possuem veneno nas suas espinhas, e portanto devem ser manuseadas com cuidado.

Alguns membros da família Acanthuridae são briguentos quando há dois peixes da mesma espécie ou de espécie similar num tanque, todavia eles se relacionam bem em grupos de quatro ou mais indivíduos. Todos os membros da família Acanthuridae têm um espigão na base da cauda. A área ao redor desta espinha caudal é normalmente em cores brilhantes como um aviso, uma vez que numa luta, o peixe pode curvar seu espigão para fora de modo ela se sobressaia e golpeie o oponente.

Os membros maiores da família Acanthuridae são especialmente territoriais para com os da mesma espécie e algumas vezes para com os de outras espécies também. Isto é particularmente verdadeiro no gênero Acanthurus. Por essa razão é recomendável observar se há agressão quando se coloca um novo peixe em um tanque. Se houver algum problema, remova a espécie *Acanthurus* e reintroduza-a após alguns dias. O peixe agressor poderá também ser isolado em um compartimento de plástico dentro do tanque. Outra opção seria acomodar todos os outros peixes que você desejar no aquário e introduzir os membros do gênero *Acanthurus* por último. A maioria dos membros desta família são fáceis de manter num ambiente de aquário, embora alguns poucos da espécie sejam particularmente sensíveis ao parasita *Cryptocarion irritans* (que causa Ictio Marinho) e ao *Amyloodinium* (que causa Oodinum). *Paracanthuruss hepatus* ("Hepatus Tang") e *Naso lituratus* ("Naso Tang") têm veneno em suas espinhas dorsais, assim como todos os membros da família Siganidae ("Rabbitfish"). Eles podem causar um ferimento doloroso quando manuseados impropriamente, embora a dor não seja tão grande como a que um membro da família Scorpaenidae (Peixe-Escorpião) pode causar.

O *Acanthurus pyroferus* jovem tem a habilidade de imitar a coloração do gênero *Centropyge* (Peixes-Anjo Anões) para proteção. Isto é porque os membros do gênero *Centropyge* não são um alvo favorito para os predadores. Eles costumam ser espinhosos e rápidos.

Muitas espécies pertencentes ao gênero *Zebrasoma* são ideais num ambiente de tanque de recife, pois não irão prejudicar corais ou outros invertebrados.

Family: Acanthuridae

(Famiglia: Acanthuridae) I membri della famiglia Acanthuridae sono caratterizzati da un corpo alto e una pinna dorsale che, come quella anale, si estende in modo continuo lungo il corpo. Inoltre, gli occhi sono collocati nella parte superiore della testa. Alcune specie presentano aculei velenosi e, per questo motivo, devono essere maneggiate con cautela.

Alcuni membri della famiglia Acanthuridae manifestano aggressività quando due pesci della stessa specie o di due specie simili sono presenti in acquario, ma sono più pacifici in gruppi di 4 o più individui. Tutte le specie della famiglia Acanthuridae hanno uno o più aculei alla base della coda (da qui il nome comune "pesce chirurgo"). La zona circostante la pinna caudale è di colore vivace, utile come segnale di avvertimento, dal momento che durante i combattimenti questi pesci possono piegare l'aculeo verso l'esterno, in modo che sporga, e ferire l'avversario.

I più grandi Acanturidi hanno un forte senso della territorialità verso i conspecifici e talvolta anche verso altre specie. Questo fatto è particolarmente sviluppato nel genere *Acanthurus*. Per questo motivo è buona norma controllare il comportamento quando si aggiungono pesci nuovi in acquario. Se si riscontra un problema, è necessario rimuovere la specie di *Acanthurus* e reintrodurla dopo alcuni giorni. E' possibile anche isolare momentaneamente i pesci aggressivi in un recinto di plastica all'interno dell'acquario di comunità. Un'altra soluzione è introdurre tutti gli altri pesci desiderati nell'acquario e aggiungere gli *Acanthurus* per ultimi.

E' facile mantenere la maggior parte dei membri di questa famiglia in acquario, benché alcune specie siano particolarmente sensibili al parassita *Cryptocaryon irritans* (che causa l'Ittio marino) e al parassita *Amyloodinium* (che causa Oodiniasi). *Paracanthurus hepatus* e *Naso lituratus*, come anche tutti i membri della famiglia Siganidae, secernono del veleno nella pinna dorsale. Possono infliggere dolorose ferite quando vengono maneggiati incautamente, benché il dolore non sia forte quanto quello che possono provocare alcuni Scorpaenidae.

Giovani esemplari di *Acanthurus pyroferus* hanno la capacità di imitare la colorazione del genere *Centropyge* per autodifesa. Questo perché i *Centropyge* non sono tra i bersagli favoriti dei predatori visto che generalmente sono pericolosi (per i loro aculei) e rapidi nuotatori.

Molte delle specie che appartengono al genere *Zebrasoma* sono ideali per l'acquario da barriera perché non danneggiano i coralli o gli altri invertebrati.

FAM: Acanthuridae
Acanthurus japonicus
Gold Rimmed Tang

**General
Aggression**

**Color
Maintenance**

**Dietary
Requirements**

**Con-Species
Compatibility**

Collected: Indonesia
Aquarium: Reef (Caution)
Survivability: Moderate
Size: 4" (10 cm.) – 8" (20 cm.)

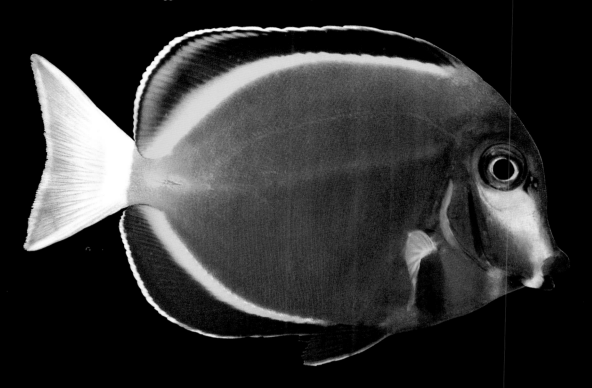

FAM: Acanthuridae
Acanthurus leucosternon
Powder Blue Tang

**General
Aggression**

**Color
Maintenance**

**Dietary
Requirements**

**Con-Species
Compatibility**

Collected: Indonesia
Aquarium: Reef (Caution)
Survivability: Moderate
Size: 4" (10 cm.) – 8" (20 cm.)

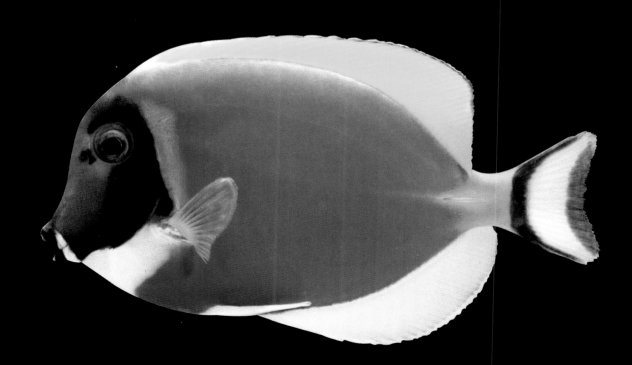

27

FAM: Acanthuridae
Acanthurus lineatus
Clown Surgeonfish

General
Aggression

Color
Maintenance

Dietary
Requirements

Con-Species
Compatibility

Collected: Indonesia
Aquarium: Reef (Caution)
Survivability: Moderate
Size: 4" (10 cm.) – 8" (20 cm.)

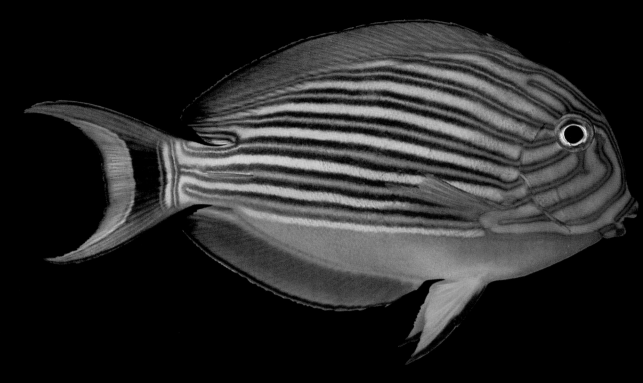

FAM: Acanthuridae
Acanthurus olivaceus
Orange-shoulder Surgeonfish

General
Aggression

Color
Maintenance

Dietary
Requirements

Con-Species
Compatibility

Collected: Philippines
Aquarium: Reef (Caution)
Survivability: Moderate
Size: 4" (10 cm.) – 8" (20 cm

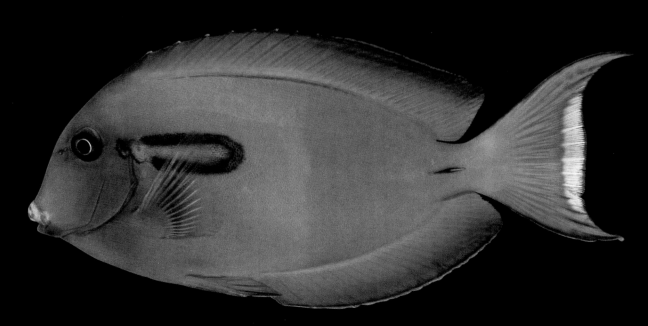

FAM: Acanthuridae
Acanthurus pyroferus (Gold)
Mimic Tang (Gold)
FORM: Juvenile

General
Aggression

Color
Maintenance

Dietary
Requirements

Con-Species
Compatibility

Collected: Indonesia
Aquarium: Reef (Caution)
Survivability: Moderate
Size: 4" (10 cm) – 8" (20 cm)

FAM: Acanthuridae
Acanthurus pyroferus (Half Black)
Mimic Tang (Half Black)
FORM: Juvenile

General
Aggression

Color
Maintenance

Dietary
Requirements

Con-Species
Compatibility

Collected: Indonesia
Aquarium: Reef (Caution)
Survivability: Moderate
Size: 4" (10 cm) – 8" (20 cm)

FAM: Acanthuridae
Acanthurus pyroferus (Yellow)
Mimic Tang (Yellow)
FORM: Juvenile

General Aggression | **Color Maintenance** | **Dietary Requirements** | **Con-Species Compatibility**

Collected: Indonesia
Aquarium: Reef (Caution)
Survivability: Moderate
Size: 4" (10 cm.) – 8" (20 cm.)

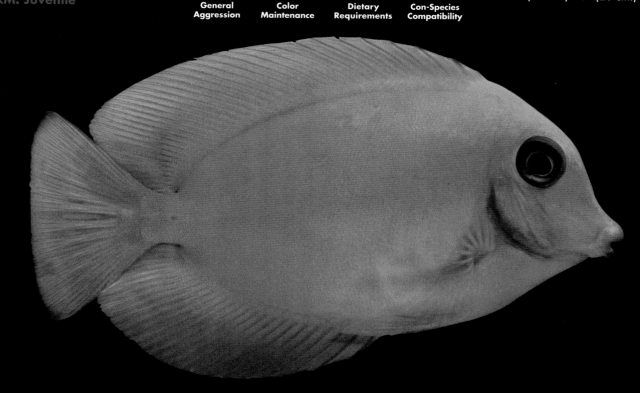

FAM: Acanthuridae
Acanthurus triostegus
Convict Tang

General Aggression | **Color Maintenance** | **Dietary Requirements** | **Con-Species Compatibility**

Collected: Indonesia
Aquarium: Reef (Caution)
Survivability: Easy
Size: 4" (10 cm.) – 8" (20 cm.)

FAM: Acanthuridae
Naso lituratus
Naso Tang

**General
Aggression**

**Color
Maintenance**

**Dietary
Requirements**

**Con-Species
Compatibility**

Collected: Philippines
Aquarium: Reef
Survivability:Easy
Size: More than 8" (20 cm)

 FAM: Acanthuridae
Naso lituratus (Blonde)
Blonde Naso Tang

**General
Aggression**

**Color
Maintenance**

**Dietary
Requirements**

**Con-Species
Compatibility**

Collected: Indonesia
Aquarium: Reef
Survivability: Moderate
Size: More than 8" (20 cm)

31

FAM: Acanthuridae
Paracanthurus hepatus
Blue Tang

General
Aggression

Color
Maintenance

Dietary
Requirements

Con-Species
Compatibility

Collected: Indonesia
Aquarium: Reef
Survivability: Easy
Size: 4" (10 cm) – 8" (20 cm)

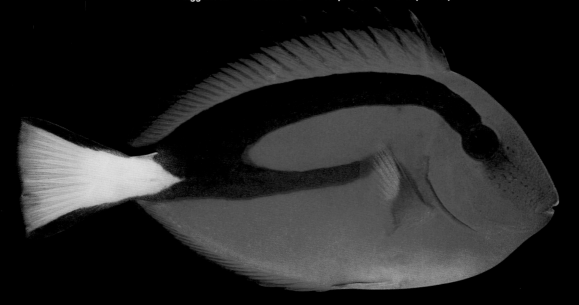

FAM: Acanthuridae
Zebrasoma scopas
Brown Tang

General
Aggression

Color
Maintenance

Dietary
Requirements

Con-Species
Compatibility

Collected: Indonesia
Aquarium: Reef
Survivability: Easy
Size: 4" (10 cm) – 8" (20 cm)

Family: Anomalopidae

(Flashlightfish) This deep-water fish is adapted to low-light conditions and has light-producing organs beneath the eyes. The light from these organs flash intermittently. They are not particularly attractive, but when a group of these fish is kept in a dark tank the blinking displays resemble a field full of fiereflies on a summer night.

(Famille: Anomalopidae) Ces poissons vivant en eau profonde se sont adaptés à des conditions de lumière tr réduite, ils ont développé des organes spécifiques, placés sous les yeux, qui produisent de la lumière. Ces poissons, en eux mêmes, ne sont pas particulièrement attirants mais lorsque le groupe se trouve dans un aquarium sombre, le spectacle ressemble à un champ rempli de lucioles par une nuit d'été.

(Pez Linterna) Estos peces de aguas profundas se encuentran adaptados a condiciones de poca iluminación y poseen órganos productores de luz debajo de su ojos. Estos peces no resultan especialmente atractivos, per si se mantiene un grupo de ellos en un tanque a oscuras, la muestra asemeja un prado lleno de luciérnagas en una noche de verano.

(Peixe Lanterna) Estes peixes de águas profundas estão adaptados a condições de pouca luminosidade e têm órgãos produtores de luz sob seus olhos. Os peixes eles mesmos não são particularmente atraentes, mas quando um grupo é mantido num tanque escuro, o espetáculo assemelha-se a um campo cheio de vaga-lumes numa noite de verão.

(Famiglia: Anomalopidae) Questi pesci originari delle grandi profondità richiedono condizioni di scarsa luminosità e possiedono degli organi, sotto gli occhi, che producono luce fredda. Questi pesci non sono particolarmente attraenti, ma quando se ne mantiene un gruppo in un acquario poco illuminato, l'effetto può essere paragonato a un campo pieno di lucciole in una bella notte d'estate.

FAM: Anomalopidae
Anomalops katoptron
Flashlightfish

General Aggression

Color Maintenance

Dietary Requirements

Con-Species Compatibility

Collected: Philippines
Aquarium: Reef
Survivability: Difficult
Size: 4" (10 cm) – 8" (20 cm)

Family: Antennaridae

(Frogfishes) Members of the *Antennaridae* family are masters of disguise and deception. They take on the appearance of sponges, corals or rocks in their environment, and many attract their prey with artificial lures. Most species in this family have a "lure," mounted on a stalk, that looks like a worm or crustacean in front of their mouth. This bait is waved back and forth so that it seems to be alive. Members of the *Antennaridae* family have large mouths and stomachs, and can swallow very large fishes in relation to their size. Therefore, they should be kept with fishes of their own size or larger.

Another interesting characterisitic of these fishes are their pectoral fins that are shaped like hands. Using both pectoral and pelvic fins, they can crawl around effectively, but are poor swimmers. Also unlike other fishes, members of the *Antennaridae* family don't have large gill openings. They have small openings below their pectoral fins so that they can breath without being detected by their prey or being hunted by a predator. Frogfishes are easy to keep when provided with live fishes as food.

(Famille: Antennaridae) Les membres de la famille des *Antennaridae* sont maîtres du déguisement et de illusion. Ils prennent l'aspect des éponges, du corail ou des pierres les environnant et attirent leur proie omme un pêcheur avec un appât artificiel ! Grâce à leurs caractéristiques de caméléon, il est très ossible que de nombreuses variétés proposées soient en fait la même espèce. La plupart des individus le cette famille possèdent un «appât», ressemblant à un ver ou à un crustacé, monté sur un bâtonnet et lacé devant leur bouche. Le poisson agite cet appât de manière à ce qu'il paraisse nager et happe tout ndividu ayant eu le malheur de s'intéresser à ce leurre. Les membres de la famille des *Antennaridae* ont ne bouche et un estomac très extensibles et peuvent avaler de très gros poissons par rapport à leur ropre taille; ils devront donc être placés avec des poissons d'une taille au moins équivalente.

Leur nageoire pectorale en forme de main est une autre caractéristique intéressante de ces oissons. Ce sont de bien piètres nageurs, mais grâce à leurs nageoires pectorales et pelviennes, ils euvent très bien ramper sur le sol. A l'inverse des autres poissons, les membres de cette famille n'ont as de grandes ouvertures pour les ouïes, mais de petits orifices situés sous leurs nageoires pectorales, e qui leur permet de respirer sans être détectés par leur proie potentielle ou sans être poursuivis par n prédateur. En ce qui concerne la maintenance, ils sont faciles à garder lorsqu'on les nourrit de oissons vivants.

(Pez Piedra) Los miembros de la familia Antennaridae son maestros del encubrimiento y de la ecepción. Estos peces asumen la forma de esponjas, corales o rocas en su medio ambiente y atraen a us presas con cebos artificiales. Debido a atributos de tipo camaleón, es muy posible que muchas de as especies actualmente detectadas sean en realidad una sola especie. La mayoría de las especies de sta familia poseen un "cebo" que se parece a un gusano o crustáceo en la parte anterior de sus bocas, nontado sobre una vara. Esta "carnada" se mueve de un lado hacia el otro de forma tal que parece ue esta nadando. Los miembros de la familia Antennaridae poseen bocas y estómagos muy grandes y ueden tragarse peces muy grandes en comparación con su tamaño y, por tanto, deben mantenerse unto a peces de su mismo tamaño o más grandes.

Otra característica interesante de estos peces son sus aletas pectorales en forma de manos. Utilizando anto las aletas pectorales como las pélvicas, estos peces pueden arrastrarse efectivamente pero son nalos nadadores. También a diferencia de otros peces, los miembros de la familia Antennaridae no ienen grandes aperturas de agallas. Poseen pequeñas aperturas debajo de sus aletas pectorales para oder respirar sin ser detectados por su presa o ser cazados por un predator. Los peces piedra son áciles de mantener en acuario cuando se les proporciona peces vivos como alimento.\

Family: Antennaridae

(Família: Antennaridae) Os membros da família *Antennaridae* são mestres do disfarce e da ilusão. Tomam a aparência de esponjas, corais ou rochas em seu meio ambiente e atraem suas presas com chamarizes artificiais. Devido aos seus atributos, semelhantes aos do camaleão, é bem possível que as muitas variedades disponíveis sejam na verdade uma única espécie. A maioria das espécies nesta família têm um chamariz que se parece com um verme ou crustáceo em frente à sua boca, fixado em uma haste. Esta isca é movimentada de um lado para o outro de modo que pareça estar nadando. Os membros da família *Antennaridae* têm bocas e estômagos grandes e podem engolir peixes muito grandes em relação aos seus tamanhos, devendo, portanto ser mantidos com peixes de seu tamanho ou maiores.

Outra característica interessante desses peixes são suas barbatanas peitorais em forma de mãos. Usando ambas as barbatanas peitorais e pélvicas, eles podem se arrastar com eficiência, mas são maus nadadores. Diferentemente de outros peixes, os membros da família *Antennaridae* não têm grandes aberturas das guelras. Têm pequenas aberturas sob suas barbatanas peitorais, de modo que possam respirar sem serem detectados por sua presa ou caçados por um predador. Os peixes-pescadores são fáceis de manter quando supridos com peixe vivo como alimento.

(Famiglia: Antennaridae) I membri della famiglia Antennaridae sono maestri nel mimetismo e nell'inganno. Assumono le fattezze di spugne, coralli o pietre tipiche del loro ambiente e attirano le loro prede con esche fittizie. E' molto probabile che, a causa delle capacità camaleontiche, le molte varietà finora conosciute appartengano in realtà a un numero limitato di specie. La maggior parte dei pesci di questa famiglia possiede "un'esca" che assomiglia a un verme o un crostaceo nella parte anteriore della bocca, in cima a una sottile protuberanza. Questa esca viene agitata in avanti e in dietro in modo da simulare il nuoto. Gli Antennaridae hanno bocca e stomaco grandi e possono inghiottire prede molto grandi rispetto alle loro dimensioni. Per questo motivo, è consigliabile mantenerli con pesci della stessa taglia o, meglio, con esemplari più grandi.

Un'altra caratteristica interessante di questi pesci è che le loro pinne pettorali assomigliano a delle mani. Utilizzando le pinne pettorali e quelle ventrali, riescono a spostarsi sul fondo trascinandosi, ma sono cattivi nuotatori. Diversamente da altri pesci, gli Antennaridae non hanno grandi opercoli branchiali, ma possiedono piccole aperture sotto le pinne pettorali in modo da respirare senza essere notati dalle loro prede o divenire a loro volta facili bersagli. I "pesci pescatori" sono semplici da allevare e vengono nutriti con pesci vivi.

FAM: Antennaridae
Antennarius commersoni (Green Marble)
Green Marble Frogfish

General
Aggression

Color
Maintenance

Dietary
Requirements

Con-Species
Compatibility

Collected: Philippines
Aquarium: Non-Reef
Survivability: Moderate
Size: Less than 4" (10

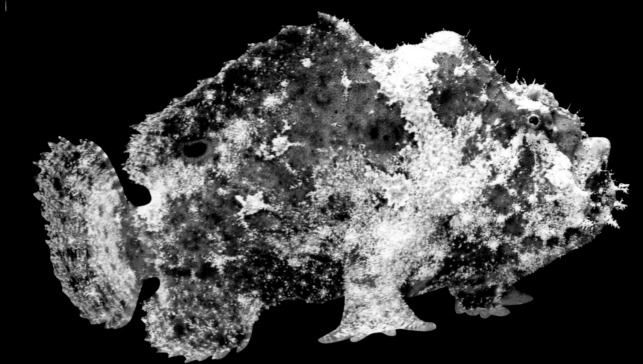

FAM: Antennaridae
Antennarius commersoni (Yellow)
Yellow Frogfish

General
Aggression

Color
Maintenance

Dietary
Requirements

Con-Species
Compatibility

Collected: Philippines
Aquarium: Non-Reef
Survivability: Moderate
Size: 4" (10 cm.) – 8" (20 cr

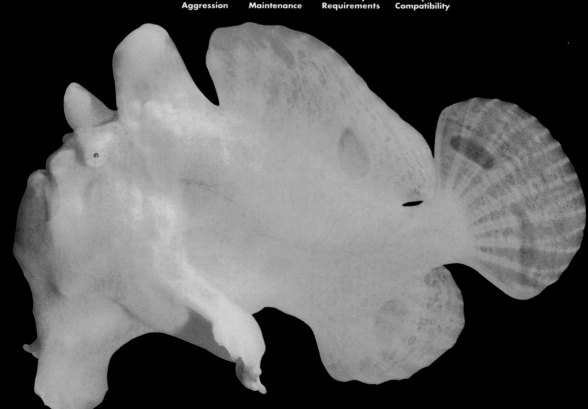

FAM: Antennaridae
Antennarius maculatus (White)
White Wartskin Frogfish

General
Aggression

Color
Maintenance

Dietary
Requirements

Con-Species
Compatibility

Collected: Philippines
Aquarium: Non-Reef
Survivability: Moderate
Size: 4" (10 cm.) – 8" (20 cm.)

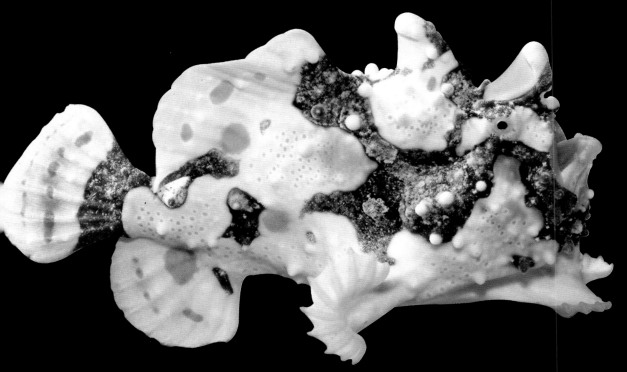

FAM: Antennaridae
Antennarius maculatus (Yellow)
Yellow Wartskin Frogfish

General
Aggression

Color
Maintenance

Dietary
Requirements

Con-Species
Compatibility

Collected: Indonesia
Aquarium: Non-Reef
Survivability: Moderate
Size: 4" (10 cm.) – 8" (20 cm.)

39

FAM: Antennaridae
Antennarius sp. "Mustard"*
Mustard Frogfish

General Aggression

Color Maintenance

Dietary Requirements

Con-Species Compatibility

Collected: Philippines
Aquarium: Non-Reef
Survivability: Moderate
Size: 4" (10 cm.) – 8" (20 cm.)

FAM: Antennaridae
Antennarius sp. "Redhead Dwarf"*
Redhead Dwarf Frogfish

General Aggression

Color Maintenance

Dietary Requirements

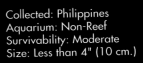

Con-Species Compatibility

Collected: Philippines
Aquarium: Non-Reef
Survivability: Moderate
Size: Less than 4" (10 cm.)

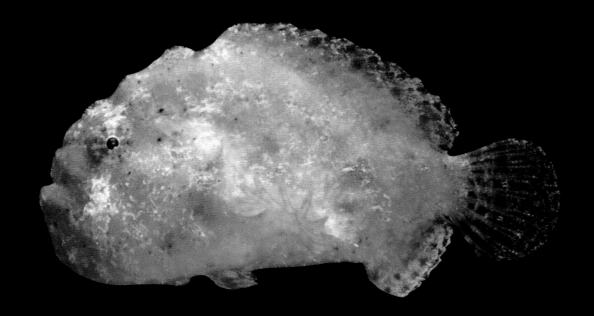

40

FAM: Apogonidae
Apogon melas
Black Cardinalfish

**General
Aggression**   **Color
Maintenance**   **Dietary
Requirements**   **Con-Species
Compatibility**

Collected: Philippines
Aquarium: Reef
Survivability: Moderate
Size: Less than 4" (10 cm)

FAM: Apogonidae
Apogon talboti
Talbot's Cardinalfish

**General
Aggression**   **Color
Maintenance**   **Dietary
Requirements**   **Con-Species
Compatibility**

Collected: Philippines
Aquarium: Reef
Survivability: Moderate
Size: Less than 4" (10 cm)

45

FAM: Apogonidae
Pseudamia amblyuroptera
False-eye Cardinalfish

General Aggression **Color Maintenance** **Dietary Requirements** **Con-Species Compatibility**

Collected: Philippines
Aquarium: Reef
Survivability: Moderate
Size: Less than 4" (10 cm)

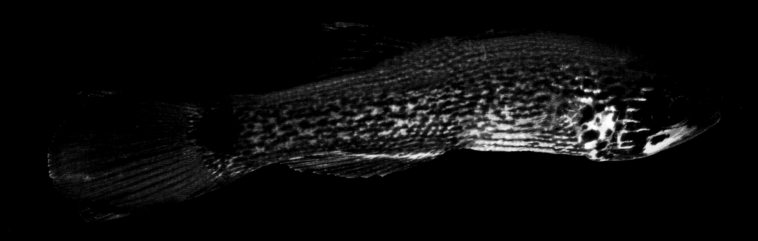

FAM: Apogonidae
Pterapogon kauderni
Milky Way Cardinalfish

General Aggression **Color Maintenance** **Dietary Requirements** **Con-Species Compatibility**

Collected: Indonesia
Aquarium: Reef
Survivability: Easy
Size: Less than 4" (10 cm)

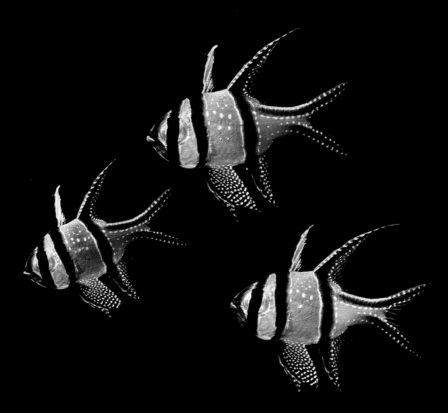

46

FAM: Apogonidae
Sphaeramia nematoptera
Pajama Cardinalfish

General Aggression Color Maintenance Dietary Requirements Con-Species Compatibility

Aquarium: Reef
Survivability: Easy
Size: Less than 4" (10 cm)

FAM: Apogonidae
Sphaeramia orbicularis
Orbiculate Cardinalfish

   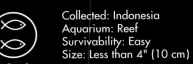

General Aggression Color Maintenance Dietary Requirements Con-Species Compatibility

Collected: Indonesia
Aquarium: Reef
Survivability: Easy
Size: Less than 4" (10 cm)

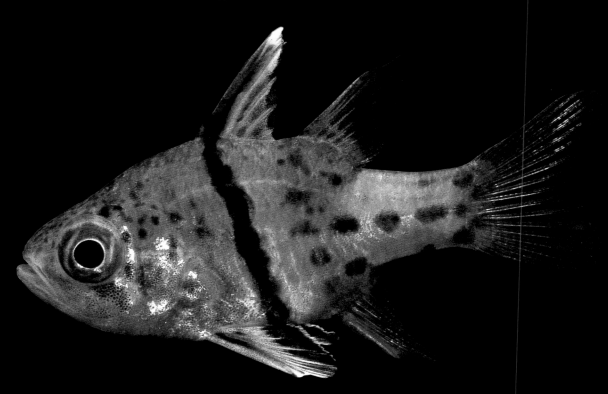

Family: Balistidae

(Triggerfishes) Members of the family Balistidae have some distinctive traits. One odd characteristic is the ability to produce sound when they are out of the water. Another interesting trait is their divided, spine-like front dorsal fin. The front dorsal fin of the fishes in this family is divided by multiple spines; including a larger front spine and a less prominent rear spine. The rear spine serves as a controlling mechanism for the front spine. In essence, the smaller spine is a "trigger" whose position controls its larger counterpart. Hence the name "Triggerfish."

These fishes use the spiny dorsal fin to wedge themselves into crevices so that they cannot be taken or eaten. Triggerfishes have tough, leathery hides sporting fine scales. They are extremely hardy and are recommended for the beginning hobbyist.

A warning to unsuspecting aquarists: Members of the Balistidae family can bite when handled! They have very sharp teeth which — in the wild — are used to break sea urchins, starfishes or crabs. They blow sea urchins and starfishes upside-down to expose their soft underbellies. Triggerfishes (along with their relatives in the Monocanthidae family (Filefishes) have a distinctive, undulating motion when swimming. This is because they lack a pelvic fin and instead use their second dorsal and anal fins to swim.

In an aquarium situation, these fishes are very aggressive. The species best known for aggression is the *Balistapus undulatus* (Undulated Triggerfish). The least aggressive is the *Odonus niger* (Niger Triggerfish).

(Famille: Balistidae) Les individus de la famille des Balistidae possèdent certaines caractéristiques remarquables, dont celle de produire un son lorsqu'ils se trouvent hors de l'eau. Leur système de nageoire dorsale avant, divisée en de multiples rayons épineux autoblocants est également remarquable. L'épine arrière, moins proéminente, sert de mécanisme de contrôle à l'épine avant, plus large et érectile. L'épine la plus petite sert essentiellement de «gâchette» dont l'angle contrôle la position de l'épine la plus grande. Ces poissons utilisent ce système de verrouillage pour se bloquer dans des crevasses et éviter ainsi d'être capturés ou dévorés. Les membres de la famille des Balistidae ont des peaux robustes faites de fines écailles, ressemblant à du cuir ; ils sont extrêmement résistants et recommandés aux aquariophiles débutants.

Un avertissement à l'aquariophile sans méfiance : ces poissons peuvent mordre lorsqu'on les manipule ! Ils ont en effet des dents très pointues qu'ils utilisent dans leur habitat naturel pour casser les oursins, les étoiles de mer ou les crabes. Ils soufflent sur les oursins et les étoiles de mer pour les retourner et exposer leur parties non protégées. Parce qu'ils leur manque une nageoire pelvienne et qu'ils utilisent leur deuxième nageoire dorsale et anale pour nager, les membres de la famille des Balistidae et leurs cousins, les Monocanthidae, ont un mouvement ondulatoire très particulier lorsqu'ils nagent.

En aquarium, ces poissons peuvent être très agressifs. L'espèce la plus connue pour son agressivité est le *Balistapus undulatus*. La moins agressive est l'*Odonus niger*.

Family: Balistidae

(Pez Ballesta) La familia Balistidae (Pez Ballesta) poseen algunas características distintivas. Una característica es la habilidad de producir sonidos cuando se encuentran dentro y fuera del agua. Otra característica interesante es su aleta dorsal anterior dividida en varia secciones. La aleta dorsal anterior de los peces de esta familia esta dividida por varias espinas, entre ellas una espina anterior mas grande y una espina posterior menos prominente. La espina posterior sirve de mecanismo de control para la espina anterior. En esencia, la espina más pequeña es un "gatillo" cuya posición controla su contraparte más grande. Estos peces usan sus aletas espinosas para insertarse dentro de grietas para evitar ser apresados y comidos. Los miembros de la familia Balistidae poseen un piel dura, tipo cuero, con escamas finas. Los ejemplares de esta especie son extremadamente fuertes y recomendables para el aficionado principiante.

¡Una advertencia a los aficionados ingenuos de acuarios: los miembros de la familia Balistidae pueden morder cuando se manipulan! Estos peces poseen dientes muy afilados que en su ambiente natural utilizan para quebrar erizos de mar, estrellas de mar o cangrejos. Ellos soplan contra los erizos de mar y estrellas de mar para virarlos boca arriba para exponer la parte inferior suave de sus cuerpos. Los miembros de la familia Balistidae (Pez Ballesta), conjuntamente con sus parientes de la familia Monocanthidae, presentan un movimiento ondulatorio distintivo cuando nadan. Esto es porque carecen de aleta pélvica y, en su lugar, emplean su segunda aleta dorsal y las aletas anales para nadar.

En una pecera, estos peces son muy agresivos. La especie mejor conocida por su agresividad es la Balistapus undulatus (Ballesta Ondulada). La menos agresiva es la Odonus Niger (Ballesta Niger).

(Peixes-Gatilho) Os peixes da família *Balistidae* (Peixes-Gatilho) têm algumas características peculiares. Uma delas é a habilidade de produzir som quando estão fora d'água. Outra característica interessante é sua barbatana dorsal frontal em forma de espinha e dividida. A barbatana dorsal frontal dos peixes dessa família é dividida em múltiplas espinhas; incluindo uma espinha frontal maior e uma espinha traseira menos saliente. A espinha traseira funciona como um mecanismo de controle da espinha frontal. Em resumo, a espinha menor é o "gatilho" cuja posição controla sua contraparte maior. Esses peixes usam suas barbatanas espinhosas para se introduzirem em frestas, de modo que não possam ser apanhados ou devorados. Os membros da família *Balistidae* têm pele de couro resistente ostentando finas escamas. São extremamente resistentes, sendo recomendados para os iniciantes.

Um aviso para os aquaristas confiantes: os membros da família *Balistidae* podem morder quando manuseados! Eles têm dentes muito afiados que, na vida selvagem, são usados para quebrar ouriços-do-mar, estrelas-do-mar ou caranguejos. Eles viram ouriços-do-mar e estrelas-do-mar de cabeça para baixo para expor seus macios ventres inferiores. Os Balistidae (Peixes Gatilho), juntamente com seus parentes da família Monocanthidae, têm um movimento ondulatório característico quando estão nadando. Isto é porque lhes falta uma barbatana pélvica e em substituição usam sua segunda barbatana dorsal e anal para nadar. Em um ambiente de aquário, esses peixes são muito agressivos. A espécie mais conhecida por ser agressiva é a *Balistapus undulatus* (Peixe-Gatilho Ondulado). A menos agressiva é a *Odonus niger* (Peixe-Gatilho Niger).

Family: Balistidae

(Famiglia: Balistidae) I membri della famiglia Balistidae presentano alcune caratteristiche molto particolari. Una è la capacità di produrre suoni quando si trovano fuori dall'acqua. Un altro aspetto interessante è la pinna dorsale, la cui parte anteriore è trasformata in un grande aculeo. La parte posteriore della dorsale è sorretta da numerosi raggi, ma è meno prominente della parte anteriore. Nella parte anteriore esiste un meccanismo costituito da diversi raggi che controlla la posizione dell'aculeo a mo' di "grilletto", da qui il nome comune "pesce balestra". Questi pesci utilizzano i loro aculei per incastrarsi nelle fessure in modo da non essere catturati. I membri della famiglia Balistidae hanno una pelle dura con squame sottili. Sono molto robusti e sono molto indicati per l'acquariofilo principiante.

Un'avvertenza per l'acquariofilo incauto: i membri della famiglia Balistidae possono mordere quando vengono maneggiati! Hanno denti molto affilati che, nell'ambiente naturale, sono utilizzati per rompere i ricci, le stelle marine o i granchi. Soffiando e sollevando della sabbia i pesci balestra riescono a capovolgere ricci e stelle marine attaccando poi la parte soffice del loro ventre. I Balistidae insieme ai loro parenti della famiglia Monacanthidae si distinguono per un movimento ondulatorio del corpo quando nuotano. Questo dipende dal fatto che mancando le pinne ventrali, trasformate in un aculeo, utilizzano la seconda parte della pinna dorsale e l'anale per nuotare. In acquario questi pesci sono assai aggressivi. La specie più bellicosa è *Balistapus undulatus*, quella più pacifica *Odonus niger*.

FAM: Balistidae
Balistapus undulatus
Undulated Triggerfish

General Aggression

Color Maintenance

Dietary Requirements

Con-Species Compatibility

Collected: Philippines
Aquarium: Non-Reef
Survivability: Easy
Size: More than 8" (20 cm)

FAM: Balistidae
Balistoides conspicillum
Clown Triggerfish

General Aggression

Color Maintenance

Dietary Requirements

Con-Species Compatibility

Collected: Philippines
Aquarium: Non-Reef
Survivability: Easy
Size: More than 8" (20 cm)

FAM: Balistidae
Melichthys niger
Black Durgeon Triggerfish

General Aggression

Color Maintenance

Dietary Requirements

Con-Species Compatibility

Collected: Philippines
Aquarium: Non-Reef
Survivability: Easy
Size: More than 8" (20 cm)

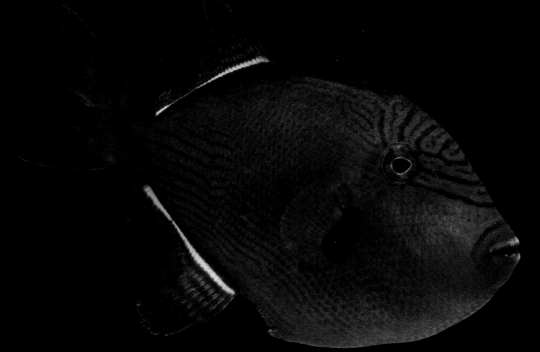

FAM: Balistidae
Melichthys vidua
Pinktail Triggerfish

General Aggression

Color Maintenance

Dietary Requirements

Con-Species Compatibility

Collected: Philippines
Aquarium: Non-Reef
Survivability: Easy
Size: More than 8" (20 cm)

54

Family: Batrachoididae*

(Pacific Toadfish) Although it is interestingly shaped, this fish is not common in the Marine Aquarium trade because of its lack of spectacular color. According to Richard Pyle of the *Bishop Museum*, Honolulu, this family of fishes (Batrachoididae) is under revision. Therefore, the genus (and needless to say the species) of the members of this family is not formally known as of 1996.

(Famille: Batrachoididae) Bien que sa forme soit intéressante, ce poisson n'est pas courant dans le commerce de l'aquariophilie marine parce qu'il manque de couleur spectaculaire. D'après Richard Pyle du Musée Bishop, à Honolulu, cette famille de poissons (les *Batrachoididae*) est en cours de révision. Le genre (et cela va sans dire l'espèce) des membres de cette famille n'est donc pas officiellement connue en 1996.

(Pez Sapo) Aunque posee una forma muy interesante, este pez no es común en el comercio de acuario marino debido a su carencia de un colorido espectacular. Según Richard Pyle del Museo "Bishop" en Honolulú, esta familia de peces (Batrachoididae) se encuentra sujeta a revisión. Por consiguiente, el género (y huelga decir, las especies) de los miembros de esta familia aún no han sido formalmente reconocida hasta la fecha (1996).

(Peixe-Sapo) Apesar de seu formato interessante, este peixe não é comum no comércio de Aquários Marinhos, devido à sua falta de cores espetaculares. De acordo com Richard Pyle do *Bishop Museum*, Honolulu, essa família de peixes (Batrachoididae) está sob revisão. Portanto, o gênero (e desnecessário dizer a espécie) dos membros dessa família não é formalmente conhecido em 1996.

(Famiglia: Batrachoididae) Benché abbia una forma interessante, questo pesce si trova raramente sul mercato acquariofilo a causa della livrea poco spettacolare. Secondo Richard Pyle del Museo Bishop a Honolulu, la classificazione di questa famiglia è sotto revisione. Per questo motivo, il numero dei generi (e certamente anche delle specie) di questa famiglia a tutt'oggi non è noto con precisione.

FAM: Batrachoididae*
Batrachoididae (Pacific Toadfish)*
Pacific Toadfish

General
Aggression

 Color
Maintenance

 Dietary
Requirements

 Con-Species
Compatibility

Collected: Philippines
Aquarium: Non-Reef
Survivability: Easy
Size: More than 8" (20 cm)

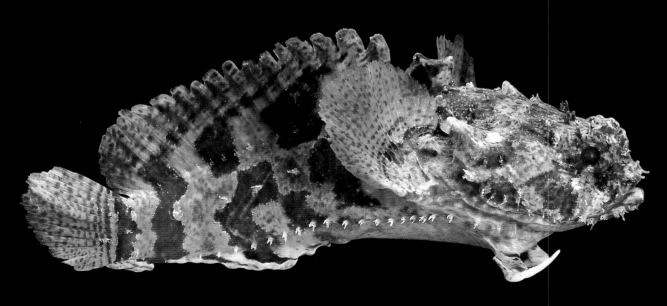

Family: Blenniidae

(Blennies) Species in the family Blenniidae are small fishes which use their pelvic fin to rest on rocks. They have a continuous dorsal and anal fin and an elongated body. Their heads are generally blunt with 2 bristle-like structures over the eyes called *cirri*. These are active fishes among which territorial disputes are quite common. A species to watch out for is the *Aspidontus taeniatus*, which masquerades as a *Labroides dimidiatus* (Cleaner Wrasse) and takes a bite out of unsuspecting victims. They have the potential of doing a lot of harm in an aquarium. Blenniidae are easy to feed and ideal subjects for a reef aquarium.

(Famille: Blenniidae) La famille des Blenniidae est constituée de petits poissons qui utilisent souvent leurs nageoires pelviennes pour se reposer sur les rochers. Leurs nageoires dorsales et anales sont continues et leur corps est allongé. La tête, en général carrée, porte au dessus des yeux deux éléments appelés *cirri* ressemblant à des poils. Ce sont des poissons actifs chez lesquels les disputes territoriales se produisent fréquemment. Une espèce à surveiller, l'*Aspidontus taeniatus*, dont la robe est très proche du *Labroides dimidiatus* (poisson infirmier) déchiquette ses victimes venues là en toute confiance. On distingue cette espèce par sa bouche située non pas dans le prolongement du corps, mais légèrement en dessous de la ligne centrale noire. Les Blenniidae sont faciles à nourrir et sont des spécimens idéaux pour un aquarium récifal.

(Pez Blenio) La familia Blenniidae son peces pequeños que utilizan su aleta pélvica para descansar sobre rocas. Poseen una aleta dorsal y anal continua y un cuerpo elongado. Sus cabezas son generalmente redondas con dos estructuras parecidas a cerdas de cepillos sobre los ojos llamadas "cirri". Estos son peces activos entre los cuales son bastante comunes las disputas territoriales. Una especie que vigilar es la *Aspidontus taeniatus*, que se disfraza de *Labroides dimidiatus* (Labro Limpiador) y muerde sus víctimas ingenuas. Estos peces potencialmente pueden hacer mucho daño en una pecera. Los miembros de la familia Blenniidae son fáciles de alimentar y sujetos ideales para una pecera de arrecife.

(Blênios) A família Blenniidae é constituída de peixes pequenos que usam sua barbatana pélvica para descansar nas rochas. Eles têm uma barbatana dorsal e anal contínua e um corpo alongado. Suas cabeças são geralmente ásperas com duas estruturas semelhantes a cerdas sobre os olhos chamadas cirro. Estes são peixes ativos entre os quais as disputas territoriais são bastante comuns. Uma espécie para ficar atento é a *Aspidontus taeniatus*, que se disfarça como a *Labroides dimidiatus* (Labros Limpador) e morde vítimas confiantes. Eles têm a capacidade de causar muito dano em um aquário. Os Blenniidae são fáceis de alimentar e ideais para um aquário de recife.

(Famiglia: Blenniidae) La famiglia Blenniidae è composta da pesciolini che utilizzano le pinne ventrali per riposarsi su rocce e sassi. Il loro corpo è allungato e sia la pinna ventrale sia quella anale non presentano interruzioni. Generalmente la testa ha forma affusolata con due protuberanze, ritte sopra gli occhi, chiamate cirri. Sono pesci attivi, tra i quali le liti territoriali sono molto comuni. Una specie da controllare accuratamente è Aspidontus taeniatus, che si camuffa in modo da risultare simile a *Labroides dimidiatus* e quindi morde le vittime ignare. Questo pesce può provocare molti danni in acquario. I Blennidi sono facili da nutrire e sono ospiti ideali per un acquario da barriera.

FAM: Blenniidae
Aspidontus taeniatus
Mimic Cleaner Wrasse Blenny

General Aggression

Color Maintenance

Dietary Requirements

Con-Species Compatibility

Collected: Philippines
Aquarium: Non-Reef
Survivability: Moderate
Size: Less than 4" (10 cm.)

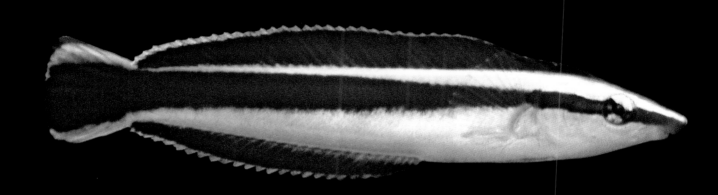

FAM: Blenniidae
Atrosalarias fuscus (Black)*
High-finned Blenny

General Aggression

Color Maintenance

Dietary Requirements

Con-Species Compatibility

Collected: Indonesia
Aquarium: Reef
Survivability: Easy
Size: Less than 4" (10 cm.)

61

FAM: Blenniidae
Atrosalarias fuscus (Yellow)*
High-finned Blenny (Yellow)

General Aggression

Color Maintenance

Dietary Requirements

Con-Species Compatibility

Collected: Indonesia
Aquarium: Reef
Survivability: Easy
Size: Less than 4" (10 cm.)

FAM: Blenniidae
Blenniid sp. "Blue Midas"*
Midas Blenny (Blue)

General Aggression

Color Maintenance

Dietary Requirements

Con-Species Compatibility

Collected: Indonesia
Aquarium: Reef
Survivability: Easy
Size: Less than 4" (10 cm.)

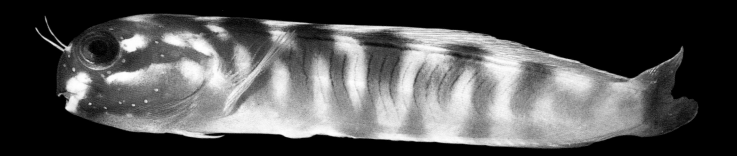

FAM: Blenniidae
Blenniid **sp. "Gold & White"***
Gold & White Blenny

General
Aggression

Color
Maintenance

Dietary
Requirements

Con-Species
Compatibility

Collected: Indonesia
Aquarium: Reef
Survivability: Easy
Size: Less than 4" (10 cm)

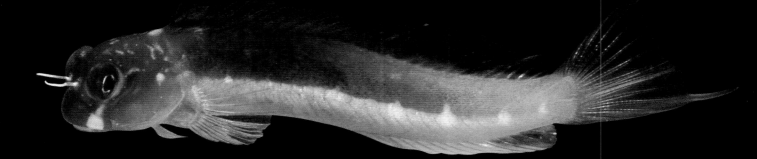

FAM: Blenniidae
Blenniid **sp. "Striped"***
Striped Blenny

General
Aggression

Color
Maintenance

Dietary
Requirements

Con-Species
Compatibility

Collected: Indonesia
Aquarium: Reef
Survivability: Easy
Size: Less than 4" (10 cm)

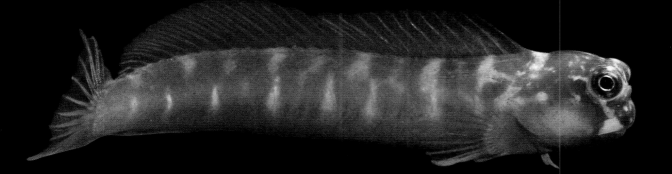

63

FAM: Blenniidae
Ecsenius bicolor
Bicolor Blenny

General
Aggression

Color
Maintenance

Dietary
Requirements

Con-Species
Compatibility

Collected: Philippines
Aquarium: Reef
Survivability: Easy
Size: Less than 4" (10 cm.)

FAM: Blenniidae
Ecsenius midas
Midas Blenny (Yellow)

General
Aggression

Color
Maintenance

Dietary
Requirements

Con-Species
Compatibility

Collected: Indonesia
Aquarium: Reef
Survivability: Easy
Size: Less than 4" (10 cm.)

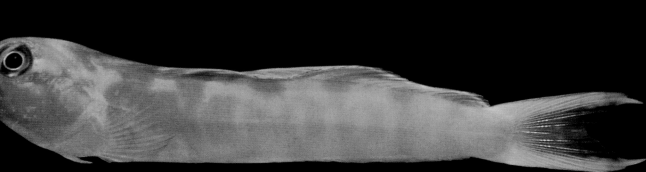

FAM: Blenniidae
Exallias brevis
Leopard Blenny

**General
Aggression**

**Color
Maintenance**

**Dietary
Requirements**

**Con-Species
Compatibility**

Collected: Indonesia
Aquarium: Non-Reef
Survivability: Difficult
Size: Less than 4" (10 cm)

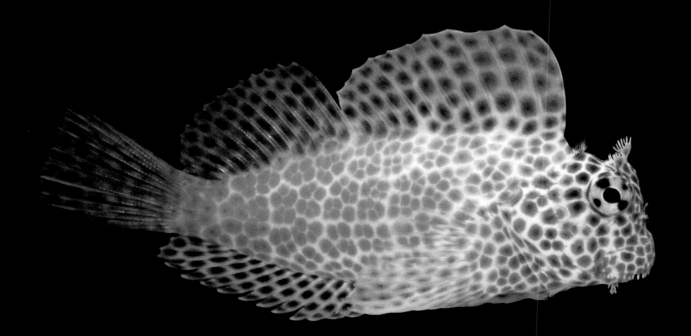

FAM: Blenniidae
Meiacanthus atrodorsalis (Cream)
Poison-fang Blenny (Cream)

**General
Aggression**

**Color
Maintenance**

**Dietary
Requirements**

**Con-Species
Compatibility**

Collected: Philippines
Aquarium: Reef
Survivability: Moderate
Size: Less than 4" (10 cm)

65

FAM: Blenniidae
Meiacanthus atrodorsalis (Yellow)
Poison-fang Blenny (Yellow)

General Aggression

Color Maintenance

Dietary Requirements

Con-Species Compatibility

Collected: Philippines
Aquarium: Reef
Survivability: Moderate
Size: Less than 4" (10 cm

FAM: Blenniidae
Meiacanthus grammistes
Cat Blenny

General Aggression

Color Maintenance

Dietary Requirements

Con-Species Compatibility

Collected: Indonesia
Aquarium: Reef
Survivability: Moderate
Size: Less than 4" (10 cm.)

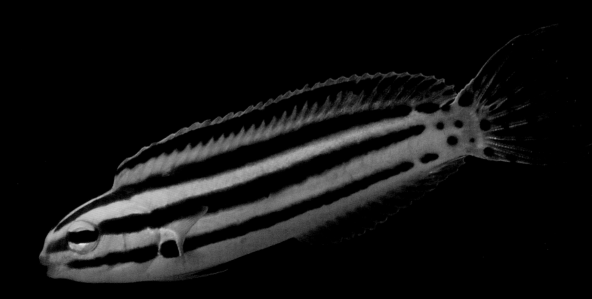

FAM: Blenniidae
Plagiotremus rhinorhynchos
Sabertooth Blenny

General Aggression   Color Maintenance   Dietary Requirements   Con-Species Compatibility

Collected: Indonesia
Aquarium: Non-Reef
Survivability: Easy
Size: Less than 4" (10 cm.)

FAM: Blenniidae
Salarias fasciatus
Striped Sailfin Blenny

General Aggression   Color Maintenance   Dietary Requirements   Con-Species Compatibility

Collected: Philippines
Aquarium: Reef
Survivability: Easy
Size: Less than 4" (10 cm.)

67

Family: Bythitidae

(Knifefishes) Although most people in the aquarium trade refer to this as a "Lycopod Goby" these fishes do not belong in any way to the Family Gobiidae. This is why we are not using the common name "Lycopod Goby" for these fishes. Because it looks like a freshwater knifefish such as the *Apteronotus albifrons* (Black Ghost Knifefish), this is the term we are using.

(Famille: Bythitidae) Bien que la plupart des gens dans le commerce de l'aquariophilie appellent ce poisson le «Goby lycopode», il n'appartient en aucun cas à la famille des Gobiidae. C'est la raison pour laquelle nous n'utilisons pas le nom «Goby lycopode» pour ce poisson. Il ressemble au *Apteronotus albifrons* d'eau douce et c'est pourquoi nous utilisons ce terme.

(Pez Cuchillo o Pez Viuda) Aunque la mayoría de las personas que se dedican al comercio de acuarios se refieren a este ejemplar como un *"Lycopod Goby,"* estos peces no pertenecen de modo alguno a la familia Gobiidae. Dada esta razón, no utilizamos el nombre común de *"Lycopod Goby"* para este pez y ya que se parece al pez cuchillo de agua dulce denominado *Apteronotus albifrons* (Pez Cuchillo Fantasma Negro), éste es el término que utilizaremos.

(Família: Bythitidae) Apesar de a maioria das pessoas no comércio de aquários se referirem a estes peixes como "Gobião Licopódio" eles não pertencem de maneira alguma à Família Gobiidae. É por isso que não estamos usando a denominação comum "Gobião Licopódio" para este peixe. Uma vez que ele se parece com o "knifefish" de água doce, assim como o *Apteronotus albifrons* ("Black Ghost Knifefish"), este é o termo que estamos usando.

(Famiglia: Bythitidae) Benché molti acquariofili si riferiscano a questo pesce come al "ghiozzo licopodio," questi pesci non appartengono affatto alla famiglia dei Gobidi e pertanto non usiamo questo nome comune, ma, assomigliando al pesce coltello di acqua dolce *Apteronotus albifrons*, proponiamo il nome "pesce coltello fantasma."

FAM: Bythitidae
Dinematichthys* sp. "Knife"
Knifefish

General Aggression

Color Maintenance

Dietary Requirements

Con-Species Compatibility

Collected: Philippines
Aquarium: Reef
Survivability: Moderate
Size: 4" (10 cm) – 8" (20 cm)

Family: Callionymidae

(Dragonetfishes) Of the members of the Callionymidae family, the *Synchiropus splendidus* (Mandarin Dragonetfish) is the most spectacular. It should be kept in mind, however, that this species is a poor choice for a community tank, as they are so slow moving that they starve to death when there is competition for food. It is best to keep the Mandarin Dragonetfish in a reef aquarium where they can feed all day long on microorganisms. When threatened, a Mandarin Dragonetfish secretes a mucus that is presumably distasteful and prevents them from being eaten.

(Famille: Callionymidae) Parmi les membres de la famille des Callionymidae, le *Synchiropus splendidus* (poisson-mandarin) est le plus spectaculaire. Il est cependant important de ne pas oublier que c'est un très mauvais choix pour un aquarium communautaire, car il se déplace si lentement qu'il meurt régulièrement de faim lorsqu'il y a compétition pour la nourriture. Il est préférable de garder le *Synchiropus splendidus* dans un aquarium d'invertébrés où il pourra se nourrir de micro-organismes tout au long de la journée. Lorsqu'il se sent menacé, le *Synchiropus splendidus* sécrète un mucus, probablement repoussant, qui lui évite d'être importuné.

(Pez Dragón o Dragoncillo) Entre los miembros de la familia Callionymidae, el *Synchiropus splendidus* (Pez Mandarín) es el más espectacular. Sin embargo, debemos tener presente que resultan una mala selección para un tanque de comunidad, ya que se mueven tan lentamente que se mueren de hambre cuando hay competencia por alimentos. Lo mejor es mantener los *Synchiropus splendidus* (Pez Mandarín) en un acuario de arrecife donde se puedan alimentar todo el día de microorganismos. Cuando amenazados, el *Synchiropus splendidus* (Pez Mandarín) segrega una mucosidad que supuestamente tiene un sabor desagradable e impide que sean comidos por otros peces.

(Peixes Dragonetes) Dos membros da família Callionymidae, o *Synchiropus splendidus* (Peixe-Mandarim) é o mais espetacular. Deve-se ter em mente, entretanto, que eles são uma má escolha para um tanque comunitário, pois se movem tão lentamente que morrem de fome quando há competição por comida. É melhor manter o *Synchiropus splendidus* (Peixe Mandarim) em um aquário de recife onde eles possam se alimentar o dia todo de micro-organismos. Quando ameaçado, um *Synchiropus splendidus* (Peixe Mandarim) secreta um muco que é presumivelmente desagradável e evita que sejam comidos.

(Famiglia: Callionymidae) Dei membri della famiglia Callionymidae, *Synchiropus splendidus* è il più spettacolare. E' necessario ricordare, però, che rappresenta una cattiva scelta per un acquario di comunità, perché questi pesci si muovono tanto lentamente da morire per fame, quando c'è una forte concorrenza alimentare in acquario. E' consigliabile mantenere *Synchiropus splendidus* in un acquario con invertebrati dove possa nutrirsi di microrganismi tutto il giorno. Quando viene minacciato, *Synchiropus splendidus* produce un muco presumibilmente disgustoso che gli consente di evitare di essere divorato.

FAM: Callionymidae
Synchiropus morrisoni
Scooter Dragonetfish

 General Aggression

 Color Maintenance

Dietary Requirements

 Con-Species Compatibility

Collected: Philippines
Aquarium: Reef
Survivability: Difficult
Size: Less than 4" (10 cm.)

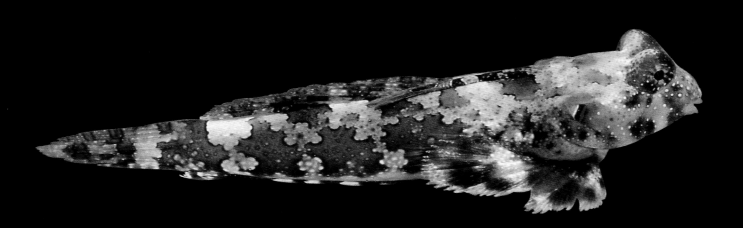

FAM: Callionymidae
Synchiropus picturatus
Spotted Mandarinfish

 General Aggression

 Color Maintenance

Dietary Requirements

 Con-Species Compatibility

Collected: Philippines
Aquarium: Reef
Survivability: Difficult
Size: Less than 4" (10 cm.)

70

FAM: Callionymidae
Synchiropus splendidus
Mandarinfish

General
Aggression

Color
Maintenance

Dietary
Requirements

Con-Species
Compatibility

Collected: Philippines
Aquarium: Reef
Survivability: Difficult
Size: Less than 4" (10 cm)

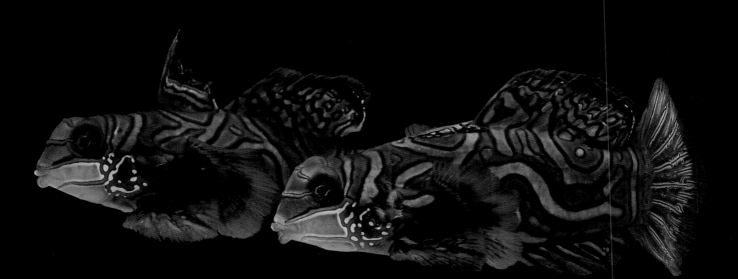

Family: Carangidae

(Trevallys) Members of this group are hardy but not particularly colorful. Therefore, they are not very popular aquarium fishes. Almost all of them can get quite large and —in fact — are considered food fishes in Southeast Asia. Members of the Carangidae family tend to be more colorful when they are juveniles than when they are adults.

(Famille: Carangidae) Ce groupe de poissons est robuste mais pas particulièrement coloré et donc pas particulièrement prisé pour l'aquarium. Considéré comme un « poisson de consommation » en Asie du Sud-Est, les membres de cette famille peuvent devenir assez gros. Les jeunes poissons de la famille des Carangidae ayant tendance à être plus colorés que les adultes, ceux-ci sont généralement vendus dans le commerce de l'aquariophilie sous leur forme juvénile.

(Pez Piloto) Miembros de este grupo son fuertes pero no poseen mucho colorido. Por tanto, no resultan muy populares para peceras. Casi todos pueden crecer hasta un tamaño bastante grande y, de hecho, son considerados pescado de alimento en el Sudeste Asiático. Los miembros de la familia Carangidae tienden a ser más coloridos en su estado juvenil que cuando llegan a adultos.

(Família: Carangidae) Este grupo é robusto, porém não particularmente colorido. Entretanto, não é um peixe de aquário muito popular. Quase todos eles podem ficar bem grandes e, na verdade, são considerados peixe para comida no Sudeste Asiático. Os membros da família Carangidae tendem a ser mais coloridos quando jovens que quando adultos.

(Famiglia: Carangidae) I pesci di questo gruppo sono robusti ma non presentano una colorazione particolarmente vivace. Per questo motivo, non sono molto ricercati dagli acquariofili. Quasi tutti raggiungono grandi dimensioni e infatti vengono considerati pesci commestibili nel Sudest asiatico. I giovani Carangidi hanno una livrea più vivace degli adulti e di conseguenza, i pesci di questa famiglia vengono venduti sul mercato acquariologico allo stadio giovanile.

FAM: Carangidae
Carangoides dinema
Shadow Trevally

 General Aggression

 Color Maintenance

 Dietary Requirements

 Con-Species Compatibility

Collected: Philippines
Aquarium: Non-Reef
Survivability: Easy
Size: More than 8" (20 cm)

FAM: Carangidae
Carangoides oblongus
Disk Trevally

General Aggression

Color Maintenance

Dietary Requirements

Con-Species Compatibility

Collected: Philippines
Aquarium: Non-Reef
Survivability: Moderate
Size: More than 8" (20 cm)

FAM: Carangidae
Gnathanodon speciosus
Golden Trevally

General Aggression

Color Maintenance

Dietary Requirements

Con-Species Compatibility

Collected: Philippines
Aquarium: Non-Reef
Survivability: Moderate
Size: More than 8" (20 cm)

Family: Centriscidae

(Shrimpfish) Members of this family are characterized by a rigid body and their habit of swimming in a vertical, heads-down positison. They are among the most difficult fish to transport and maintain. This is the reason they are not seen often in the aquarium trade, though in nature they are very common.

(Famille: Centriscidae) Les membres de cette famille sont caractérisés par un corps rigide et par le fait qu'ils nagent à la verticale, la tête en bas (poisson-rasoir). Ils sont parmi les poissons les plus difficiles à transporter et à maintenir. C'est la raison pour laquelle on les voit rarement dans les magasins d'aquarium bien que très communs en liberté.

(Pez Camarón) Los miembros de esta familia se caracterizan por un cuerpo rígido y su hábito de nadar en una posición vertical, con la cabeza para abajo. Estos peces se encuentran entre las especies más difíciles de transportar y mantener y por esto no se ven muy a menudo en el comercio de peceras, aunque en la naturaleza son muy comunes.

(Família: Centriscidae) Os membros dessa família são caracterizados por um corpo rígido e hábitos de nadar em uma posição vertical e de cabeça para baixo. Eles estão entre os peixes mais difíceis de transportar e de manter. Esta é a razão pela qual eles não muito vistos no comércio de aquário, apesar de serem bem comuns na natureza.

(Famiglia: Centriscidae) I membri di questa famiglia sono caratterizzati da un corpo poco flessuoso e dall'abitudine di nuotare in posizione verticale con la testa rivolta verso il basso. Sono tra i pesci più difficili da trasportare e da allevare e per questo motivo sono piuttosto rari sul mercato acquariologico, benché in natura siano molto comuni.

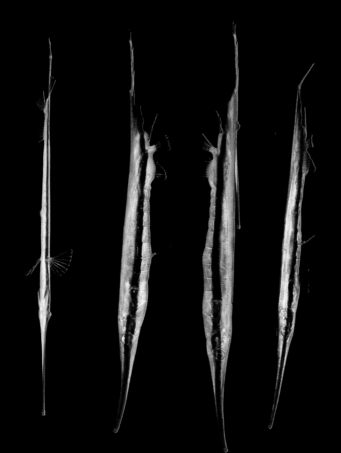

FAM: Centriscidae
Aeoliscus strigatus
Shrimpfish

General Aggression

Color Maintenance

Dietary Requirements

Con-Species Compatibility

Collected: Philippines
Aquarium: Reef
Survivability: Doomed
Size: Less than 4" (10 cm)

FAM: Chaetodontidae
Chaetodon collare
Collare Butterflyfish

General Aggression

Color Maintenance

Dietary Requirements

Con-Species Compatibility

Collected: Indonesia
Aquarium: Non-Reef
Survivability: Moderate
Size: 4" (10 cm) – 8" (20 cm)

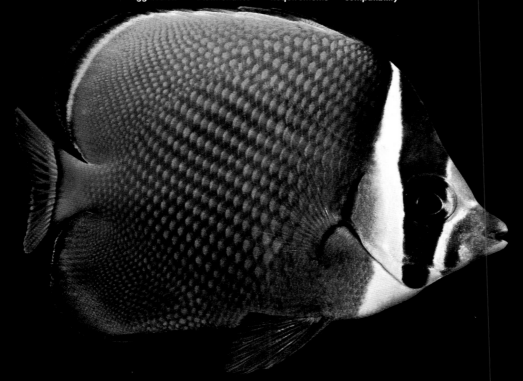

FAM: Chaetodontidae
Chaetodon **ephippium**
Saddleback Butterflyfish

General Aggression

Color Maintenance

Dietary Requirements

Con-Species Compatibility

Collected: Philippines
Aquarium: Non-Reef
Survivability: Moderate
Size: More than 8" (20 cm)

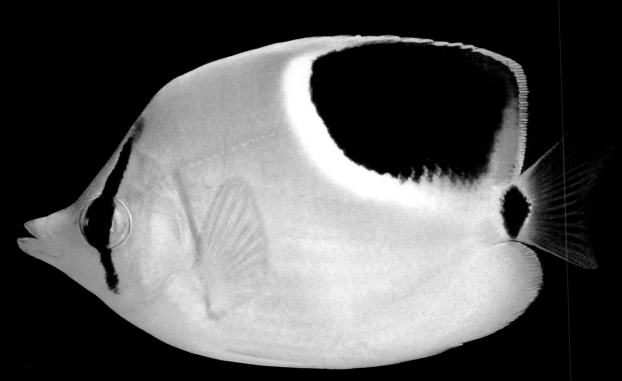

79

FAM: Chaetodontidae
Chaetodon falcula
Double Saddle Butterflyfish

General Aggression **Color Maintenance** **Dietary Requirements** **Con-Species Compatibility**

Collected: Indonesia
Aquarium: Non-Reef
Survivability: Moderate
Size: 4" (10 cm) – 8" (20 cm)

FAM: Chaetodontidae
Chaetodon kleinii
Klein's Butterflyfish

General Aggression **Color Maintenance** **Dietary Requirements** **Con-Species Compatibility**

Collected: Philippines
Aquarium: Non-Reef
Survivability: Easy
Size: Less than 4" (10 cm)

FAM: Chaetodontidae
Chaetodon lineolatus
Lined Butterflyfish

General Aggression **Color Maintenance** **Dietary Requirements** **Con-Species Compatibility**

Collected: Philippines
Aquarium: Non-Reef
Survivability: Difficult
Size: More than 8" (20 cm)

FAM: Chaetodontidae
Chaetodon lunula
Racoon Butterflyfish

General Aggression **Color Maintenance** **Dietary Requirements** **Con-Species Compatibility**

Collected: Philippines
Aquarium: Non-Reef
Survivability: Easy
Size: More than 8" (20 cm)

81

FAM: Chaetodontidae
Chaetodon lunula
Racoon Butterflyfish
FORM: Juvenile

   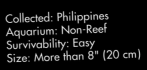

General Aggression **Color Maintenance** **Dietary Requirements** **Con-Species Compatibility**

Collected: Philippines
Aquarium: Non-Reef
Survivability: Easy
Size: More than 8" (20 cm)

FAM: Chaetodontidae
Chaetodon melannotus
Black-backed Butterflyfish

General Aggression **Color Maintenance** **Dietary Requirements** **Con-Species Compatibility**

Collected: Philippines
Aquarium: Non-Reef
Survivability: Difficult
Size: 4" (10 cm) – 8" (20 cm)

82

FAM: Chaetodontidae
Chaetodon meyeri
Meyer's Butterflyfish

General Aggression

Color Maintenance

Dietary Requirements

Con-Species Compatibility

Collected: Philippines
Aquarium: Non-Reef
Survivability: Doomed
Size: More than 8" (20 cm)

FAM: Chaetodontidae
Chaetodon ocellicaudus
Spot-tail Butterflyfish

General Aggression

Color Maintenance

Dietary Requirements

Con-Species Compatibility

Collected: Philippines
Aquarium: Non-Reef
Survivability: Doomed
Size: 4" (10 cm) – 8" (20 cm)

83

FAM: Chaetodontidae
Chaetodon octofasciatus
Eight Banded Butterfly

General Aggression **Color Maintenance** **Dietary Requirements** **Con-Species Compatibility**

Collected: Philippines
Aquarium: Non-Reef
Survivability: Difficult
Size: Less than 4" (10 cm)

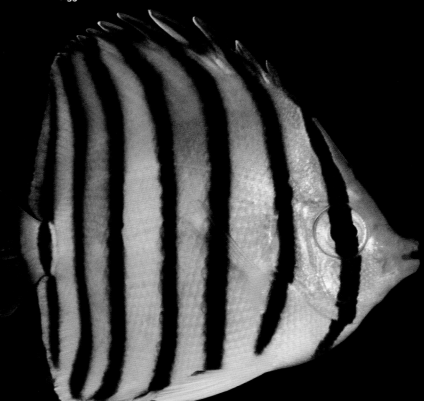

FAM: Chaetodontidae
Chaetodon ornatissimus
Ornate Butterflyfish

General Aggression **Color Maintenance** **Dietary Requirements** **Con-Species Compatibility**

Collected: Philippines
Aquarium: Non-Reef
Survivability: Doomed
Size: Less than 8" (20 cm)

General Aggression

Color Maintenance

Dietary Requirements

Con-Species Compatibility

Collected: Philippines
Aquarium: Non-Reef
Survivability: Doomed
Size: 4" (10 cm) – 8" (20 cm)

FAM: Chaetodontidae
Chaetodon punctatofasciatus
Spot & Bands Butterflyfish

General Aggression

Color Maintenance

Dietary Requirements

Con-Species Compatibility

Collected: Philippines
Aquarium: Non-Reef
Survivability: Moderate
Size: Less than 4" (10 cm)

85

FAM: Chaetodontidae
Chaetodon quadrimaculatus
Four-spot Butterflyfish

General
Aggression

Color
Maintenance

Dietary
Requirements

Con-Species
Compatibility

Collected: Philippines
Aquarium: Non-Reef
Survivability: Difficult
Size: 4" (10 cm) – 8" (20 cm)

FAM: Chaetodontidae
Chaetodon rafflesi
Latticed Butterflyfish

General
Aggression

Color
Maintenance

Dietary
Requirements

Con-Species
Compatibility

Collected: Indonesia
Aquarium: Non-Reef
Survivability: Doomed
Size: 4" (10 cm) – 8" (20 cm)

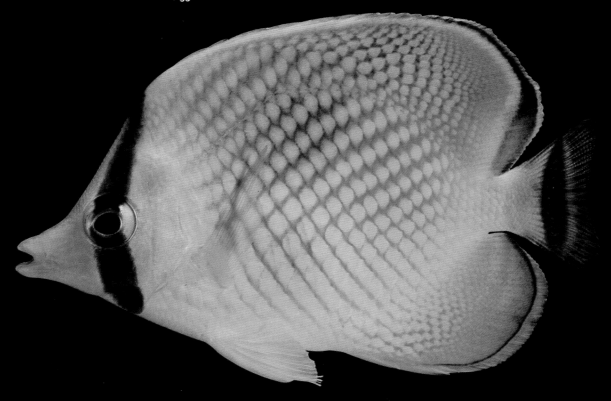

FAM: Chaetodontidae
Chaetodon reticulatus
Reticulated Butterflyfish

 General Aggression
 Color Maintenance
 Dietary Requirements
Con-Species Compatibility

Collected: Philippines
Aquarium: Non-Reef
Survivability: Doomed
Size: 4" (10 cm) – 8" (20 cm)

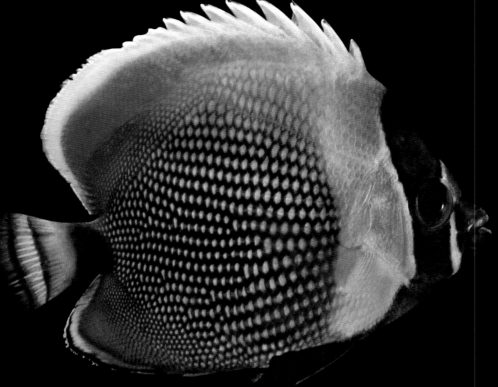

FAM: Chaetodontidae
Chaetodon speculum
Oval-spot Butterflyfish

 General Aggression
 Color Maintenance
 Dietary Requirements
Con-Species Compatibility

Collected: Philippines
Aquarium: Non-Reef
Survivability: Doomed
Size: 4" (10 cm) – 8" (20 cm)

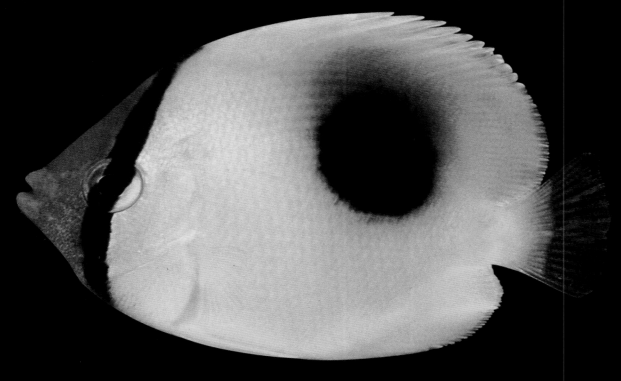

FAM: Chaetodontidae
Chaetodon triangulum
Triangular Butterflyfish

General Aggression

Color Maintenance

Dietary Requirements

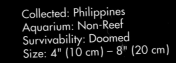
Con-Species Compatibility

Collected: Philippines
Aquarium: Non-Reef
Survivability: Doomed
Size: 4" (10 cm) – 8" (20 cm)

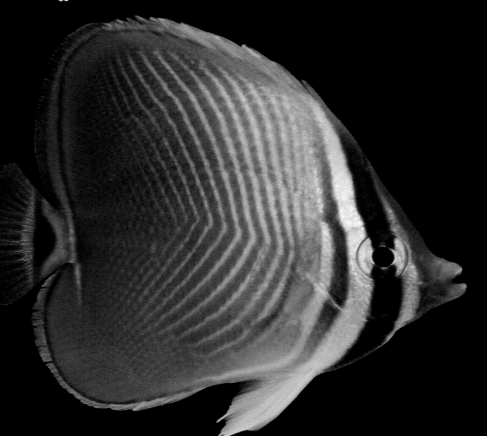

FAM: Chaetodontidae
Chaetodon trifascialis
Chevron Butterflyfish

General Aggression

Color Maintenance

Dietary Requirements

Con-Species Compatibility

Collected: Philippines
Aquarium: Non-Reef
Survivability: Doomed
Size: 4" (10 cm) – 8" (20 cm)

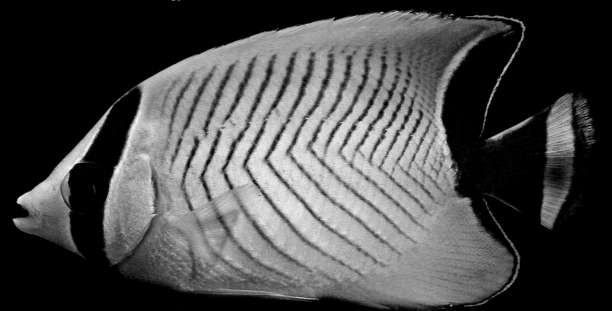

FAM: Chaetodontidae
Chaetodon trifasciatus
Melon Butterflyfish

General
Aggression

Color
Maintenance

Dietary
Requirements

Con-Species
Compatibility

Collected: Philippines
Aquarium: Non-Reef
Survivability: Doomed
Size: 4" (10 cm) – 8" (20 cm)

FAM: Chaetodontidae
Chaetodon ulietensis
Pacific Double-saddle Butterflyfish

General
Aggression

Color
Maintenance

Dietary
Requirements

Con-Species
Compatibility

Collected: Philippines
Aquarium: Non-Reef
Survivability: Moderate
Size: 4" (10 cm) – 8" (20 cm)

89

FAM: Chaetodontidae
Chaetodon unimaculatus
Teardrop Butterflyfish

General Aggression **Color Maintenance** **Dietary Requirements** **Con-Species Compatibility**

Collected: Philippines
Aquarium: Non-Reef
Survivability: Difficult
Size: 4" (10 cm) – 8" (20 cm)

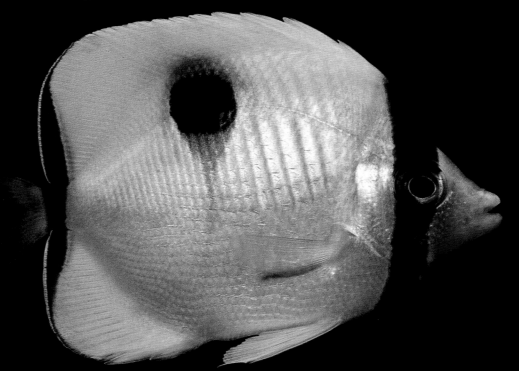

FAM: Chaetodontidae
Chaetodon xanthurus (Red)
Pearlscale Butterflyfish (Red)

General Aggression **Color Maintenance** **Dietary Requirements** **Con-Species Compatibility**

Collected: Philippines
Aquarium: Non-Reef
Survivability: Moderate
Size: 4" (10 cm) – 8" (20 cm)

General Aggression

Color Maintenance

Dietary Requirements

Con-Species Compatibility

Collected: Indonesia
Aquarium: Non-Reef
Survivability: Moderate
Size: 4" (10 cm) – 8" (20 cm)

General Aggression

 Color Maintenance

 Dietary Requirements

 Con-Species Compatibility

Collected: Philippines
Aquarium: Non-Reef
Survivability: Moderate
Size: 4" (10 cm) – 8" (20 cm)

Family: Cirrhitidae

(Hawkfishes) Family Cirrhitidae is not generally a good addition to a reef aquarium, because they re carnivorous and hunt small fishes and crustaceans. Exceptions are the *Neocirrhites armatus* (Flame Hawkfish) nd the *Oxycirrhites typus* (Longnose Hawkfish), which have gentler temperments. Like the Gobiidae family, most members of the Cirrhitidae familly are bottom-dwellers that spend most of their time perching on coral branches r rocks, looking for prey. Almost all member species have hair-like structures at the end of the dorsal spine. They are also territorial fishes that defend against any intruder. Beginners can have confidence that the members of the family Cirrhitidae (Hawkfish) will do well for them, as they are hardy and easy to keep.

(Famille: Cirrhitidae) La famille des Cirrhitidae n'est en général pas conseillée en aquarium récifal parce que c'est un carnivore qui chasse petits poissons et crustacés. Parmi les exceptions, on compte le *Neocirrhites armatus* et l'*Oxycirrhites typus* qui a des dispositions plus sympathiques. Comme les Gobiidae, la plupart des membres de la famille des Cirrhitidae sont des poissons de fond qui passent le plus clair de leur temps sur des branches de corail ou sur des roches en surplomb à la recherche d'une proie. La majorité de ses espèces membres possède es appendices ressemblant à des poils à l'extrémité de leur épine dorsale. Ce sont également des poissons erritoriaux qui se défendent contre tout intrus. Poissons robustes et faciles à garder, ils sont conseillés aux débutants.

(Pez Halcón) Los miembros de la familia Cirrhitidae generalmente no constituyen buenos ejemplares para na pecera de arrecife ya que son carnívoros y cazan pequeños peces y crustáceos. Las excepciones son el *Neocirrhites armatus* (Halcón de fuego) y el *Oxycirrhites typus* (Halcón Nariz Larga), que son de un temperamento más docil. Como la familia Gobiidae, la mayoría de los miembros de la familia Cirrhitidae viven en los fondos marinos y pasan la mayor parte del tiempo sentados sobre ramas de coral o rocas, en busca de sus presas. Casi todos los miembros de la especie poseen estructuras que parecen pelos al final de la espina dorsal. También son peces territoriales que se defienden contra cualquier intruso. Los principiantes pueden sentirse confiados de que no tendrán problemas con los miembros de la familia Cirrhitidae (Pez Halcón) ya que son uertes y fáciles de mantener.

(Família: Cirrhitidae) A família Cirrhitidae não é geralmente um bom acréscimo a um aquário de recife, orque são carnívoros e caçam pequenos peixes e crustáceos. Exceções são os *Neocirrhites armatus* "(Flame Hawkfish") e os *Oxycirrhites typus* ("Longnose Hawkfish"), que têm temperamentos mais dóceis. Assim como família Gobiidae, a maioria dos membros da família Cirrhitidae são habitantes do fundo que passam a maior arte do seu tempo pousados em corais ou rochas, procurando por presas. Quase todos os membros da spécie têm estruturas que se assemelham a cabelos no fim da espinha dorsal. São também peixes territoriais que se defendem contra qualquer intruso. Os iniciantes podem estar seguros que os membros da família Cirrhitidae "(Hawkfishes") irão agradar, pois são resistentes e fáceis de manter.

(Famiglia: Cirrhitidae) Generalmente, la famiglia Cirrhitidae non rappresenta una felice aggiunta ll'acquario da barriera, perché i suoi membri sono carnivori e predano pesci piccoli e crostacei. Le ccezioni sono *Neocirrhites armatus* e *Oxycirrhites typus*, che hanno un atteggiamento più mite. Come i Gobidi, molti Cirritidi occupano la zona di fondo dell'acquario e passano la maggior parte del tempo ppoggiati sui rami di corallo o sulle pietre, cercando le loro prede. Quasi tutte le specie hanno ppendici simili a capelli all'estremità della pinna dorsale. Sono pesci territoriali che si difendono nergicamente dagli invasori. I principianti possono confidare nel fatto che i membri della famiglia Cirrhitidae vivranno bene in acquario, perché sono robusti e facilmente allevabili.

FAM: Cirrhitidae
Cirrhitichthys aprinus
Threadfin Hawkfish

General Aggression

Color Maintenance

Dietary Requirements

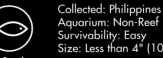
Con-Species Compatibility

Collected: Philippines
Aquarium: Non-Reef
Survivability: Easy
Size: Less than 4" (10 cm)

FAM: Cirrhitidae
Cirrhitichthys falco
Dwarf Hawkfish

General Aggression

Color Maintenance

Dietary Requirements

Con-Species Compatibility

Collected: Philippines
Aquarium: Non-Reef
Survivability: Easy
Size: Less than 4" (10 cm)

FAM: Cirrhitidae
Cyprinocirrhites polyactis
Lyretail Hawkfish

General Aggression

Color Maintenance

Dietary Requirements

Con-Species Compatibility

Collected: Philippines
Aquarium: Reef (Caution)
Survivability: Easy
Size: 4" (10 cm) – 8" (20 cm)

FAM: Cirrhitidae
Oxycirrhites typus
Longnose Hawkfish

General Aggression

Color Maintenance

Dietary Requirements

Con-Species Compatibility

Collected: Philippines
Aquarium: Reef
Survivability: Easy
Size: Less than 4" (10 cm)

FAM: Cirrhitidae
Paracirrhites arcatus
Arc-eyed Hawkfish

General
Aggression

Color
Maintenance

Dietary
Requirements

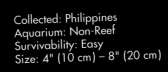

Con-Species
Compatibility

Collected: Philippines
Aquarium: Non-Reef
Survivability: Easy
Size: 4" (10 cm) – 8" (20 cm)

FAM: Cirrhitidae
Paracirrhites fosteri
Freckle-face Hawkfish

General
Aggression

Color
Maintenance

Dietary
Requirements

Con-Species
Compatibility

Collected: Philippines
Aquarium: Non-Reef
Survivability: Easy
Size: 4" (10 cm) – 8" (20 cm)

Family: Dactylopteridae

(Flying Gunard) This fish glides through the water using its extremely large, wing-like pectoral fins. In addition, these pectoral fins form a structure similar to a claw that it uses to scratch along the bottom in search of crustaceans to eat, and its pelvic fins can be used to crawl along the bottom of the ocean. These features make this an interesting fish.

(Famille: Dactylopteridae) Les nageoires de ces poissons sont extrêmement larges; elles ressemblent à des ailes et donnent l'impression que les poissons volent dans l'eau. De plus, leurs nageoires pectorales forment une structure ressemblant à une griffe qu'ils utilisent pour gratter le fond à la recherche de crustacés dont ils se nourrissent; ils peuvent également utiliser leurs nageoires pelviennes pour ramper au fond de l'océan. Ces caractéristiques en font des poissons intéressants.

(Familia: Dactylopteridae) Este pez se desliza por el agua usando sus aletas pectorales extremadamente grandes en forma de alas. Además, estas aletas pectorales conforman una estructura similar a una garra que utiliza para raspar el fondo marino en busca de crustáceos de que comer, y sus aletas pélvicas pueden utilizarse para arrastrarse por el fondo del océano. Estas características lo convierten en un pez en extremo interesante

(Família: Dactylopteridae) Este peixe desliza pela água usando suas barbatanas peitorais extremamente grandes, em formato de asas. Além disso, estas barbatanas peitorais formam uma estrutura similar a uma garra, que ele usa para arranhar o fundo do oceano em busca de crustáceos para comer e suas barbatanas pélvicas podem ser usadas para rastejar pelo fundo do oceano. Estas características o tornam um peixe bem interessante.

(Famiglia: Dactylopteridae) Questo pesce fluttua nell'acqua utilizzando le pinne pettorali, estremamente grandi, che assomigliano a delle ali. Inoltre, queste pinne possono assumere una forma simile a una chela di certi granchi permettendo al pesce di muoversi lentamente sul fondo alla ricerca di crostacei da predare. Questa caratteristica li rende molto interessanti.

FAM: Dactylopteridae
Dactyloptena orientalis*
Flying Gunard

General Aggression | Color Maintenance | Dietary Requirements | Con-Species Compatibility

Collected: Philippines
Aquarium: Non-Reef
Survivability: Difficult
Size: 4" (10 cm) – 8" (20 cm)

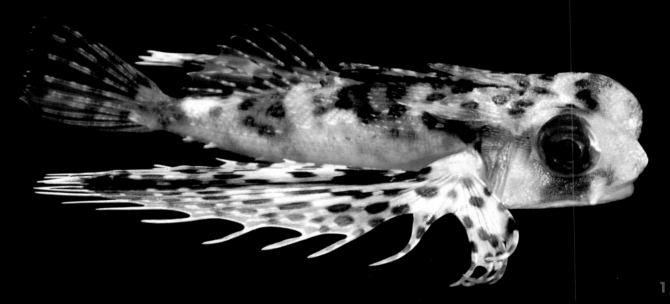

Family: Dasyatididae

(Rays) Members of the Dasyatididae family share some common traits: they are carnivorous, have cartilaginous skeletons, and reproduce via internal fertilization. They should be handled with care, as members of this family have a poisonous spike at the tip of the tail. Dasyatididae species are bottom dwelling scavengers which do not prey on fishes swimming above them. Their main diet is crustaceans. When threatened, they bury themselves.

(Famille: Dasyatididae) Les membres de la famille des Dasyatididae (raies) partagent certains traits communs : ce sont des carnivores qui ont un squelette cartilagineux et se reproduisent par fertilisation interne. Ils doivent être manipulés avec beaucoup de précaution car les membres de cette famille possèdent une pointe empoisonnée à la base de leur queue.
Les poissons de l'espèce des Dasyatididae vivent sur les fonds marins qu'ils fouillent pour y trouver leur nourriture. Ils ne chassent pas les poissons nageant autour d'eux, leur régime alimentaire principal étant fait de crustacés. Ils s'ensablent lorsqu'ils se sentent menacés.

(Rayas) Los miembros de la familia Dasyatididae comparten algunos rasgos comunes: son carnívoros, poseen esqueletos cartilaginosos y se reproducen por medio de fertilización interna. Deben manipularse con cuidado, pues los miembros de esta familia poseen un espolón venenoso en la base de la cola. Los miembros de la especie Dasyatididae son peces carroñeros que viven en los fondos marinos y no cazan los peces que nadan arriba de ellas. Su dieta principal consiste de crustáceos. Estos peces cuando se ven amenazados, se entierran en la arena.

(Raias) Os membros da família Dasyatididae compartilham alguns traços comuns: são carnívoros, têm esqueletos cartilaginosos, e se reproduzem através de fertilização interna. Eles devem ser manuseados com cuidado, pois os membros dessa família têm um espigão venenoso na base da cauda. As espécies Dasyatdidae alimentam-se de deritos orgânicos e habitam o fundo, não caçando peixes que nadam acima deles. Sua dieta principal são crustáceos. Quando ameaçados, eles se enterram.

(Famiglia: Dasyatididae) I membri della famiglia Dasyatididae hanno alcune caratteristiche in comune: sono carnivori, hanno scheletri cartilaginei e si riproducono mediante fecondazione interna. E' necessario maneggiarli con cautela, perché possiedono un aculeo velenoso alla base della coda. Le specie Dasyatidae che vivono sul fondo sono saprofaghe e non predano i pesci che nuotano vicino a loro. L'alimento principale sono i crostacei. Quando vengono minacciati, si insabbiano.

FAM: Ephippidae
Platax batavianus
Zebra Batfish
FORM: Juvenile

General
Aggression

Color
Maintenance

Dietary
Requirements

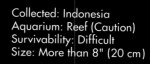
Con-Species
Compatibility

Collected: Indonesia
Aquarium: Reef (Caution)
Survivability: Difficult
Size: More than 8" (20 cm)

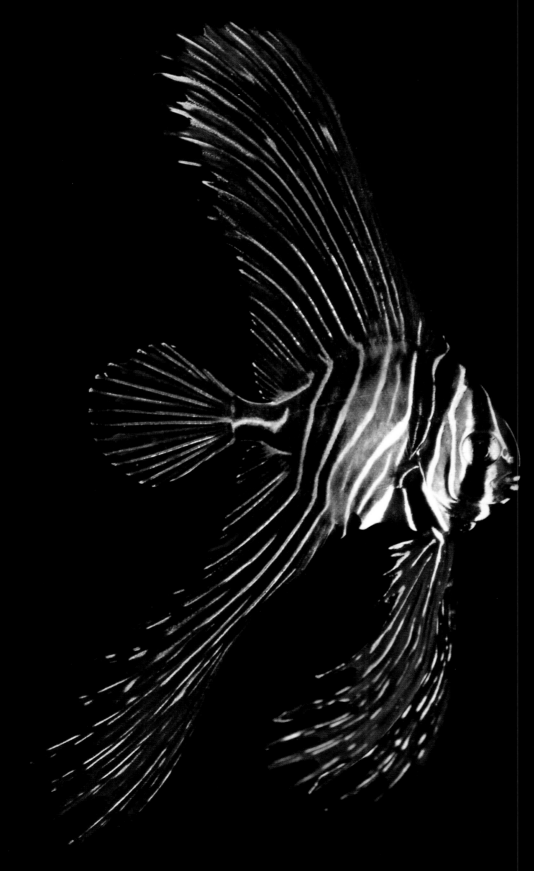

107

FAM: **Ephippidae**
Platax orbicularis
Orbic Batfish
FORM: **Juvenile**

 General Aggression

Color Maintenance

 Dietary Requirements

 Con-Species Compatibility

Collected: Philippines
Aquarium: Reef (Caution)
Survivability: Easy
Size: More than 8" (20 cm)

FAM: Ephippidae
Platax pinnatus
Pinnatus Batfish
FORM: Juvenile

General Aggression

Color Maintenance

Dietary Requirements

Con-Species Compatibility

Collected: Philippines
Aquarium: Reef (Caution)
Survivability: Doomed
Size: More than 8" (20 cm)

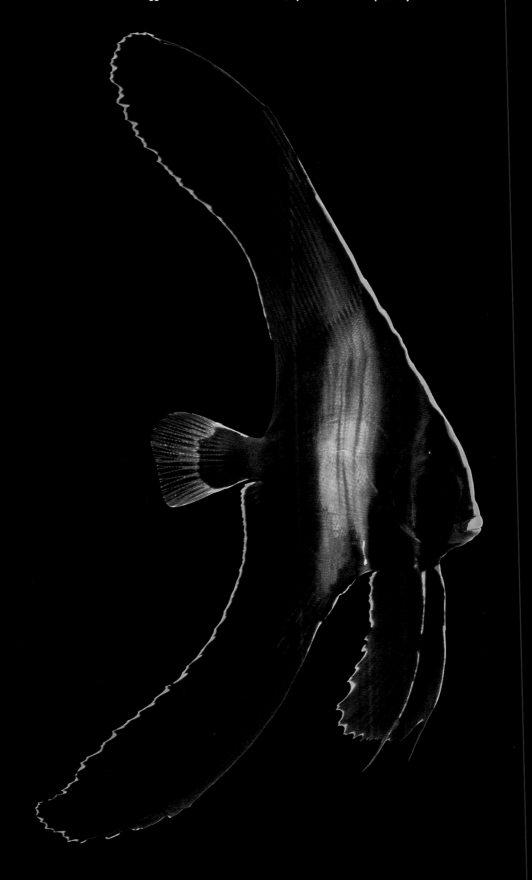

FAM: Ephippidae
Platax teira
Teira Batfish
FORM: Juvenile

General
Aggression

Color
Maintenance

Dietary
Requirements

Con-Species
Compatibility

Collected: Indonesia
Aquarium: Reef (Caution)
Survivability: Moderate
Size: More than 8" (20 cm)

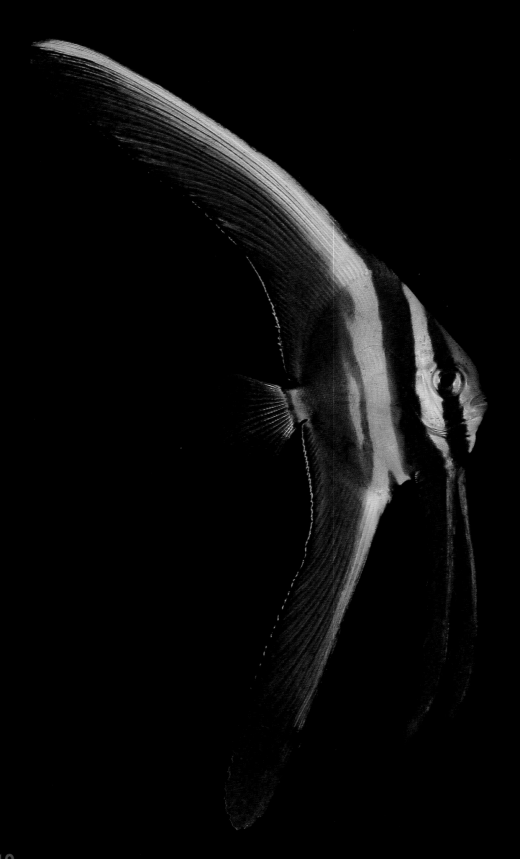

110

Family: Gobiidae

(Gobies) The members of this group of fishes will appreciate living in a reef aquarium with plenty of rock for hiding places. They are generally good reef aquarium fishes. In the wild, many members of the Gobiidae family (Gobies) share burrows with shrimp. This symbiotic relationship may also occur in an aquarium (and is very interesting to watch!). In some cases, members of this family may bury themselves at night for protection. Family Gobiidae (Gobies) are bottom dwellers and are ideal subjects for a reef aquarium. They are mainly carnivorous in the wild. In an aquarium, they can be fed frozen Brine Shrimp and many will also eat flakes. This makes them easy fishes to maintain.

(Famille: Gobiidae) Les membres de ce groupe de poissons apprécieront la vie de récif en aquarium et évolueront parmi les nombreuses pierres qui leur permettront de se cacher. En liberté, de nombreux membres de cette famille partagent leurs terriers avec des crevettes. Cette relation symbiotique peut également se produire en aquarium et elle est très intéressante à observer! Dans certains cas, les membres de cette famille peuvent s'enterrer la nuit par mesure de protection. Les Gobiidae sont des poissons de fond et sont des sujets idéaux pour un aquarium d'invertébrés.

(Góbios) Los miembros de este grupo de peces apreciarán vivir en una pecera de arrecife con muchas piedras que le sirvan de escondites. Generalmente son buenos peces para peceras de arrecife. En su estado natural, muchos miembros de la familia Gobiidae (Góbios) comparten su madrigueras con camarones. ¡Esta relación simbiótica puede también ocurrir en una pecera y resulta muy interesante de observar! En algunos casos, miembros de esta familia pueden enterrarse de noche para protegerse. Los miembros de la familia Gobiidae (Góbios) viven en los fondos marinos y son ejemplares ideales para una pecera de arrecife. En una pecera se les puede alimentar artemia congelada y muchos también comerán hojuelas de pescado. Esto hace que sean peces fáciles de mantener en cautiverio.

(Gobiões) Os membros desse grupo de peixes apreciarão viver em um aquário de recife com muita rocha e lugares para se esconder. São geralmente bons peixes para aquários de recife. Na vida selvagem muitos membros da família Gobiidae (Gobiões) compartilham as tocas com o camarão. Esta relação simbiótica também pode ocorrer em um aquário, sendo muito interessante de se observar! Em alguns casos, os membros dessa família podem se enterrar à noite para proteção. A família Gobiidae é constituída de habitantes do fundo, sendo ideais para um aquário de recife. Eles são primariamente carnívoros na vida selvagem. Em um aquário, podem ser alimentados com camarão em salmoura congelado e muitos também comerão flocos. Isso os torna peixes fáceis de se manter.

(Famiglia: Gobiidae) I membri di questo gruppo vivono volentieri nell'acquario da barriera, con un'abbondanza di rocce che permettano loro di nascondersi. In natura molti Gobidi condividono le tane con dei gamberetti. Questa relazione simbiotica può avvenire anche in acquario ed è molto interessante da osservare! In alcuni casi, i membri di questa famiglia possono insabbiarsi durante la notte per proteggersi. I Gobidi prediligono la zona più bassa dell'acquario e sono soggetti ideali per l'acquario da barriera. In natura sono principalmente carnivori. In un acquario, è possibile nutrirli con Artemia congelati e molti si cibano anche di mangimi in fiocchi; per questa ragione sono facili da allevare.

FAM: Gobiidae
Amblyeleotris sp. "Flame Stripe"*
Flame Stripe Goby

General Aggression **Color Maintenance** **Dietary Requirements** **Con-Species Compatibility**

Collected: Indonesia
Aquarium: Reef
Survivability: Easy
Size: Less than 4" (10 cm)

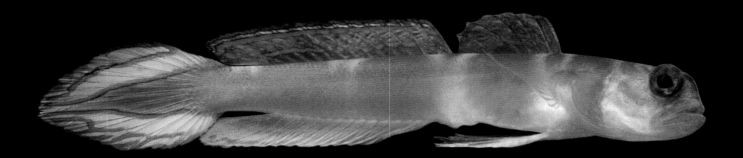

FAM: Gobiidae
Amblyeleotris guttata
Spotted Shrimp Goby

General Aggression **Color Maintenance** **Dietary Requirements** **Con-Species Compatibility**

Collected: Indonesia
Aquarium: Reef
Survivability: Easy
Size: Less than 4" (10 cm)

FAM: Gobiidae
Amblyeleotris latifasciatus
Blue-spot Shrimp Goby

General Aggression

Color Maintenance

Dietary Requirements

Con-Species Compatibility

Collected: Indonesia
Aquarium: Reef
Survivability: Easy
Size: Less than 4" (10 cm)

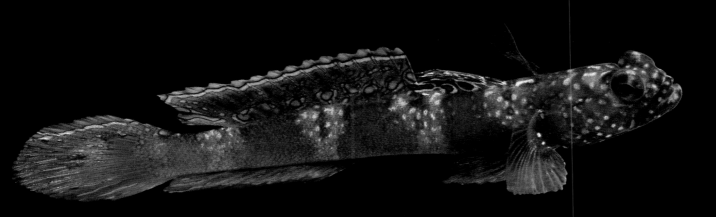

FAM: Gobiidae
Amblyeleotris periopthalma
Banded Shrimp Goby

General Aggression

Color Maintenance

Dietary Requirements

Con-Species Compatibility

Collected: Indonesia
Aquarium: Reef
Survivability: Easy
Size: Less than 4" (10 cm)

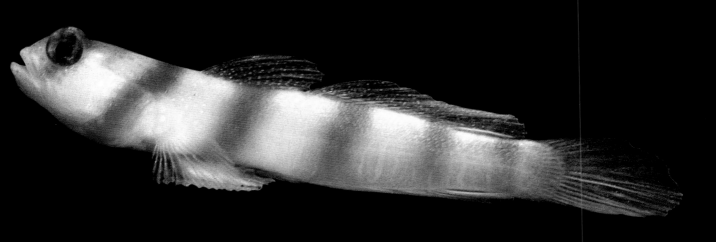

113

FAM: Gobiidae
Amblyeleotris randalli
Randall's Shrimp Goby

General Aggression

Color Maintenance

Dietary Requirements

Con-Species Compatibility

Collected: Indonesia
Aquarium: Reef
Survivability: Easy
Size: Less than 4" (10 cm)

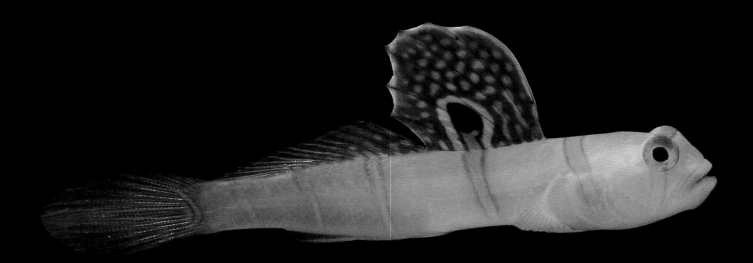

FAM: Gobiidae
Amblyeleotris sungami
Magnus' Shrimp Goby

General Aggression

Color Maintenance

Dietary Requirements

Con-Species Compatibility

Collected: Philippines
Aquarium: Reef
Survivability: Easy
Size: Less than 4" (10 cm)

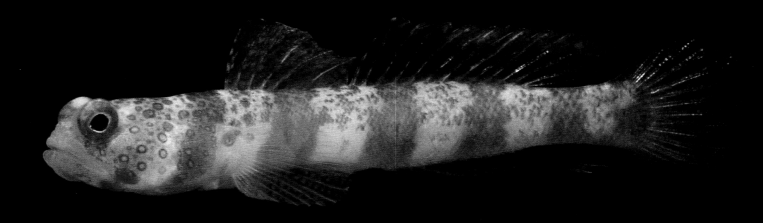

FAM: Gobiidae
Amblyeleotris wheeleri
Wheeler's Shrimp Goby

General Aggression   Color Maintenance   Dietary Requirements   Con-Species Compatibility

Collected: Philippines
Aquarium: Reef
Survivability: Easy
Size: Less than 4" (10 cm)

FAM: Gobiidae
Amblygobius hectori
Hector's Goby

General Aggression   Color Maintenance   Dietary Requirements   Con-Species Compatibility

Collected: Philippines
Aquarium: Reef
Survivability: Moderate
Size: Less than 4" (10 cm)

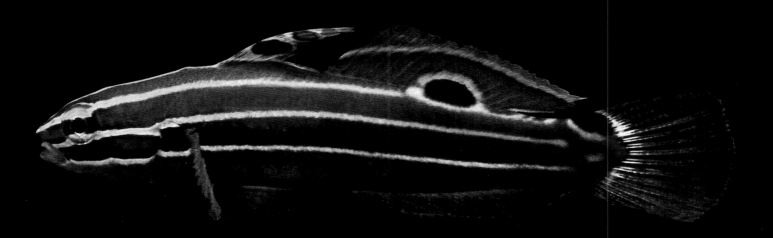

115

FAM: Gobiidae
Amblygobius phalaena
Bullet Goby

General Aggression **Color Maintenance** **Dietary Requirements** **Con-Species Compatibility**

Collected: Philippines
Aquarium: Reef
Survivability: Easy
Size: Less than 4" (10 cm)

FAM: Gobiidae
Cryptocentrus caeruleopunctatus
Harlequin Shrimp Goby

General Aggression **Color Maintenance** **Dietary Requirements** **Con-Species Compatibility**

Collected: Philippines
Aquarium: Reef
Survivability: Easy
Size: Less than 4" (10 cm)

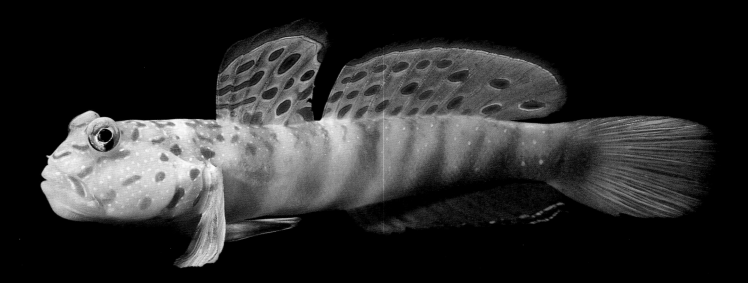

116

FAM: Gobiidae
Cryptocentrus cinctus (Grey)
Grey Shrimp Goby

General Aggression

Color Maintenance

Dietary Requirements

Con-Species Compatibility

Collected: Indonesia
Aquarium: Reef
Survivability: Easy
Size: Less than 4" (10 cm)

FAM: Gobiidae
Cryptocentrus cinctus (Yellow)
Yellow Shrimp Goby

General Aggression

Color Maintenance

Dietary Requirements

Con-Species Compatibility

Collected: Indonesia
Aquarium: Reef
Survivability: Easy
Size: Less than 4" (10 cm)

117

FAM: Gobiidae
Gobiodon sp. "Black Clown"*
Black Clown Goby

General Aggression   Color Maintenance   Dietary Requirements   Con-Species Compatibility

Collected: Philippines
Aquarium: Reef
Survivability: Moderate
Size: Less than 4" (10 cm)

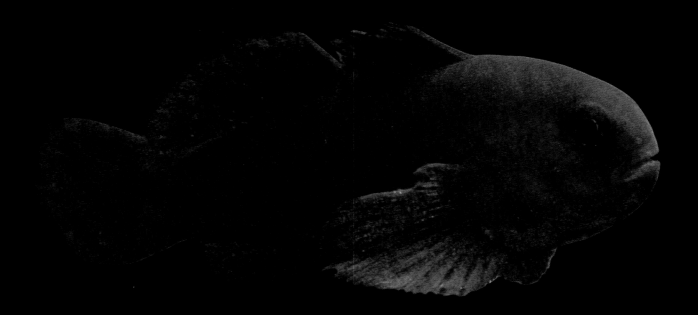

FAM: Gobiidae
Gobiodon sp. "Blue-stripe"*
Blue-stripe Clown Goby

General Aggression   Color Maintenance   Dietary Requirements   Con-Species Compatibility

Collected: Philippines
Aquarium: Reef
Survivability: Moderate
Size: Less than 4" (10 cm)

FAM: Gobiidae
Gobiodon sp. "Burgundy"*
Burgundy Clown Goby

General Aggression   Color Maintenance   Dietary Requirements   Con-Species Compatibility

Collected: Philippines
Aquarium: Reef
Survivability: Easy
Size: Less than 4" (10 cm)

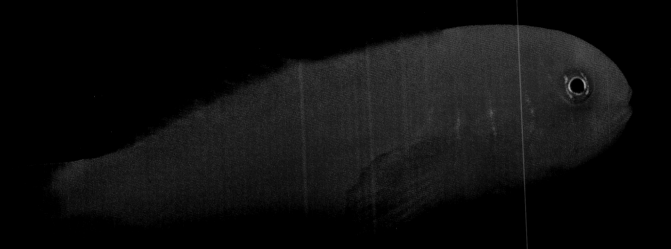

FAM: Gobiidae
Gobiodon okinawae
Yellow Clown Goby

General Aggression   Color Maintenance   Dietary Requirements   Con-Species Compatibility

Collected: Philippines
Aquarium: Reef
Survivability: Easy
Size: Less than 4" (10 cm)

119

FAM: Gobiidae
Gobiodon rivulatus
Green Clown Goby

General Aggression **Color Maintenance** **Dietary Requirements** **Con-Species Compatibility**

Collected: Philippines
Aquarium: Reef
Survivability: Moderate
Size: Less than 4" (10 cm)

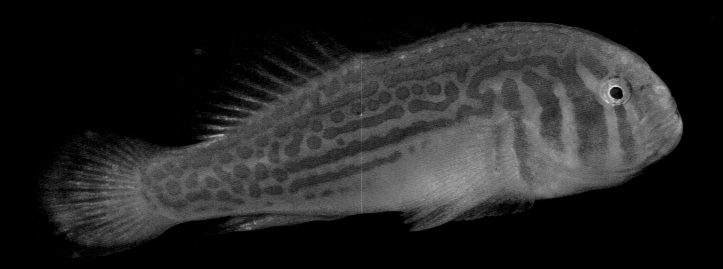

FAM: Gobiidae
Signigobius biocellatus
Crab-eye Goby

General Aggression **Color Maintenance** **Dietary Requirements** **Con-Species Compatibility**

Collected: Indonesia
Aquarium: Reef
Survivability: Moderate
Size: Less than 4" (10 cm)

120

FAM: *Gobiidae*
Stonogobiops nematodes
Barber Post Goby

General
Aggression

Color
Maintenance

Dietary
Requirements

Con-Species
Compatibility

Collected: Philippines
Aquarium: Reef
Survivability: Easy
Size: Less than 4" (10 cm)

FAM: *Gobiidae*
Valenciennea puellaris
Orange-spotted Sleeper Goby

General
Aggression

Color
Maintenance

Dietary
Requirements

Con-Species
Compatibility

Collected: Philippines
Aquarium: Reef
Survivability: Easy
Size: Small 4" (10 cm)

121

FAM: Gobiidae
Valenciennea strigata
Goldenhead Sleeper Goby

General
Aggression

Color
Maintenance

Dietary
Requirements

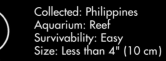
Con-Species
Compatibility

Collected: Philippines
Aquarium: Reef
Survivability: Easy
Size: Less than 4" (10 cm)

FAM: Gobiidae
Yeongeichthys nebulosus
Nebulosus Poison Goby

General
Aggression

Color
Maintenance

Dietary
Requirements

Con-Species
Compatibility

Collected: Philippines
Aquarium: Reef
Survivability: Easy
Size: Less than 4" (10 cm)

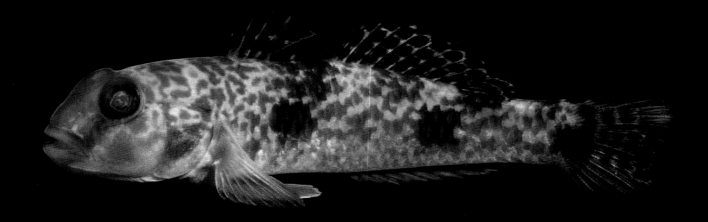

FAM: Haemulidae
*Plectorhinchus lineatus**
Lined Sweetlips
FORM: Juvenile

 General Aggression
 Color Maintenance
 Dietary Requirements
 Con-Species Compatibility

Collected: Philippines
Aquarium: Non-Reef
Survivability: Difficult
Size: More than 8" (20 cm)

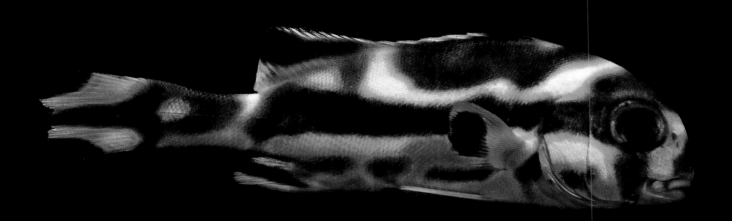

FAM: Haemulidae
*Plectorhinchus orientalis**
Oriental Sweetlips
FORM: Juvenile

 General Aggression
 Color Maintenance
 Dietary Requirements
 Con-Species Compatibility

Collected: Philippines
Aquarium: Non-Reef
Survivability: Doomed
Size: More than 8" (20 cm)

FAM: *Haemulidae*
Plectorhinchus picus* (Black & White)
Black & White Sweetlips
FORM: Juvenile

General Aggression   **Color Maintenance**   **Dietary Requirements**   **Con-Species Compatibility**

Collected: Philippines
Aquarium: Non-Reef
Survivability: Difficult
Size: More than 8" (20 cm)

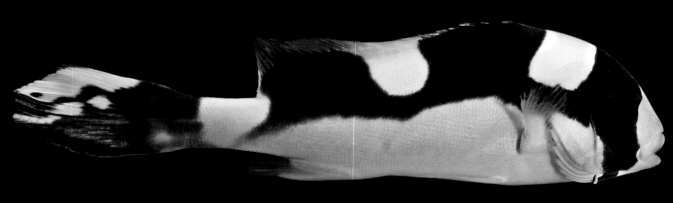

FAM: *Haemulidae*
Plectorhinchus pictus* (Slately)
Slately Sweetlips
FORM: Juvenile

General Aggression   **Color Maintenance**   **Dietary Requirements**   **Con-Species Compatibility**

Collected: Philippines
Aquarium: Non-Reef
Survivability: Difficult
Size: More than 8" (20 cm)

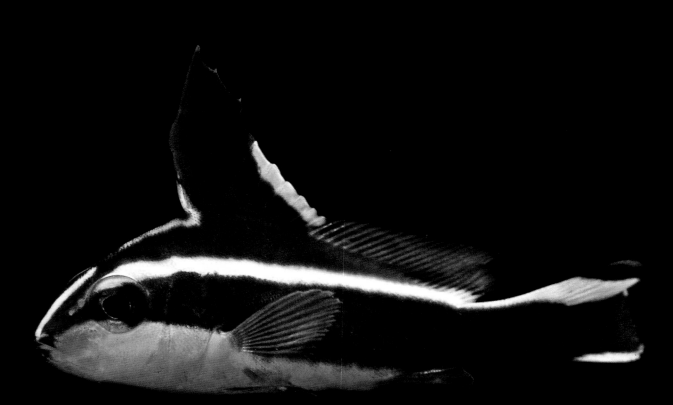

Family: Hemiscylliidae

(Bamboo Sharks) People are fascinated by sharks. If you set up a tank filled with beautiful fishes and another with sharks, people's attention will generally be immediately drawn to the shark tank. The shark's killing-machine efficiency — I believe — accounts for much of this interest. This ancient creature is such an efficient predator that its design has remained virtually unchanged since prehistoric times. Sharks do not have the same bony structure found in most other fishes. Instead, they sport a cartiliginous skeleton which gives them extreme flexibility. Also unlike most other fishes, Sharks fertilize their eggs through *internal* fertilization. Sharks tend to have sharp teeth and can inflict nasty wounds. Aquarists should handle them with care.

(Famille: Hemiscylliidae) Le public est particulièrement fasciné par les requins. Si vous installez un aquarium rempli de poissons magnifiques et un autre contenant des requins, en général, l'attention se portera immédiatement sur l'aquarium de requins. L'efficacité de cette machine à tuer ainsi que sa réputation expliquent l'intérêt qu'il suscite ! Cette créature est un prédateur d'une telle efficacité que sa forme n'a presque pas changé depuis les temps préhistoriques. Les requins n'ont pas la même structure osseuse que celle trouvée chez la plupart des autres poissons, ils possèdent à la place un squelette cartilagineux qui leur donne leur extrême souplesse. Vivipares ou ovipares et contrairement à la majorité des poissons, les requins ont besoin de réellement s'accoupler pour la fécondation de leurs oeufs. Même de petite taille, ils ont tendance à posséder des dents acérées qui peuvent infliger des blessures douloureuses. Les aquariophiles devraient les manipuler prudemment.

(Tiburón Bambú) La mayoría de las personas se sienten fascinados con los tiburones. Si uno llena una pecera de peces bellos y otra con tiburones, las personas generalmente se sentirán atraídos al tanque de tiburones. En mi opinión, gran parte de este interés se explica por la eficiencia del tiburón como maquinaria letal. Esta criatura milenaria es un predador tan eficiente que su diseño corporal se ha mantenido de hecho sin variación desde la época prehistórica. Los tiburones no poseen la misma estructura osea que encontramos en la mayoría de los demás peces. En su lugar, gozan de un esqueleto cartilaginoso que les da extrema flexibilidad. También a diferencia de la mayoría de los demás peces, los tiburones fertilizan sus huevos mediante fertilización interna. Los tiburones tienden a tener dientes afilados y pueden infligir heridas peligrosas. Los aficionados del acuarismo deben manipularlos con cuidado.

Family: Hemiscylliidae

(Família: Hemiscylliidae) As pessoas são fascinadas por tubarões. Se você montar um tanque com lindos peixes e outro com tubarões, a atenção das pessoas se voltará imediatamente para o tanque de tubarões. A eficiência da máquina mortífera do Tubarão, creio, é responsável por grande parte desse interesse. Essa antiga criatura é um predador tão eficiente, que sua estrutura permaneceu virtualmente inalterada desde os tempos pré-históricos. Os Tubarões não têm a mesma estrutura óssea encontrada na maioria dos outros peixes. Em vez disso, eles ostentam um esqueleto cartilaginoso que lhes oferece extrema flexibilidade. Também diferentemente da maioria dos outros peixes, os Tubarões fertilizam seus ovos através de fertilização interna. Os Tubarões tendem a ter dentes afiados e podem infligir graves ferimentos. Os aquaristas devem manuseá-los com cuidado.

(Famiglia: Hemiscyllidae) Moltissime persone sono affascinate dai pescicani. Se si sistema un acquario pieno di pesci bellissimi e un altro di pescicani, generalmente l'attenzione delle persone sarà attratta dall'acquario con i pescicani. Credo che sia la micidiale efficacia del pescecane il motivo principale di questo interesse. Questa antica creatura è un così abile predatore che la forma del corpo è rimasta quasi inalterata dai tempi preistorici. I pescicani non hanno la stessa struttura ossea riscontrata nella maggior parte degli altri pesci. Invece, hanno uno scheletro cartilagineo che consente loro una grande flessibilità. Inoltre, a differenza della maggioranza degli altri pesci, i pescicani si riproducono mediante fecondazione interna. I pescicani possiedono generalmente una dentatura affilata e possono infliggere profonde ferite. Gli appassionati devono maneggiarli con molta cautela.

FAM: Hemiscylliidae
Chiloscyllium griseum
Brown Bamboo Shark
FORM: Juvenile

General
Aggression

Color
Maintenance

Dietary
Requirements

Con-Species
Compatibility

Collected: Philippines
Aquarium: Non-Reef
Survivability: Moderate
Size: More than 8" (20 cm)

FAM: Hemiscylliidae
Chiloscyllium plagiosum
Whitespotted Bamboo Shark
FORM: Juvenile

General
Aggression

Color
Maintenance

Dietary
Requirements

Con-Species
Compatibility

Collected: Philippines
Aquarium: Non-Reef
Survivability: Moderate
Size: More than 8" (20 cm)

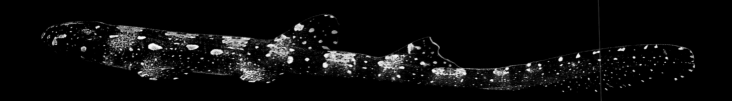

FAM: Hemiscylliidae
Chiloscyllium punctatum
Banded Bamboo Shark
FORM: Juvenile

General
Aggression

Color
Maintenance

Dietary
Requirements

Con-Species
Compatibility

Collected: Philippines
Aquarium: Non-Reef
Survivability: Moderate
Size: More than 8" (20 cm)

131

Family: Holocentridae

(Squirrelfishes & Soilderfishes) Family Holocentridae consists of nocturnal predators. Their large eyes attest to these nocturnal habits. In the wild, they eat primarily small fishes and crustaceans. They eat readily in an aquarium and are not particularly finicky about what you feed them. Because they are used to lowlight conditions, either supply them with plenty of dark crevices where they can avoid the light, or set up a low-light aquarium.

(Famille: Holocentridae) Les membres de la famille des *Holocentridae* sont des prédateurs nocturnes. Leurs grands yeux attestent de leurs habitudes nocturnes. Dans leur habitat naturel, leur repas est principalement constitué de petits poissons et de crustacés, mais ils se nourrissent facilement en aquarium et ne sont pas particulièrement difficiles. Il est important de leur procurer des endroits ombrés où ils pourront se cacher de la lumière.

(Pez Soldado y Pez Candil) Los miembros de la familia Holocentridae son predadores nocturnos. Sus ojos grandes atestiguan a sus hábitos nocturnos. En estado natural, comen principalmente pequeños peces y crustáceos. Comen sin dificultad en una pecera y no son particularmente melindrosos de lo que se alimentan. Como están acostumbrados a condiciones de poca iluminación, se les debe proporcionar un ambiente con bastantes grietas oscuras donde pueden guarnecerse de la luz o diseñar una pecera de poca iluminación.

(Família: Holocentridae) Os componentes da família Holocentridae são predadores noturnos. Seus grandes olhos comprovam seus hábitos noturnos. Em seu estado natural de existência, comem principalmente pequenos peixes e crustáceos. Comem facilmente em aquário, não sendo particularmente enjoados sobre o tipo de comida que recebem. Uma vez que estão acostumados a condições de pouca luminosidade, devem ser colocados em aquário com muitas frestas escuras, onde eles possam evitar a luz, ou aquário com pouca luminosidade.

(Famiglia: Holocentridae) Gli Holocentridae sono predatori notturni come mostrano anche i loro occhi grandi. In natura si nutrono principalmente di piccoli pesci e crostacei. In acquario accettano cibo facilmente e non sono particolarmente esigenti per quanto riguarda il tipo di alimenti. Poiché sono abituati a condizioni di scarsa luminosità, si deve predisporre molti anfratti bui in cui possano sfuggire la luce e sistemare l'acquario in una zona non troppo intensamente illuminata.

FAM: Holocentridae
Sargocentron caudimaculatum
Tailspot Squirrelfish

General Aggression

Color Maintenance

Dietary Requirements

Con-Species Compatibility

Aquarium: Non-Reef
Survivability: Moderate
Size: 4" (10 cm) – 8" (20 cm

FAM: Holocentridae
Sargocentron melanospilos
Three Spot Squirrelfish

   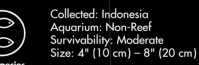

General Aggression

Color Maintenance

Dietary Requirements

Con-Species Compatibility

Collected: Indonesia
Aquarium: Non-Reef
Survivability: Moderate
Size: 4" (10 cm) – 8" (20 cm)

Family: Labridae

(Wrasses) Wrasses represent perhaps the largest number of species in the aquarium trade. Most of them are colorful. As juveniles their coloration is often different from that of adults, and the changes are dramatic. It is com on for members of this family to change sex when only one sex is present in an environment (usually from fema o male). The majority of species in the Labridae family can be highly recommended for the beginner because they re easy to keep.

Most of these fishes swim with their pectoral fin, using their tail fin for steering and bursts of speed o escape danger. A number of species serve as cleaner fishes. Some of them bury themselves in the sand when ightened or to sleep at night. Most members of the Labridae family are bottom-feeders, and will eat just about nything. This makes the majority of them quite easy to keep in a tank since they don't require any particular diet.

The coloration of the males, females, and juveniles of a single species in this family are often all distinct from one nother. Therefore, we have frequently included separate entries for each of the different forms (male, female and juven

(Famille: Labridae) La famille des Labridae représente peut-être le plus grand nombre d'espèces proposées dans e commerce de l'aquariophilie. La plupart d'entre eux sont des poissons aux teintes chatoyantes. Les couleurs de ujets juvéniles diffèrent souvent de celles des adultes et les changements sont saisissants. Il est courant pour les nembres de cette famille de changer de sexe lorsque l'un des deux sexes est absent; ils se transforment énéralement de femelle en mâle.

a majorité des espèces dans la famille des Labridae peuvt être tout à fait recommandée pour le novice parce qu'ils ont faciles à garder. La plupart de ces poissons nagent avec leurs nageoires pectorales et utilisent leur nageoire audale pour se diriger et pour les pointes de vitesse qui leur permettent d'échapper au danger. Un certain nomb 'espèces servent de poissons nettoyeurs (ou poissons infirmiers). Certains d'entre eux s'enterrent dans le sable orsqu'ils sont effrayés ou pour dormir la nuit. La majorité des membres de la famille des Labridae se nourrit au ond et mange à peu près n'importe quoi, ce qui en fait des poissons faciles à garder en aquarium, puisque n'exige aucun régime particulier.

Les formes mâles, femelles et juvéniles d'une même espèce dans cette famille sont souvent de couleurs différentes, ous avons donc souvent inclus des paragraphes séparés pour chaque différent lorsqu'ils sont distincts les uns des autre

(Pez Labro) La familia Labridae quizás representa el número más grande de especies en el comercio de acuario. mayoría poseen colores brillantes. Presentan una coloración diferente en estado juvenil en comparación a la que oseen como adultos y a menudo, los cambios resultan dramáticos. Los miembros de esta familia comúnmente camb e sexo cuando sólo se encuentran presentes ejemplares de un sólo sexo, usualmente de hembra a macho. La nayoría de las especies en la familia Labridae pueden ser altamente recomendadas para el principiante porque sor íciles de mantener.

La mayoría de estos peces nadan con su aleta pectoral, utilizando su aleta de cola para maniobrar un curso o rranques de velocidad para escapar del peligro. Un número de especies sirve como peces limpiadores. Algunos e entierran en la arena cuando asustados o para dormir por la noche. Esta familia puede ser identificada por la resencia de 2 barbillas en sus mandíbulas que emplean para cavar y localizar alimento en el substrato marino. Estos eces se alimentan esencialmente de carroña y crustaceos, por lo qual son útiles en una pecera para limpiar el fondo ablandar el substrato. El problema en mantener estos peces es que con frecuencia no hay suficiente restos de omida en el fondo del tanque para que se puedan alimentar. En una pecera los peces que nadan libremente eneralmente agarran los alimentos antes que se lleguen al fondo. Estos peces suelen sentirse perfectamente onfortables en un tanque de arrecife. Esto se debe a que las peceras de arrecife generalmente están pobladas de eces más pequeños, menos agresivos y corales que no se alimentan de una manera particularmente minuciosa. E ste ambiente, los miembros de la familia Mullidae pueden no solamente prosperar sino cumplir una función valios n el mantenimiento del acuario.

FAM: Labridae
Bodianus anthoides
Lyretail Hogfish

 General Aggression

 Color Maintenance

 Dietary Requirements

 Con-Species Compatibility

Collected: Indonesia
Aquarium: Reef
Survivability: Moderate
Size: 4" (10 cm) – 8" (20 cm)

FAM: Labridae
Bodianus axillaris
Axilspot Hogfish

 General Aggression

 Color Maintenance

 Dietary Requirements

 Con-Species Compatibility

Collected: Indonesia
Aquarium: Non-Reef
Survivability: Easy
Size: 4" (10 cm) – 8" (20 cm)

139

FAM: Labridae
Bodianus diana
Diana's Hogfish
FORM: Adult

General Aggression

Color Maintenance

Dietary Requirements

Con-Species Compatibility

Collected: Indonesia
Aquarium: Non-Reef
Survivability: Easy
Size: 4" (10 cm) – 8" (20 cm)

FAM: Labridae
Bodianus diana
Diana's Hogfish
FORM: Juvenile

General Aggression

Color Maintenance

Dietary Requirements

Con-Species Compatibility

Collected: Indonesia
Aquarium: Non-Reef
Survivability: Easy
Size: 4" (10 cm) – 8" (20 cm)

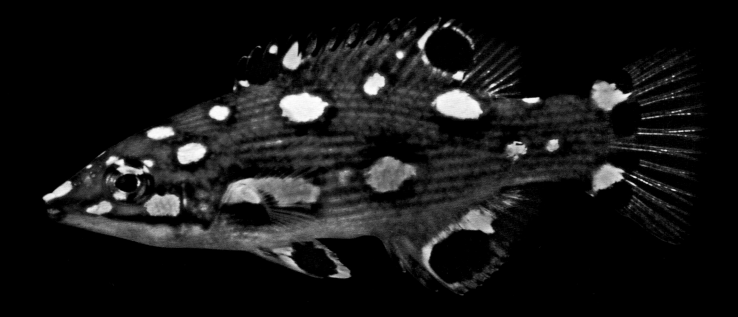

FAM: Labridae
Bodianus loxozonus
Pacific Saddle Hogfish
FORM: Adult

**General
Aggression**

**Color
Maintenance**

**Dietary
Requirements**

**Con-Species
Compatibility**

Collected: Indonesia
Aquarium: Non-Reef
Survivability: Easy
Size: 4" (10 cm) – 8" (20 cm)

FAM: Labridae
Bodianus loxozonus
Pacific Saddle Hogfish
FORM: Juvenile

**General
Aggression**

**Color
Maintenance**

**Dietary
Requirements**

**Con-Species
Compatibility**

Collected: Indonesia
Aquarium: Non-Reef
Survivability: Easy
Size: 4" (10 cm) – 8" (20 cm)

FAM: Labridae
Bodianus mesothorax
Coral Hogfish
FORM: Adult

 General Aggression

 Color Maintenance

 Dietary Requirements

 Con-Species Compatibility

Collected: Indonesia
Aquarium: Non-Reef
Survivability: Easy
Size: 4" (10 cm) – 8" (20 cm)

FAM: Labridae
Bodianus mesothorax
Coral Hogfish
FORM: Juvenile

 General Aggression

 Color Maintenance

 Dietary Requirements

 Con-Species Compatibility

Collected: Indonesia
Aquarium: Non-Reef
Survivability: Easy
Size: 4" (10 cm) – 8" (20 cm)

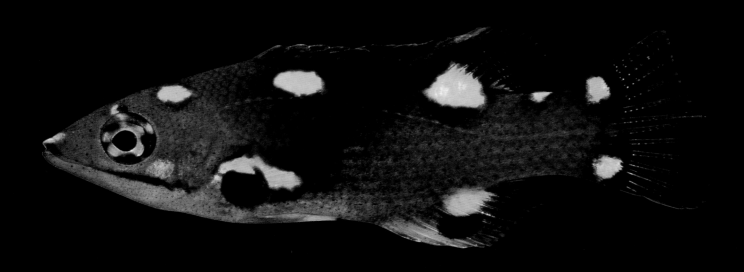

142

FAM: Labridae
Bodianus mesothorax
Coral Hogfish
FORM: Subadult

 General Aggression

 Color Maintenance

 Dietary Requirements

 **Con-Species Compatibility**

Collected: Indonesia
Aquarium: Non-Reef
Survivability: Easy
Size: 4" (10 cm) – 8" (20 cm)

FAM: Labridae
Cheilinus oxycephalus
Red Hog Wrasse

 General Aggression

 Color Maintenance

 Dietary Requirements

 Con-Species Compatibility

Collected: Indonesia
Aquarium: Non-Reef
Survivability: Moderate
Size: 4" (10 cm) – 8" (20 cm)

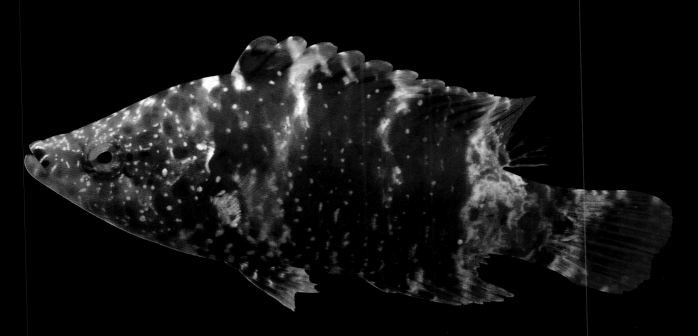

FAM: Labridae
Cheilinus **sp. "Redtail Hog"***
Redtail Hog Wrasse

General Aggression **Color Maintenance** **Dietary Requirements** **Con-Species Compatibility**

Collected: Indonesia
Aquarium: Non-Reef
Survivability: Moderate
Size: 4" (10 cm) – 8" (20 cm)

FAM: Labridae
Cheilio inermis
Cigar Wrasse

General Aggression **Color Maintenance** **Dietary Requirements** **Con-Species Compatibility**

Collected: Indonesia
Aquarium: Non-Reef
Survivability: Doomed
Size: 4" (10 cm) – 8" (20 cm)

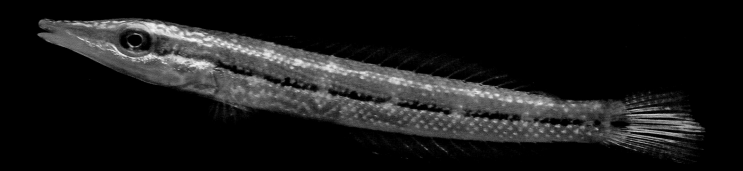

FAM: Labridae
Choerodon fasciatus
Harlequin Tuskfish

General Aggression

Color Maintenance

Dietary Requirements

Con-Species Compatibility

Collected: Philippines
Aquarium: Non-Reef
Survivability: Moderate
Size: More than 8" (20 cm)

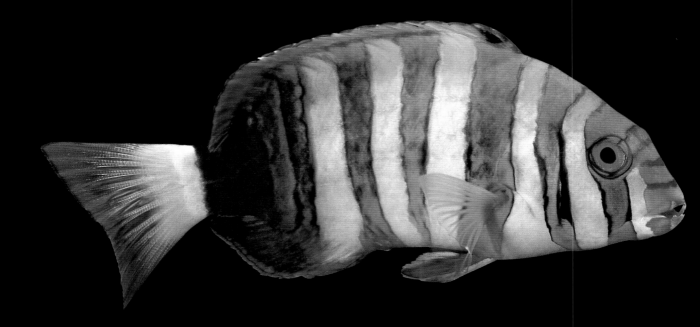

FAM: Labridae
Cirrhilabrus cyanopleura
Blueside Fairy Wrasse

General Aggression

Color Maintenance

Dietary Requirements

Con-Species Compatibility

Collected: Indonesia
Aquarium: Reef (Caution)
Survivability: Moderate
Size: 4" (10 cm) – 8" (20 cm)

145

FAM: Labridae
Cirrhilabrus exquisitus
Exquisite Fairy Wrasse

General Aggression

Color Maintenance

Dietary Requirements

Con-Species Compatibility

Collected: Indonesia
Aquarium: Reef (Caution)
Survivability: Moderate
Size: 4" (10 cm) – 8" (20 cm)

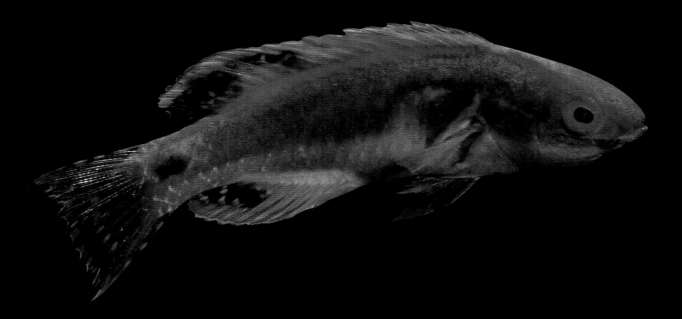

FAM: Labridae
Cirrhilabrus lubbocki
Lubbock's Fairy Wrasse

General Aggression

Color Maintenance

Dietary Requirements

Con-Species Compatibility

Collected: Indonesia
Aquarium: Reef (Caution)
Survivability: Moderate
Size: 4" (10 cm) – 8" (20 cm)

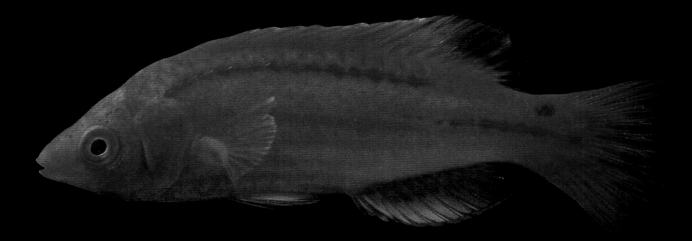

146

FAM: Labridae
Cirrhilabrus luteovitatus
Velvet Fairy Wrasse
FORM: Female

General Aggression

Color Maintenance

Dietary Requirements

Con-Species Compatibility

Collected: Indonesia
Aquarium: Reef (Caution)
Survivability: Moderate
Size: 4" (10 cm) – 8" (20 cm)

FAM: Labridae
Cirrhilabrus luteovitatus
Velvet Fairy Wrasse
FORM: Male

General Aggression

Color Maintenance

Dietary Requirements

Con-Species Compatibility

Collected: Indonesia
Aquarium: Reef (Caution)
Survivability: Moderate
Size: 4" (10 cm) – 8" (20 cm)

FAM: Labridae
Cirrhilabrus rubrimarginatus
Red-margin Fairy Wrasse
FORM: Female

General Aggression

Color Maintenance

Dietary Requirements

Con-Species Compatibility

Collected: Indonesia
Aquarium: Reef (Caution)
Survivability: Moderate
Size: 4" (10 cm) – 8" (20 cm)

FAM: Labridae
Cirrhilabrus rubrimarginatus
Red-margin Fairy Wrasse
FORM: Male

General Aggression

Color Maintenance

Dietary Requirements

Con-Species Compatibility

Collected: Indonesia
Aquarium: Reef (Caution)
Survivability: Moderate
Size: 4" (10 cm) – 8" (20 cm)

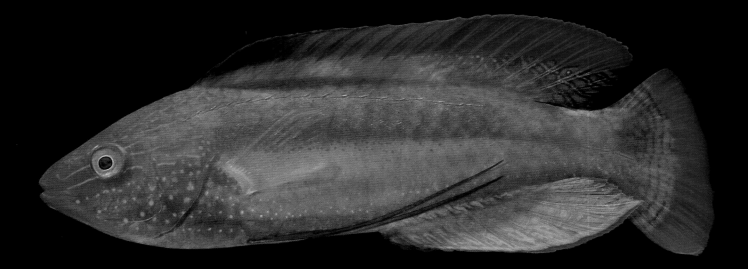

FAM: Labridae
Cirrhilabrus rubripinnis
Scarlet-finned Fairy Wrasse

General Aggression

Color Maintenance

Dietary Requirements

Con-Species Compatibility

Collected: Indonesia
Aquarium: Reef (Caution)
Survivability: Moderate
Size: 4" (10 cm) – 8" (20 cm)

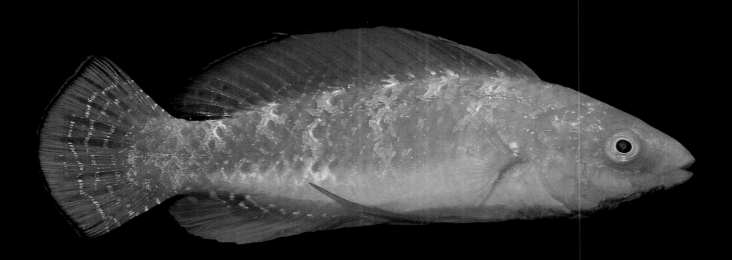

FAM: Labridae
Cirrhilabrus solorensis
Violet-bellied Fairy Wrasse
FORM: Female

General Aggression

Color Maintenance

Dietary Requirements

Con-Species Compatibility

Collected: Indonesia
Aquarium: Reef (Caution)
Survivability: Moderate
Size: 4" (10 cm) – 8" (20 cm)

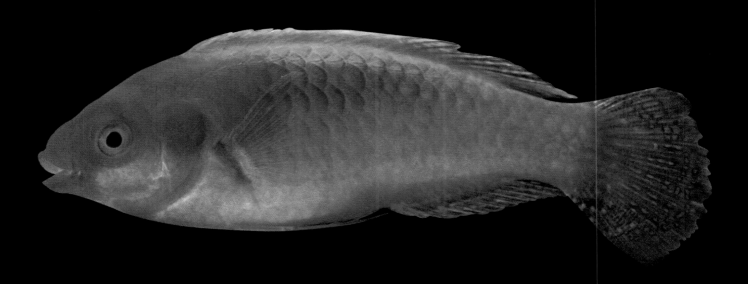

149

FAM: Labridae
Cirrhilabrus sp. "Spot-tail"*
Spot-tail Fairy Wrasse

General Aggression Color Maintenance Dietary Requirements Con-Species Compatibility

Collected: Indonesia
Aquarium: Reef (Caution)
Survivability: Moderate
Size: 4" (10 cm) – 8" (20

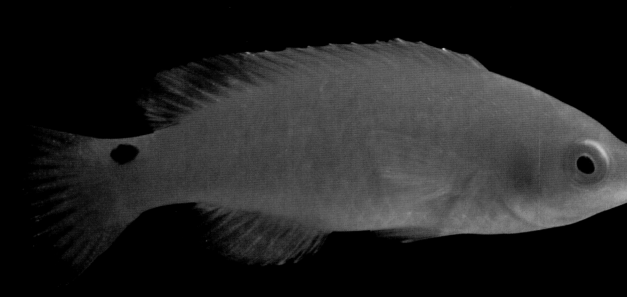

FAM: Labridae
Coris aygula
Twinspot Wrasse
FORM: Juvenile

General Aggression Color Maintenance Dietary Requirements Con-Species Compatibility

Collected: Phillipines
Aquarium: Reef (Caution)
Survivability: Difficult
Size: More than 8" (20 cm)

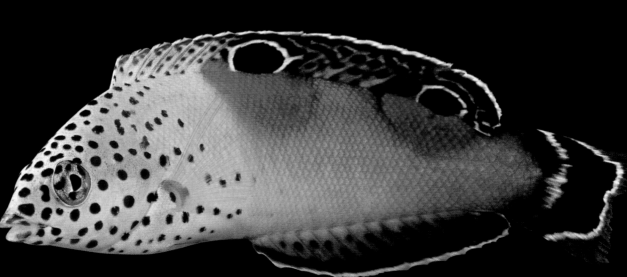

FAM: Labridae
Halichoeres biocellatus
Noel Wrasse

General Aggression

Color Maintenance

Dietary Requirements

Con-Species Compatibility

Collected: Indonesia
Aquarium: Non-Reef
Survivability: Moderate
Size: 4" (10 cm) – 8" (20 cm)

FAM: Labridae
Halichoeres chloropterus
Green Coris
FORM: Adult

General Aggression

Color Maintenance

Dietary Requirements

Con-Species Compatibility

Collected: Indonesia
Aquarium: Non-Reef
Survivability: Moderate
Size: 4" (10 cm) – 8" (20 cm)

FAM: Labridae
Halichoeres chloropterus
Green Coris
FORM: Juvenile

General
Aggression

Color
Maintenance

Dietary
Requirements

Con-Species
Compatibility

Collected: Indonesia
Aquarium: Non-Reef
Survivability: Doomed
Size: 4" (10 cm) – 8" (20 cm)

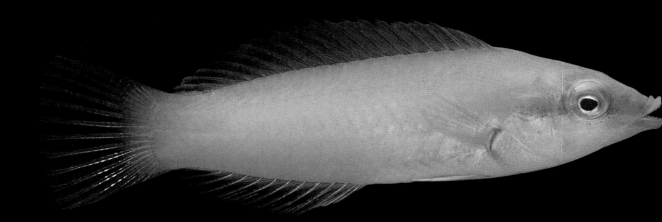

FAM: Labridae
Halichoeres chrysus
Yellow Coris
FORM: Juvenile

General
Aggression

Color
Maintenance

Dietary
Requirements

Con-Species
Compatibility

Collected: Philippines
Aquarium: Reef (Caution)
Survivability: Moderate
Size: 4" (10 cm) – 8" (20 cm)

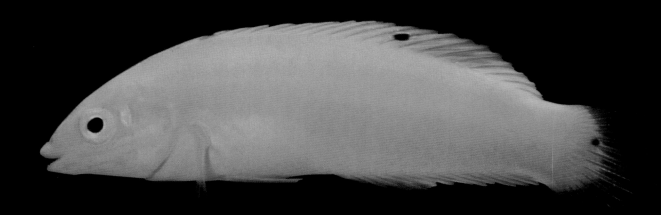

FAM: Labridae
Halichoeres hortulanus
Marble Wrasse
FORM: Juvenile

General Aggression

Color Maintenance

Dietary Requirements

Con-Species Compatibility

Collected: Philippines
Aquarium: Non-Reef
Survivability: Moderate
Size: 4" (10 cm) – 8" (20 cm)

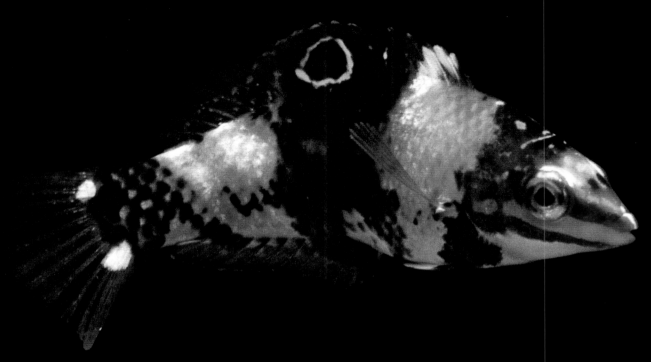

FAM: Labridae
Halichoeres hortulanus
Marble Wrasse
FORM: Subadult

General Aggression

Color Maintenance

Dietary Requirements

Con-Species Compatibility

Collected: Philippines
Aquarium: Non-Reef
Survivability: Moderate
Size: 4" (10 cm) – 8" (20 cm)

157

FAM: Labridae
Halichoeres margaritaceus
Bleeding Heart Wrasse

General Aggression

Color Maintenance

Dietary Requirements

Con-Species Compatibility

Collected: Philippines
Aquarium: Non-Reef
Survivability: Moderate
Size: 4" (10 cm) – 8" (20 cm)

FAM: Labridae
Halichoeres marginatus
Dusky Wrasse

General Aggression

Color Maintenance

Dietary Requirements

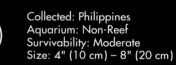
Con-Species Compatibility

Collected: Philippines
Aquarium: Non-Reef
Survivability: Moderate
Size: 4" (10 cm) – 8" (20 cm)

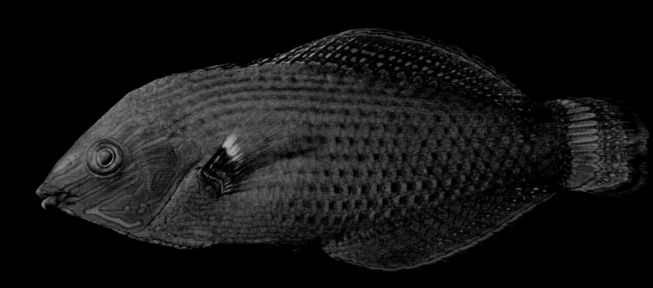

FAM: Labridae
Halichoeres melanochir
Black Wrasse

 General Aggression

 Color Maintenance

 Dietary Requirements

 Con-Species Compatibility

Collected: Philippines
Aquarium: Non-Reef
Survivability: Difficult
Size: 4" (10 cm) – 8" (20 cm)

FAM: Labridae
Halichoeres melanurus
Pinstriped Wrasse

 General Aggression

 Color Maintenance

 Dietary Requirements

 Con-Species Compatibility

Collected: Philippines
Aquarium: Non-Reef
Survivability: Difficult
Size: 4" (10 cm) – 8" (20 cm)

FAM: Labridae
Halichoeres podostigma*
Checkerboard Wrasse

 General Aggression

 Color Maintenance

 Dietary Requirements

Con-Species Compatibility

Collected: Philippines
Aquarium: Non-Reef
Survivability: Moderate
Size: 4" (10 cm) – 8" (20 cm)

FAM: Labridae
Halichoeres prosopeion
Twotone Wrasse

 General Aggression

 Color Maintenance

 Dietary Requirements

 Con-Species Compatibility

Collected: Philippines
Aquarium: Non-Reef
Survivability: Moderate
Size: 4" (10 cm) – 8" (20 cm)

160

FAM: Labridae
Halichoeres prosopeion (Dark)
Twotone Wrasse (Dark)

General Aggression

Color Maintenance

Dietary Requirements

Con-Species Compatibility

Collected: Philippines
Aquarium: Non-Reef
Survivability: Moderate
Size: 4" (10 cm) – 8" (20 cm)

FAM: Labridae
Halichoeres solorensis
Yellow-cheek Wrasse

General Aggression

Color Maintenance

Dietary Requirements

Con-Species Compatibility

Collected: Philippines
Aquarium: Non-Reef
Survivability: Moderate
Size: 4" (10 cm) – 8" (20 cm)

FAM: Labridae
Halichoeres vrolikii
Clown Face Wrasse

General Aggression

Color Maintenance

Dietary Requirements

Con-Species Compatibility

Collected: Philippines
Aquarium: Non-Reef
Survivability: Easy
Size: 4" (10 cm) – 8" (20 cm)

FAM: Labridae
Hemigymnus fasciatus
Banded Clownhead Wrasse
FORM: Adult

General Aggression

Color Maintenance

Dietary Requirements

Con-Species Compatibility

Collected: Philippines
Aquarium: Non-Reef
Survivability: Difficult
Size: 4" (10 cm) – 8" (20 cm)

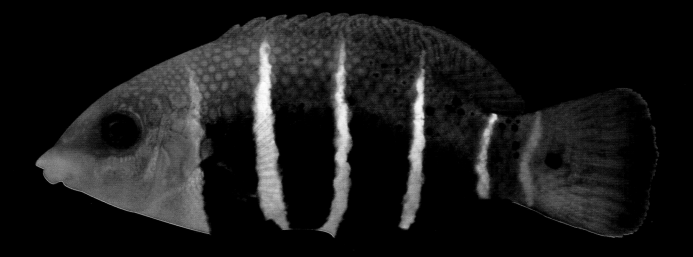

162

FAM: Labridae
Hemigymnus fasciatus
Banded Clownhead Wrasse
FORM: Juvenile

General
Aggression

Color
Maintenance

Dietary
Requirements

Con-Species
Compatibility

Collected: Philippines
Aquarium: Non-Reef
Survivability: Difficult
Size: 4" (10 cm) – 8" (20 cm)

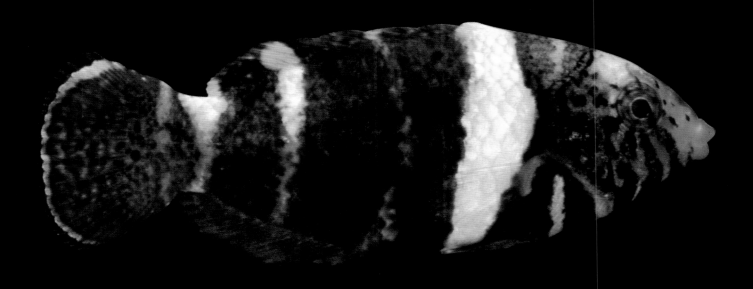

FAM: Labridae
Hemigymnus melapterus
Half & Half Wrasse

General
Aggression

Color
Maintenance

Dietary
Requirements

Con-Species
Compatibility

Collected: Philippines
Aquarium: Non-Reef
Survivability: Moderate
Size: 4" (10 cm) – 8" (20 cm)

163

FAM: Labridae
*Hologymnosus doliatus**
Candycane Wrasse

General Aggression

Color Maintenance

Dietary Requirements

Con-Species Compatibility

Collected: Philippines
Aquarium: Non-Reef
Survivability: Difficult
Size: More than 8" (20 cm)

FAM: Labridae
Labroides bicolor
Bicolor Cleaner Wrasse

General Aggression

Color Maintenance

Dietary Requirements

Con-Species Compatibility

Collected: Philippines
Aquarium: Non-Reef
Survivability: Doomed
Size: Less than 4" (10 cm)

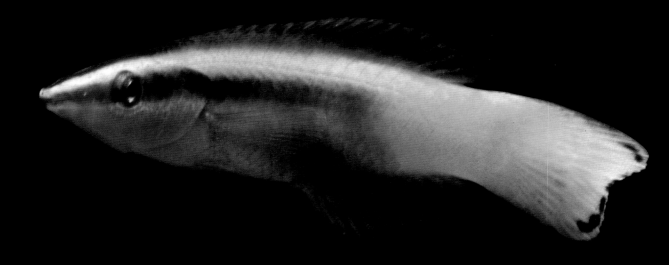

FAM: Labridae
Labroides dimidiatus
Cleaner Wrasse

 General Aggression

 Color Maintenance

 Dietary Requirements

 Con-Species Compatibility

Collected: Philippines
Aquarium: Reef
Survivability: Difficult
Size: Less than 4" (10 cm)

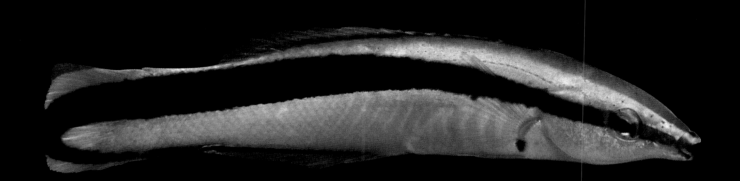

FAM: Labridae
Labroides pectoralis
Blackspot Cleaner Wrasse

 General Aggression

 Color Maintenance

 Dietary Requirements

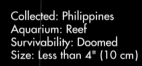 **Con-Species Compatibility**

Collected: Philippines
Aquarium: Reef
Survivability: Doomed
Size: Less than 4" (10 cm)

FAM: Labridae
Labropsis manabei
Two-line Wrasse

General Aggression

Color Maintenance

Dietary Requirements

Con-Species Compatibility

Collected: Indonesia
Aquarium: Non-Reef
Survivability: Difficult
Size: Less than 4" (10 cm)

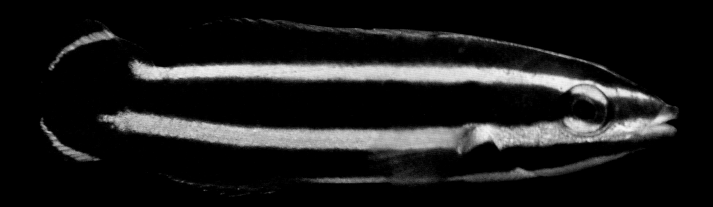

FAM: Labridae
Labropsis xanthonota
Comet Wrasse
FAM: Female

General Aggression

Color Maintenance

Dietary Requirements

Con-Species Compatibility

Collected: Philippines
Aquarium: Non-Reef
Survivability: Doomed
Size: 4" (10 cm) – 8" (20 cm)

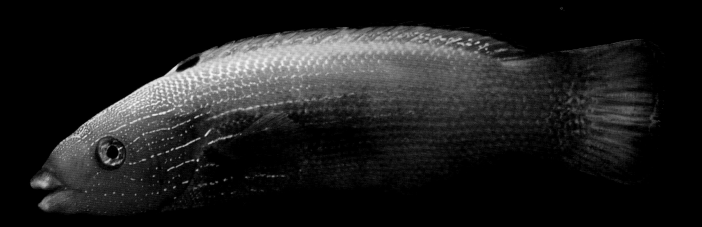

FAM: Labridae
Labropsis xanthonota
Comet Wrasse
FORM: Juvenile

General Aggression

Color Maintenance

Dietary Requirements

Con-Species Compatibility

Collected: Philippines
Aquarium: Non-Reef
Survivability: Doomed
Size: 4" (10 cm) – 8" (20 cm)

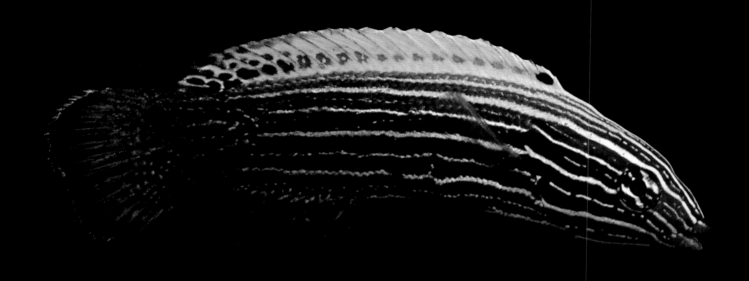

FAM: Labridae
Labropsis xanthonota
Comet Wrasse
FORM: Male

General Aggression

Color Maintenance

Dietary Requirements

Con-Species Compatibility

Collected: Philippines
Aquarium: Non-Reef
Survivability: Doomed
Size: 4" (10 cm) – 8" (20 cm)

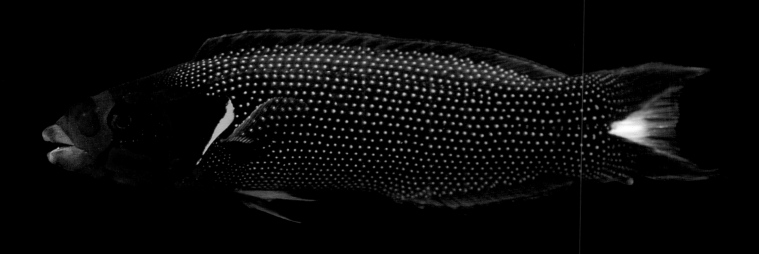

167

FAM: Labridae
Macropharyngodon meleagris
Leopard Wrasse

General Aggression   Color Maintenance   Dietary Requirements   Con-Species Compatibility

Collected: Indonesia
Aquarium: Reef (Caution)
Survivability: Difficult
Size: Less than 4" (10 cm)

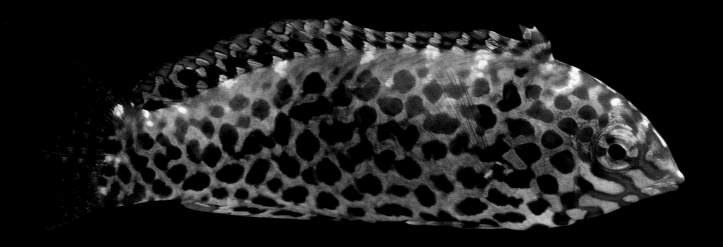

FAM: Labridae
Macropharyngodon negrosensis
Black Leopard Wrasse

General Aggression   Color Maintenance   Dietary Requirements   Con-Species Compatibility

Collected: Indonesia
Aquarium: Reef (Caution)
Survivability: Difficult
Size: Less than 4" (10 cm)

FAM: Labridae
Macropharyngodon ornatus (Green)
Ornate Leopard Wrasse (Green)

General Aggression

Color Maintenance

Dietary Requirements

Con-Species Compatibility

Collected: Indonesia
Aquarium: Reef (Caution)
Survivability: Difficult
Size: Less than 4" (10 cm)

FAM: Labridae
Macropharyngodon ornatus (Red)
Ornate Leopard Wrasse (Red)

General Aggression

Color Maintenance

Dietary Requirements

Con-Species Compatibility

Collected: Indonesia
Aquarium: Reef (Caution)
Survivability: Difficult
Size: Less than 4" (10 cm)

169

FAM: Labridae
Novaculichthys macrolepidotus
Chameleon Wrasse

General Aggression   Color Maintenance   Dietary Requirements   Con-Species Compatibility

Collected: Indonesia
Aquarium: Non-Reef
Survivability: Easy
Size: 4" (10 cm) – 8" (20 cm)

FAM: Labridae
Novaculichthys taeniourus
Dragon Wrasse
FORM: Adult

General Aggression   Color Maintenance   Dietary Requirements   Con-Species Compatibility

Collected: Philippines
Aquarium: Non-Reef
Survivability: Moderate
Size: More than 8" (20 cm)

FAM: Labridae
Novaculichthys taeniourus
Dragon Wrasse
FORM: Juvenile

General Aggression

Color Maintenance

Dietary Requirements

Con-Species Compatibility

Collected: Philippines
Aquarium: Non-Reef
Survivability: Moderate
Size: More than 8" (20 cm)

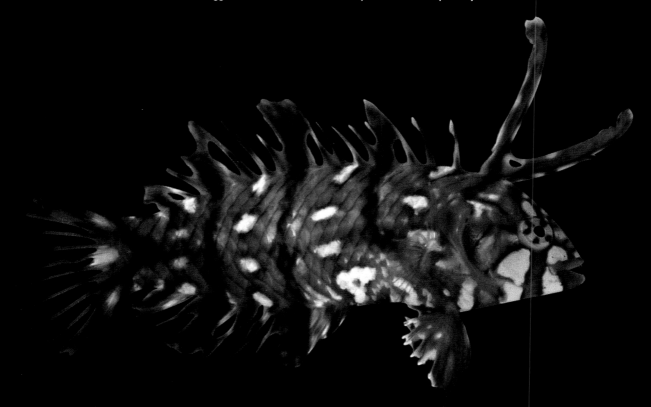

FAM: Labridae
Paracheilinus carpenteri*
Carpenter's Parrot Wrasse
FORM: Female

General Aggression

Color Maintenance

Dietary Requirements

Con-Species Compatibility

Collected: Indonesia
Aquarium: Reef (Caution)
Survivability: Moderate
Size: 4" (10 cm) – 8" (20 cm)

FAM: Labridae
Paracheilinus carpenteri
Carpenter's Parrot Wrasse
FORM: Male

General Aggression   Color Maintenance   Dietary Requirements   Con-Species Compatibility

Collected: Indonesia
Aquarium: Reef (Caution)
Survivability: Moderate
Size: 4" (10 cm) – 8" (20 cm)

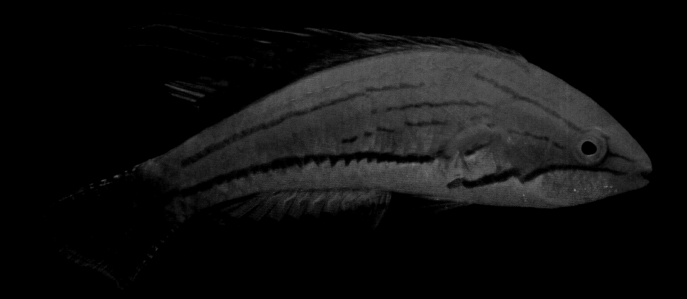

FAM: Labridae
Paracheilinus lineopunctatus
Red Parrot Wrasse

General Aggression   Color Maintenance   Dietary Requirements   Con-Species Compatibility

Collected: Indonesia
Aquarium: Reef (Caution)
Survivability: Difficult
Size: 4" (10 cm) – 8" (20 cm)

172

FAM: Labridae
Pseudojuloides sp. "Psychedelic"*
Psychedelic Pencil Wrasse

General Aggression **Color Maintenance** **Dietary Requirements** **Con-Species Compatibility**

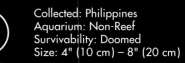

Collected: Philippines
Aquarium: Non-Reef
Survivability: Doomed
Size: 4" (10 cm) – 8" (20 cm)

FAM: Labridae
Stethojulius interrupta
Cutribbon Wrasse
FORM: Female

General Aggression **Color Maintenance** **Dietary Requirements** **Con-Species Compatibility**

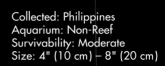

Collected: Philippines
Aquarium: Non-Reef
Survivability: Moderate
Size: 4" (10 cm) – 8" (20 cm)

17

FAM: Labridae
Stethojulius trilineata
Three-line Wrasse
FORM: Female

General Aggression

Color Maintenance

Dietary Requirements

Con-Species Compatibility

Collected: Philippines
Aquarium: Non-Reef
Survivability: Moderate
Size: 4" (10 cm) – 8" (20 cm)

FAM: Labridae
Stethojulius trilineata
Three-line Wrasse
FORM: Male

General Aggression

Color Maintenance

Dietary Requirements

Con-Species Compatibility

Collected: Philippines
Aquarium: Non-Reef
Survivability: Moderate
Size: 4" (10 cm) – 8" (20 cm)

FAM: Labridae
Thalassoma hardwicke
Sixbar Wrasse

General Aggression

Color Maintenance

Dietary Requirements

Con-Species Compatibility

Collected: Philippines
Aquarium: Non-Reef
Survivability: Easy
Size: 4" (10 cm) – 8" (20 cm)

FAM: Labridae
Thalassoma lunare
Moon Wrasse
FORM: Adult

General Aggression

Color Maintenance

Dietary Requirements

Con-Species Compatibility

Collected: Philippines
Aquarium: Non-Reef
Survivability: Easy
Size: 4" (10 cm) – 8" (20 cm)

FAM: Labridae
Thalassoma lunare
Moon Wrasse
FORM: Subadult

General
Aggression

Color
Maintenance

Dietary
Requirements

Con-Species
Compatibility

Collected: Philippines
Aquarium: Non-Reef
Survivability: Easy
Size: 4" (10 cm) – 8" (20 cm)

FAM: Labridae
Thalassoma quinquevittatum
Fivestripe Wrasse

General
Aggression

Color
Maintenance

Dietary
Requirements

Con-Species
Compatibility

Collected: Philippines
Aquarium: Non-Reef
Survivability: Moderate
Size: 4" (10 cm) – 8" (20 cm)

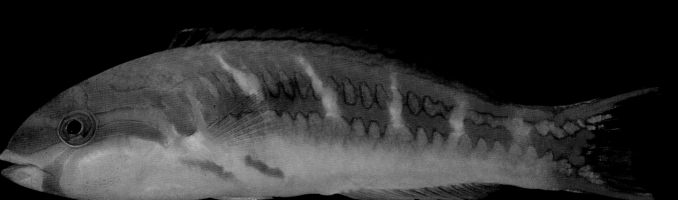

FAM. Labridae
Xyrichtys pavo
Indian Razor Wrasse

**General
Aggression**

**Color
Maintenance**

**Dietary
Requirements**

**Con-Species
Compatibility**

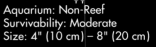

Aquarium: Non-Reef
Survivability: Moderate
Size: 4" (10 cm) – 8" (20 cm)

Family: Lutjanidae

(Snappers) The majority of these fishes — like members of the family Carangidae — are considered food fishes. In fact, only a few are attractive enough to be ornamental fish. In my opinion, most spectacular of these are *Symphorichthys spilurus* (High-finned Snapper) and *Lutjanus seabae* (Emperor Snapper). Even those that are suitable for aquariums boast their best color when juveniles. When most snappers become adults, they both lose color and become too large to comfortably fit in a home aquarium. As a consequence, this family is generally sold, within the aquarium trade, when in juvenile form. Despite these shortcomings they are good for beginning hobbyists because of their hardiness.

(Famille: Lutjanidae) La majorité de ces poissons, comme les membres de la famille des Carangidae sont, sur leur lieu de pêche, considérés comme des « poissons de consommation ». En fait, quelques spécimens seulement sont suffisamment beaux pour être classés comme des « poissons ornementaux ». A mon avis, les espèces les plus spectaculaires de cette famille sont le *Symphorichthys spilurus* et le *Lutjanus seabae*. Même les spécimens appropriés pour l'aquarium n'arborent leur plus belles couleurs que lorsqu'ils sont juvéniles. Lorsqu'ils atteignent l'âge adulte, ils perdent souvent leur éclat et deviennent trop gros et trop imposants pour rester confortablement dans un aquarium classique. De ce fait, le commerce de l'aquariophilie ne vend en général ces espèces que sous leur forme juvénile. Malgré ces inconvénients, leur robustesse en fait des poissons recommandables aux débutants.

(Pez Pargo) La mayoría de estos peces, al igual que los miembros de la familia Carangidae, se consideran como pescado de alimento. De hecho, sólo unos pocos ejemplares son lo suficientemente atractivos para ser considerados como peces ornamentales. En mi opinión, los mas espectaculares de éstos son el *Symphorichthys spilurus* (Pargo Velifero) y el *Lutjanus Sebae* (Pargo Emperador). Hasta los más apropiados para peceras ostentan sus mejores colores en su etapa juvenil. Cuando la mayoría de las pargos se convierten en adultos, a menudo pierden tanto sus colores como se hacen demasiado grandes para mantenerse cómodamente en una pecera de hogar. Como consecuencia, los miembros de esta familia generalmente se vende en estado juvenil en las tiendas de peces. A pesar de estas deficiencias, resultan buenos para aficionados principiantes debido a su fortaleza.

(Caranhos) A maioria destes peixes - como os membros da família Carangidae - são considerados peixes comestíveis. Na verdade, apenas poucos deles são atraentes o suficiente para serem peixes ornamentais. Na minha opinião, os mais fantásticos entre eles são os *Symphorichthys spilurus*. ("Hifin Snapper") e os *Lutjanus Sebae* ("Emperor Snapper"). Mesmo os que são adequados para aquários apresentam sua melhor cor enquanto jovens. Ao se tornarem adultos, a maioria dos caranhos perdem a cor e tornam-se grandes demais para caber confortavelmente em um aquário doméstico. Como conseqüência, normalmente os membros desta família são vendidos enquanto jovens no comércio de aquários. Apesar dessas desvantagens, são bons peixes para os iniciantes, devido à sua resistência.

(Famiglia: Lutjanidae) La maggior parte dei membri di questa famiglia, come quelli della famiglia Carangidae, sono pesci commestibili. Infatti, soltanto alcune specie sono abbastanza belle da poter essere considerate ornamentali. Secondo me, i più spettacolari tra questi sono *Symphorichthys spilurus* e *Lutjanus sebae*. Anche quelli idonei all'acquariofilia mostrano una livrea dai colori più vivaci quando sono giovani. Quando molti Lutjanidae diventano adulti, la loro colorazione sbiadisce e diventano troppo grandi per essere allevati negli acquari domestici. Per questo motivo, di solito questi pesci vengono venduti sul mercato dell'acquariofilia solo quando sono giovani. Nonostante questi difetti, sono indicati per il principiante perché sono robusti

FAM: Lutjanidae
Lutjanus erythropterus
Blood Red Snapper

**General
Aggression**

**Color
Maintenance**

**Dietary
Requirements**

**Con-Species
Compatibility**

Collected: Indonesia
Aquarium: Non-Reef
Survivability: Easy
Size: More than 8" (20 cm)

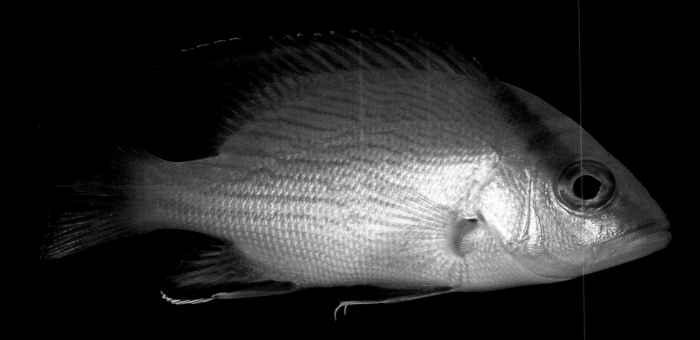

FAM: Lutjanidae
Lutjanus kasmira
Blue-lined Snapper

**General
Aggression**

**Color
Maintenance**

**Dietary
Requirements**

**Con-Species
Compatibility**

Collected: Philippines
Aquarium: Non-Reef
Survivability: Easy
Size: More than 8" (20 cm)

FAM: Lutjanidae
Lutjanus sebae
Emperor Snapper

General Aggression **Color Maintenance** **Dietary Requirements** **Con-Species Compatibility**

Collected: Indonesia
Aquarium: Non-Reef
Survivability: Easy
Size: More than 8" (20 cm)

FAM: Lutjanidae
Macolor niger
Black & White Snapper
FORM: Long Finned

General Aggression **Color Maintenance** **Dietary Requirements** **Con-Species Compatibility**

Collected: Indonesia
Aquarium: Non-Reef
Survivability: Difficult
Size: More than 8" (20 cm)

184

FAM: Lutjanidae
Macolor niger
Black & White Snapper
FORM: Short Finned

General Aggression

Color Maintenance

Dietary Requirements

Con-Species Compatibility

Collected: Indonesia
Aquarium: Non-Reef
Survivability: Difficult
Size: More than 8" (20 cm)

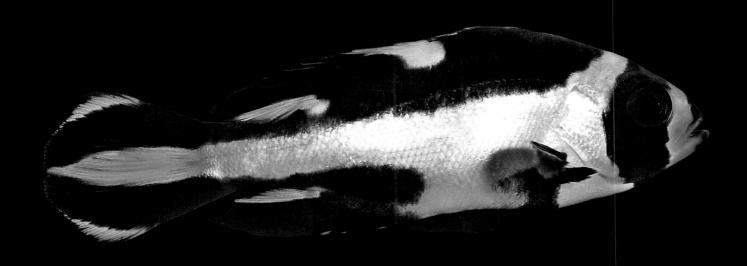

FAM: Lutjanidae
Symphorichthys nematophorus
Lemon-belly Snapper

General Aggression

Color Maintenance

Dietary Requirements

Con-Species Compatibility

Collected: Philippines
Aquarium: Non-Reef
Survivability: Easy
Size: More than 8" (20 cm)

185

General Aggression

Color Maintenance

Dietary Requirements

Con-Species Compatibility

Collected: Philippines
Aquarium: Non-Reef
Survivability: Moderate
Size: More than 8" (20 cm)

Family: Malacanthidae

(Tilefishes) Members of this family are Goby-like fishes that swim above the coral rock into which they retreat when they feel threatened. They are shy fishes that do well in a reef aquarium setup and get along with other fish. If possible, keep more than one of these fish (which seem to enjoy company).

They are very nervous, passive fishes that do not fare well in an all-fish aquarium. Therefore — in the past — they were not very popular. The increasing popularity of the reef aquarium — to which it is suited — has created a new demand for these fishes.

(Famille: Malacanthidae) Les membres de cette famille ressemblent aux Gobiidae et nagent au dessus des coraux, dans lesquels ils se réfugient lorsqu'ils se sentent menacés. Ce sont des poissons timides qui se plaisent dans un environnement récifal et qui s'entendent bien avec les autres poissons. Il est conseillé de les tenir en groupe, car ils possèdent un instinct grégaire.

Pas vraiment appréciés par le passé parce que difficiles à garder (passifs et très nerveux à la fois), ces poissons se portent bien dans un aquarium récifal. La popularité croissante de ces aquariums a créé une nouvelle demande pour ce poisson parfaitement adapté à cet environnement.

(Pez Torpedo) Los miembros de esta familia son peces como los Gobiidae que nadan sobre las rocas de coral en las cuales se esconden cuando se sienten amenazados. Son peces tímidos que prosperan en una estructura de pecera de arrecife y se llevan bien con los demás peces. Si es posible, mantenga más de uno de estos peces que parecen disfrutar de compañía.

Estos son peces muy nerviosos y dóciles que no prosperan en un tanque de peces exclusivamente. Por lo tanto, en el pasado, no eran muy populares debido a las dificultades en mantenerlos. La creciente popularidad de la pecera de arrecife, para la cual son bien apropiados, ha creado una nueva demanda para este pez.

(Lofolátilos) Os membros desta família são peixes semelhantes aos Gobiidae, que nadam acima de rochas de corais, nas quais se refugiam quando se sentem ameaçados. São peixes tímidos, que vão bem em aquários de recifes e se dão bem com outros peixes. Se possível, deve-se manter mais de um destes peixes, que parecem apreciar companhia.

São peixes muito nervosos e passivos, que não se dão bem em aquários só de peixes. Portanto, no passado, não eram muito populares devido à dificuldade de mantê-los. A crescente popularidade do aquário de recifes, adequado para estes peixes, criou uma nova demanda para eles.

(Famiglia: Malacanthidae) I membri di questa famiglia sono simili ai Gobidi e nuotano attorno alle barriere coralline in cui si rifugiano quando si sentono minacciati. Sono pesci timidi che vivono molto bene nell'acquario da barriera e coabitano pacificamente con altri pesci. Se possibile, è consigliabile tenere più di uno di questi pesci, perché sembrano preferire la compagnia.

Sono pesci molto nervosi e passivi che non si adattano agli acquari con una comunità molto varia e perciò in passato non erano molto ricercati. La popolarità crescente dell'acquario da barriera, al quale sono adatti, ha risvegliato un nuovo interesse per questi pesci.

FAM: Malacanthidae
Hoplolatilus cuniculus
Ghost Tilefish

General Aggression   Color Maintenance   Dietary Requirements   Con-Species Compatibility

Collected: Philippines
Aquarium: Reef
Survivability: Moderate
Size: 4" (10 cm) – 8" (20 cm)

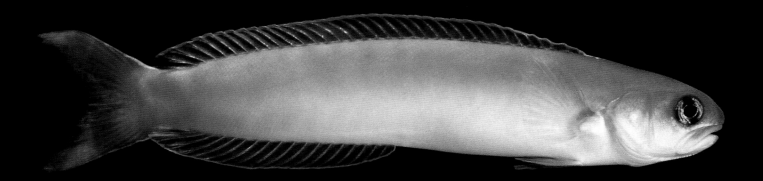

FAM: Malacanthidae
Hoplolatilus fourmanoiri
Skeleton Tilefish

General Aggression   Color Maintenance   Dietary Requirements   Con-Species Compatibility

Collected: Indonesia
Aquarium: Reef
Survivability: Moderate
Size: 4" (10 cm) – 8" (20 cm)

188

FAM: Malacanthidae
Hoplolatilus luteus
Golden Tilefish

General Aggression **Color Maintenance** **Dietary Requirements** **Con-Species Compatibility**

Collected: Indonesia
Aquarium: Reef
Survivability: Moderate
Size: 4" (10 cm) – 8" (20 cm)

FAM: Malacanthidae
Hoplolatilus marcosi
Skunk Tilefish

General Aggression **Color Maintenance** **Dietary Requirements** **Con-Species Compatibility**

Collected: Philippines
Aquarium: Reef
Survivability: Moderate
Size: 4" (10 cm) – 8" (20 cm)

189

FAM: Malacanthidae
Hoplolatilus purpureus
Purple Tilefish

General Aggression | Color Maintenance | Dietary Requirements | Con-Species Compatibility

Collected: Philippines
Aquarium: Reef
Survivability: Difficult
Size: 4" (10 cm) – 8" (20 cm)

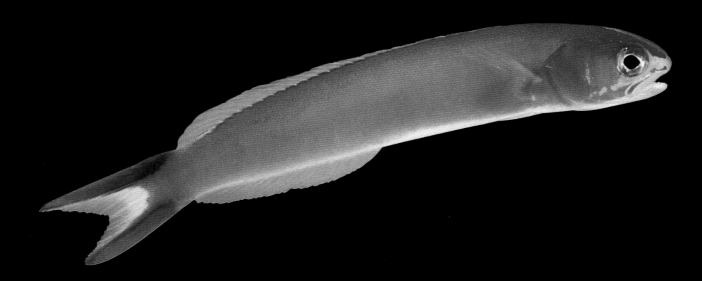

FAM: Malacanthidae
Hoplolatilus starcki
Blueface Tilefish
FORM: Adult

General Aggression | Color Maintenance | Dietary Requirements | Con-Species Compatibility

Collected: Philippines
Aquarium: Reef
Survivability: Difficult
Size: 4" (10 cm) – 8" (20 cm)

190

Hoplolatilus starcki
Blueface Tilefish
FORM: Juvenile

General Aggression **Color Maintenance** **Dietary Requirements** **Con-Species Compatibility**

Aquarium: Reef
Survivability: Moderate
Size: 4" (10 cm) – 8" (20 cm)

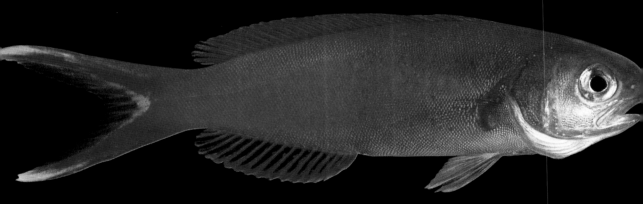

FAM: Malacanthidae
Melacanthus latovittalus
Striped Blanquillo
FORM: Juvenile

General Aggression **Color Maintenance** **Dietary Requirements** **Con-Species Compatibility**

Collected: Philippines
Aquarium: Reef (Caution)
Survivability: Difficult
Size: 4" (10 cm) – 8" (20 cm)

FAM: Malacanthidae
Melacanthus latovittalus
Striped Blanquillo
FORM: Subadult

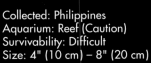

General Aggression **Color Maintenance** **Dietary Requirements** **Con-Species Compatibility**

Collected: Philippines
Aquarium: Reef (Caution)
Survivability: Difficult
Size: 4" (10 cm) – 8" (20 cm)

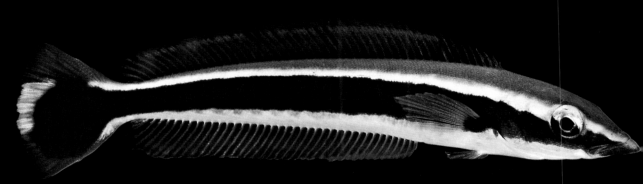

Family: Microdesmidae

(Dartfishes) This family is characterized by a long, worm-like body; hence they are often called "Worm Fishes." T
re peaceful and prefer a reef setting with plenty of hiding places. In a tank with many active, aggressive fishes these
reatures cannot compete for food. Because they have such a nervouse temperment, they tend to jump out the tan
his is particularly true in the first few days after putting them in a new tank, so it is important to keep the tank cove
nd filled with plenty of hiding spaces. *Nemateleotris decora* (Purple Flame Dartfish) and *Nemateleotris magnifica* (Fire Dartfish
re among the most sought-after fishes for the reef aquarium. They are beautiful, easy to maintain, and totally reef-compatib
Although these fishes have always been referred to as Gobies, they do not belong to the Gobiidae family. Because this bc
ters to an international audience, we chose to use the term *Dartfish* instead of "Goby."

(Famille: Microdesmidae) Cette famille est caractérisée par un corps long ressemblant à un ver; c'est pour cela que d
ertaines parties du monde on l'appelle communément le «poisson-ver». Ce sont des poissons pacifiques qui préfèr
n environnement à récifs contenant de nombreuses «cachettes». Dans un aquarium ayant un certain nombre de poisso
ctifs et agressifs, ces créatures timides ne pourraient pas se battre pour leur nourriture. Ils sont de nature nerveu
ont tendance à sauter hors de l'aquarium, en particulier les premiers jours dans un nouvel environnement.
est donc important de garder l'aquarium couvert et rempli de «cachettes».
Nemateleotris decora et *Nemateleotris magnifica* (poisson fléchette) sont parmi les espèces les plus recherchées,
sont beaux, faciles à maintenir et totalement compatibles avec un milieu récifal communautaire.

(Pez Dardo) Esta familia se caracteriza por un cuerpo largo tipo lombriz. Por tanto, a menudo se les llama "Pez
ombriz". Son apacibles y prefieren un ambiente de arrecife con muchos escondites. En un tanque con muchos
ces activos y agresivos, estas tímidas criaturas no pueden competir por sus alimentos. Al tener un temperamento
uy nervioso, tienden a saltar fuera del tanque. Esto resulta particularmente cierto en los primeros días después
e ponerlos en una pecera nueva. Así que es importante mantener la pecera cubierta y llena de muchos escondites.
El *Nemateleotris decora* (Pez Dardo de Llama Púrpura) y el *Nemateleotris magnifica* (Pez Dardo de Fuego) figuran
ntre los peces más codiciados para peceras de arrecife. Son bellos, fáciles de mantener y totalmente compatibles
on los arrecifes.

(Família: Microdesmidae) Esta família caracteriza-se por um corpo longo, tipo minhoca, por isso são
eqüentemente chamados de "Peixes Minhocas". São pacíficos e preferem aquários de recifes, com bastante lugar
ra se esconder. Em um tanque com muitos peixes ativos e agressivos, estas criaturas tímidas não conseguem
ompetir por comida. Por terem um temperamento tão nervoso, tendem a pular para fora do tanque, especialmente no
rimeiros dias após terem sido colocados em um tanque novo. Portanto, é importante manter o tanque fechado e
om bastante lugar on de possam se esconder.
Os peixes *Nemateleotris decora* ("Purple Flame Dartfish") e *Nemateleotris magnifica* ("Fire Dartfish") estão entre
mais procurados para aquários de recifes. São belos, fáceis de manter e perfeitamente compatíveis com recifes.

(Famiglia: Microdesmidae) I membri di questa famiglia sono caratterizzati da un lungo corpo, simile a un verme. Per que
otivo vengono chiamati "pesci verme". Sono pacifici e preferiscono un ambiente da barriera con abbondanza di nascondig
quari con molti pesci vivaci e aggressivi queste creature timide non possono competere per raggiungere il cibo. Dal
omento che possiedono un temperamento nervoso tendono a saltar fuori dall'acquario. Ciò si verifica in particolare dura
primi giorni di vita in un nuovo acquario. Dunque, è importante oltre ai nascondigli anche un buon coperchio per l'acquaric
Nemateleotris decora e *Nemateleotris magnifica* sono tra i pesci più ricercati per l'acquario da barriera; sono belli,
cili da tenere, e assolutamente innocui per tutti gli invertebrati.

FAM: Microdesmidae
Nemateleotris decora
Purple Flame Dartfish

General Aggression

Color Maintenance

Dietary Requirements

Con-Species Compatibility

Collected: Philippines
Aquarium: Reef
Survivability: Moderate
Size: Less than 4" (10 cm)

FAM: Microdesmidae
Nemateleotris magnifica
Fire Dartfish

General Aggression

Color Maintenance

Dietary Requirements

Con-Species Compatibility

Collected: Philippines
Aquarium: Reef
Survivability: Moderate
Size: Less than 4" (10 cm)

193

FAM: Microdesmidae
Oxymetopon cyanoctenosum
Ornate Razor Dartfish

General Aggression   **Color Maintenance**   **Dietary Requirements**   **Con-Species Compatibility**

Collected: Philippines
Aquarium: Reef (Caution)
Survivability: Difficult
Size: 4" (10 cm) – 8" (20 cm)

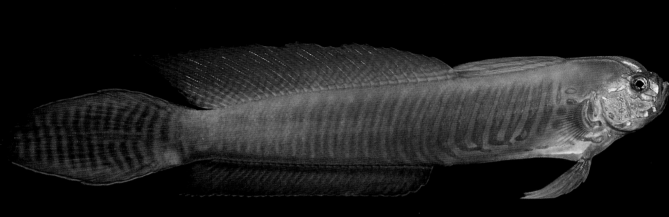

FAM: Microdesmidae
Ptereleotris evides
Scissortail Dartfish

General Aggression   **Color Maintenance**   **Dietary Requirements**   **Con-Species Compatibility**

Collected: Philippines
Aquarium: Reef
Survivability: Easy
Size: 4" (10 cm) – 8" (20 cm)

FAM: Microdesmidae
Ptereleotris hanae
Threadfin Dartfish
FORM: Female

General Aggression

Color Maintenance

Dietary Requirements

Con-Species Compatibility

Collected: Philippines
Aquarium: Reef
Survivability: Moderate
Size: 4" (10 cm) – 8" (20 cm)

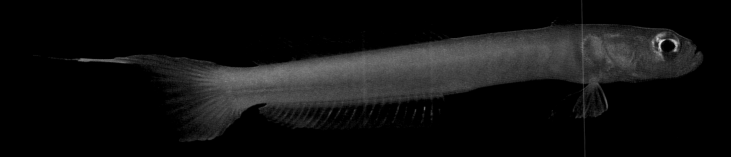

FAM: Microdesmidae
Ptereleotris hanae
Threadfin Dartfish
FORM: Male

General Aggression

Color Maintenance

Dietary Requirements

Con-Species Compatibility

Collected: Philippines
Aquarium: Reef
Survivability: Moderate
Size: 4" (10 cm) – 8" (20 cm)

FAM: Microdesmidae
Ptereleotris heteroptera
Spot-tail Dartfish

 General Aggression

 Color Maintenance

 Dietary Requirements

Con-Species Compatibility

Collected: Philippines
Aquarium: Reef
Survivability: Moderate
Size: 4" (10 cm) – 8" (20 cm)

FAM: Microdesmidae
Ptereleotris zebra
Zebra Dartfish

 General Aggression

 Color Maintenance

 Dietary Requirements

 Con-Species Compatibility

Collected: Philippines
Aquarium: Reef
Survivability: Easy
Size: 4" (10 cm) – 8" (20 cm)

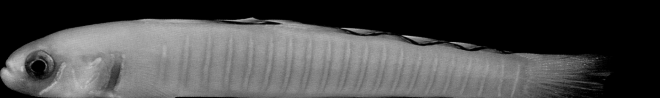

Family: Monocanthidae

(Filefishes) Family Monocanthidae share some traits with the Balistidae (Triggerfish) family. Notably, they share the ivided, spiny dorsal that serves to wedge themselves into crevices to avoid capture. The front dorsal fin of the fishes n this family is divided by multiple spines; including a larger front spine, and a less prominent rear spine. The rear spine erves as a controlling mechanism for the front spine. Unlike Balistidae (Triggerfish), they are not particularly aggressive. This o not mean, however, that they are totally passive. They are also fairly hardy and easy to keep in an aquarium. They are ot picky eaters and will eat shrimps, flakes etc. This makes them ideal fishes for the novice hobbyist. There is, however, ne notable exception to this rule. Ironically, the most beautiful member of this family — Oxymonacanthus longirostris Orange Spotted Filefish) is also the hardest to maintain.

(Famille: Monocanthidae) La famille des Monocanthidae partage certaines caractéristiques avec la famille des Balistidae. s possèdent eux aussi une nageoire dorsale épineuse divisée, qui leur sert à se glisser dans des crevasses pour éviter 'être capturés. La nageoire dorsale avant des poissons de cette famille est divisée en de multiples épines, dont une épine vant plus large et une épine arrière moins importante qui sert de mécanisme de contrôle et de blocage de l'épine avant. u contraire des Balistidae, les membres des Monocanthidae ne sont pas particulièrement agressifs, mais ceci ne veut as dire qu'ils sont totalement passifs. Ils sont également plutôt robustes et faciles à garder en aquarium. Ils ne sont as difficiles à nourrir et mangent crevettes, flocons, etc. Ce sont donc des poissons idéaux pour les aquariophiles ébutants. Il y a hélas une exception à cette règle, car le membre le plus beau de cette famille, Oxymonacanthus ongirostris, est également le plus difficile à maintenir.

(Pez Falsa Ballesta) La familia Monocanthidae (Pez Falsa Ballesta) comparten algunos rasgos con la familia Balistidae. Notablemente, comparten la espinosa aleta dorsal dividida que sirve para calzarse dentro de grietas y asi evitar ser apturados. La aleta dorsal anterior de los peces de esta familia esta dividida por espinas múltiples; entre ellas un espina anterior más grande y una espina posterior menos prominente. La espina posterior sirve de mecanismo ontrolador para la espina anterior. A diferencia de los Balistidae (Pez Ballesta), los miembros de esta familia no son articularmente agresivos. Esto no quiere decir, sin embargo, que son totalmente pasivos. También son bastante fuertes fáciles de mantener en una pecera. No son quisquillosos a la hora de alimentarse y comen camarones, hojuelas de escado, etc. Esto los hace un pez ideal para el aficionado novato. Hay, sin embargo, una notable excepción a esta regla. ónicamente, el ejemplar más bello de esta familia; Oxymonacanthus longirostris (Falsa Ballesta de Manchas Anaranjadas), es ambién el más difícil de mantaner.

(Peixes-Fantasma) A família Monocanthidae (Peixes-Fantasmas) tem algumas características da família Balistidae Peixe-Gatilho). Como é fácil observar, eles têm a mesma espinha dorsal dividida que os deixa passarem e abrirem caminho or fendas estreitas para evitar serem capturados. A barbatana dorsal dianteira dos peixes desta família é dividida por núltiplas espinhas; inclusive uma espinha frontal maior e uma espinha traseira menos saliente. A espinha traseira funciona omo um mecanismo de controle para a espinha dianteira. Ao contrário da família Balistidae (Peixe-Gatilho), os membros a família Monocanthidae não são especificamente agressivos. Isto não significa, entretanto, que os peixes desta família ejam totalmente passivos. Eles são também razoavelmente resistentes e de fácil manutenção em um aquário. Não são ifíceis de agradar quanto à alimentação e comem camarão, flocos, etc. Este fato os torna peixes ideais para os iniciantes esta atividade. Há, porém, uma clara exceção a esta regra. Ironicamente, o mais belo membro desta família — Oxymonacanthus ongirostris (Peixe-Fantasma de Manchas Laranjas) é também o que exige mais cuidados de manutenção.

(Famiglia: Monocanthidae) I Monacantidi condividono alcune caratteristiche tipiche dei Balistidi come per esempio pinna dorsale spinosa che serve loro per rintanarsi nelle fessure ed evitare la cattura. La pinna dorsale anteriore dei esci di questa famiglia è divisa da molteplici spine, inclusa una spina anteriore più grande e una pinna posteriore meno rominente. La spina posteriore serve come meccanismo di controllo della spina anteriore.
Diversamente dai Balistidi, i Monacantidi non sono particolarmente aggressivi. Questo non significa, comunque, che iano completamente passivi. Sono piuttosto robusti e facili da allevare in acquario. Si nutrono con facilità e mangeranno amberetti, mangimi in fiocchi ecc. Per questo motivo sono pesci perfetti per il principiante. Comunque, c'è un'eccezione otevole a questa regola: il membro più bello della famiglia, Oxymonacanthus longirostris, è il più difficile da allevare.

General Aggression

Color Maintenance

Dietary Requirements

Con-Species Compatibility

Collected: Indonesia
Aquarium: Non-Reef
Survivability: Moderate
Size: 4" (10 cm) – 8" (20 cm)

FAM: Monocanthidae
Oxymonacanthus longirostris
Orange-spotted Filefish

General
Aggression

Color
Maintenance

Dietary
Requirements

Con-Species
Compatibility

Collected: Philippines
Aquarium: Reef (Caution)
Survivability: Doomed
Size: Less than 4" (10 cm)

FAM: Monocanthidae
Paraluteres prionurus
Mimic Filefish

General
Aggression

Color
Maintenance

Dietary
Requirements

Con-Species
Compatibility

Collected: Philippines
Aquarium: Non-Reef
Survivability: Moderate
Size: Less than 4" (10 cm)

199

FAM: Monocanthidae
Pervagor janthinosoma
Fantail Filefish

General Aggression

Color Maintenance

Dietary Requirements

Con-Species Compatibility

Collected: Philippines
Aquarium: Non-Reef
Survivability: Moderate
Size: 4" (10 cm) – 8" (20 cm)

FAM: Monocanthidae
Pervagor melanocephalus
Red Filefish

General Aggression

Color Maintenance

Dietary Requirements

Con-Species Compatibility

Collected: Philippines
Aquarium: Non-Reef
Survivability: Moderate
Size: 4" (10 cm) – 8" (20 cm)

Family: Monocentridae

(Pineconefish) The Pineconefish is a living fossil among aquarium fishes, and is thought to have existed millior of years ago. It is encased in armor enclosing its entire body. Because it is a deep water fish, it has a light producin organ located under the jaw and requires cool water.

(Famille: Monocentridae) Les poissons de cette famille sont des fossiles vivants parmi les poissons d'aquariu et on pense qu'ils existaient déjà il y a des millions d'années. Ces curieux poissons, engoncés dans une armure protégeant entièrement leur corps, vivent en eau profonde et possèdent un organe situé sous la mâchoire qui produit de la lumière. Ils exigent une eau de basse température. Provenant des eaux profondes, ils exigent un milieu à température fraîche.

(Familia: Monocentridae) El Monocentridae es un fósil viviente entre los peces de acuario y se piensa que existe desde hace millones de años. Se encuentra cubierto por una armadura que le cubre todo el cuerpo. Debido a que es un pez de aguas profundas, posee un órgano que produce luz localizado debajo de la mandíbu y debe mantenerse en agua fría.

(Família: Monocentridae) O "pineconefish" é um fóssil vivo entre os peixes de aquário, acreditando-se que exista há milhões de anos. Ele é coberto por uma couraça que envolve seu corpo inteiro. Como é um peixe de águas profundas, ele tem um órgão que produz uma luz, localizado sob a mandíbula e exige água fria.

(Famiglia: Monocentridae) I Monocentridi sono fossili viventi; si ritiene che esistano da milioni di anni. Tutto i corpo di questi pesci è coperto di una corazza a mo' di armatura. Dal momento che vivono a grandi profondità possiedono un organo luminoso collocato sotto la mascella. I Monocentridi richiedono acqua fredda.

FAM: Monocentridae
Monocentrus japonicus
Pineconefish

General
Aggression

Color
Maintenance

Dietary
Requirements

Con-Species
Compatibility

Collected: Philippines
Aquarium: Reef (Caution)
Survivability: Difficult
Size: 4" (10 cm) – 8" (20 cm)

Family: Mullidae

(Goatfishes) The problem when keeping these fishes is that there is often not enough food debris on the bottom of the tank for them to sustain themselves. In an aquarium, the free swimming fishes generally snap-up the food before it can filter down to the bottom. One type of tank where these fish can feel perfectly at home is the reef tank. This is because reef tanks are generally populated by smaller, less aggressive fishes and corals which are not particularly thorough feeders. In this environment, members of the *Mullidae* family can not only thrive but serve a valuable housekeeping function.

(Famille: Mullidae) Il n'y a souvent pas assez de débris de nourriture au fond de l'aquarium pour que ces poissons puissent se nourrir d'eux-mêmes car, nageant librement, ils attrapent généralement devant eux la nourriture qui devrait tomber sur le fond. Les aquariums récifaux étant généralement peuplés de coraux, de roches vivantes et poissons plus petits et moins agressifs qui ne laissent pas autant de restes, c'est dans ce genre d'environnement que les membres de la famille des *Mullidae* sont le plus à leur place car, non seulement ils y prospèrent, mais ils y remplissent une fonction de nettoyage fort utile.

(Pez Chivo) El problema en mantener estos peces es que con frecuencia no hay suficiente restos de comida en el fondo del tanque para que se puedan alimentar. En una pecera los peces que nadan libremente generalmente agarran los alimentos antes que se filtran hacia el fondo. Estos peces suelen sentirse perfectamente confortables en un tanque de arrecife. Esto se debe a que las peceras de arrecife generalmente están pobladas de peces más pequeños y menos agresivos y corales que no se alimentan de una manera particularmente minuciosa. En este ambiente, los miembros de la familia Mullidae pueden no solamente prosperar sino cumplir una función valiosa en el mantenimiento de la pecera.

(Peixes-Cabras) O problema na manutenção desses peixes é que geralmente não há restos de comida suficientes no fundo do tanque para que eles se alimentem. Num aquário, os peixes nadando livremente em geral abocanham a comida antes que esta se deposite no fundo. Um tipo de tanque onde esses peixes podem sentir-se perfeitamente em casa é o tanque de recife. Isto porque os tanques de recifes geralmente são habitados por peixes e corais menores e menos agressivos, que não são alimentadores particularmente radicais. Neste ambiente, os membros da família Mullidae não só podem desenvolver-se como também exercer uma valiosa função doméstica.

(Famiglia: Mullidae) I membri di questa famiglia possono essere identificati grazie alla presenza di due barbigli sul mento che vengono utilizzati per scavare e per trovare alimenti nel materiale di fondo. Sono essenzialmente pesci saprofagi, e sono utili in acquario per pulire il fondo e rendere soffice il substrato. Il problema nel mantenimento di questi pesci consiste nel fatto che non sempre ci sono abbastanza residui di cibo sul fondo dell'acquario. In acquario, questi pesci si nutrono anche del mangime che tende a depositarsi sul fondo. Un tipo di acquario dove si sentono a loro agio è l'acquario da barriera perché questo tipo di vasca è di solito popolato da pesci più piccoli e meno aggressivi e invertebrati che si cibano molto lentamente. In questo ambiente, i Mullidi non solo prosperano, ma svolgono pure un'importante funzione di pulizia.

FAM: Mullidae
Parupeneus barberinoides
Bicolor Goatfish

General Aggression   Color Maintenance   Dietary Requirements   Con-Species Compatibility

Collected: Philippines
Aquarium: Reef
Survivability: Moderate
Size: 4" (10 cm) – 8" (20 cm)

Parupeneus barberinus
Golden-striped Goatfish

General Aggression **Color Maintenance** **Dietary Requirements** **Con-Species Compatibility**

Aquarium: Reef
Survivability: Moderate
Size: 4" (10 cm) – 8" (20 cm)

FAM: Mullidae
Parupeneus cyclostomus
Yellow Goatfish

General Aggression **Color Maintenance** **Dietary Requirements** **Con-Species Compatibility**

Collected: Philippines
Aquarium: Reef
Survivability: Moderate
Size: 4" (10 cm) – 8" (20 cm)

Family: Muraenidae

(Moray Eels) Eels look like snakes with fins. Instead of the opercular bones common on many fishe
hey have a hole for breathing. In an aquarium, they are generally easy to maintain and become tame
One of the drawbacks of eels is that they grow to be extremely large and soon outgrow their aquariur
els are the escape artists of marine fishes, so a tight-fitting tank cover is essential to have when keeping th
In their natural habitat, eels mainly eat fishes and crustaceans and are usually easy to feed in captiv
An exception is the very attractive *Rhinomuraena quaesita* (Ribbon Eel). Some *Rhinomuraena quaesita*
Ribbon Eels) can be enticed to feed on small, live fishes or shrimp. However, if this does not work,
hey cannot be kept successfully. In the wild, members of the Muraenidae family are nocturnal predato
nd, therefore, have adapted to that role. They have poor eyesight but a good sense of smell. These eel
hould be treated with caution, as they can inflict a nasty wound that might become infected if left untrea

(Famille: Muraenidae) Les murènes ressemblent à des serpents à nageoires. Au lieu des os operculair
ue portent de nombreux poissons, elles possèdent un orifice qui leur sert à respirer. En aquarium, ell
ont en général faciles à entretenir et s'apprivoisent bien. L'un des inconvénients des murènes est qu'el
randissent énormément et deviennent vite trop grandes pour leur aquarium. Ce sont les « Houdini
es poissons de mer, il est donc essentiel d'avoir un couvercle hermétique si vous voulez conserver
ype de poisson dans votre aquarium. Dans leur habitat naturel, les *muraedinae* se nourrissent principalemen
e poissons et de crustacés et sont en général faciles à nourrir en captivité. Une exception : la très
olie *Rhinomuraena quaesita*. On peut amener certaines *Rhinomuraena quaesita* (ou amboinensis) à se
ourrir de crevettes ou de petits poissons vivants (de préférence le soir dans la pénombre). Malheureuseme
i cela ne marche pas, on ne pourra pas réussir à les conserver.
En liberté, les membres de la famille des *Muraenidae* sont des prédateurs nocturnes qui se sont
daptés à ce rôle ; leur vue n'est pas bonne mais leur odorat très développé. Ces anguilles doivent
tre traitées avec précaution car certaines espèces peuvent infliger de sérieuses blessures qui
ourraient s'infecter, sans traitement pharmaceutique adéquat.

(Morena de Mar) Las morenas parecen serpientes con aletas. En vez de los agallas operculares
omunes en muchos peces, las morenas poseen un hueco para respirar. Generalmente son fáciles
e mantaner en una pecera y se tornan mansas. Una de las desventajas de las morenas es que crecen
asta alcanzar un tamaño extremadamente grande y muy pronto ya no caben en la pecera. Entre
odos los peces marinos, las morenas son expertas a la hora de escarparse, así que un tanque con
na tapa ceñidamente ajustada es esencial para mantenerlas. En su habitat natural las morenas comen
rincipalmente peces y crustáceos y por lo general son fáciles de alimentar en cautiverio. Una
xcepción es la muy atractiva *Rhinomuraena quaesita* (Cinta de Mar). Algunos ejemplares de la
Rhinomuraena quaesita (Cintas de Mar) pueden inducirse a alimentarse de pequeños peces o camarones.
in embargo, si esto no funciona, no se pueden mantener con éxito.
En su estado natural, los miembros de la familia Muraenidae son predadores nocturnos y, por
onsiguiente se han adaptado a ese papel. Poseen mala vista pero un buen olfato. Estas morenas deben
er manipuladas con cautela pues pueden infligir una herida peligrosa que se puede infectar si no se trata.

Family: Muraenidae

(Moréias) As enguias são semelhantes a cobras com barbatanas. Em vez dos ossos operculares comuns a vários peixes, elas têm um orifício para respiração. São geralmente fáceis de manter em aquário, tornando-se dóceis. Uma das desvantagens das enguias é que elas crescem muito, logo se tornando grandes demais para o aquário. As enguias são os astros da fuga entre os peixes marinhos, portanto para mantê-las é essencial uma tampa de tanque que feche muito bem. Em seu habitat natural, as enguias comem principalmente peixes e crustáceos, sendo geralmente fáceis de alimentar quando em cativeiro. Uma exceção é a atraente *Rhinomuraena quaesita* ("Ribbon Eel"). Algumas *Rhinomuraena quaesita* ("Ribbon Eel") podem ser induzidas a se alimentarem de peixes ou camarões vivos pequenos. Entretanto, se isto não funcionar, elas não podem ser mantidas com sucesso.

Em seu estado natural, os membros da família Muraenidae são predadores noturnos tendo, portanto, se adaptado ao papel. Têm pouca visão, porém excelente olfato. Essas enguias devem ser tratadas com cuidado, pois podem causar ferimentos que podem infeccionar se não forem tratados.

(Famiglia: Muraenidae) Questi pesci somigliano a serpenti dotati di pinne. Invece degli opercoli ossei, comuni in molti pesci, le Murene respirano attraverso una fessura. In acquario sono generalmente facili da allevare e diventano miti. Uno dei problemi con le Murene è che raggiungono dimensioni notevoli, tanto da non poter essere ospitate in un comune acquario. Le Murene sono particolarmente esperte in evasioni, per questo motivo è essenziale munire la vasca di un buon coperchio.

In natura, le Murene mangiano pesci e crostacei e di solito sono facili da nutrire in acquario. Un'eccezione è rappresentata dall'interessante *Rhinomuraena quaesita*. Alcune *Rhinomuraena quaesita* possono venire abituate a mangiare piccoli pesci vivi o gamberetti. Comunque, se questo sistema non funziona, sarà impossibile riuscire ad allevarle. In natura, i membri della famiglia Muraenidae sono predatori notturni, hanno una capacità visiva scarsa, ma un buon olfatto. Le Murene devono essere trattate con cautela perché con i loro denti possono infliggere profonde ferite che si infettano facilmente se non curate prontamente.

FAM: Muraenidae
Echidna nebulosa
Snowflake Eel

General
Aggression

Color
Maintenance

Dietary
Requirements

Con-Species
Compatibility

Collected: Philippines
Aquarium: Non-Reef
Survivability: Easy
Size: More than 8" (20 cm)

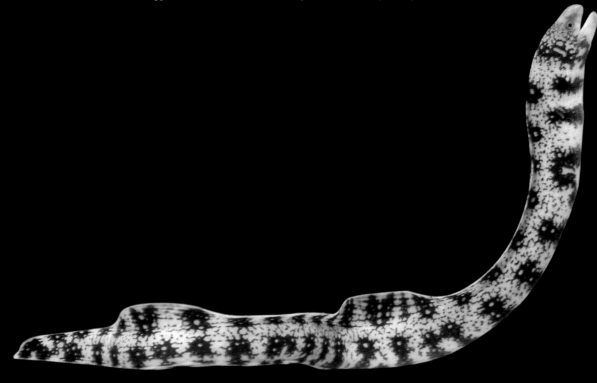

FAM: Muraenidae
Echidna polyzona
Banded Moray Eel

General
Aggression

Color
Maintenance

Dietary
Requirements

Con-Species
Compatibility

Collected: Philippines
Aquarium: Non-Reef
Survivability: Easy
Size: More than 8" (20 cm)

FAM: Muraenidae
Gymnothorax fimbriatus
Fimbriated Moray Eel

**General
Aggression**

**Color
Maintenance**

**Dietary
Requirements**

**Con-Species
Compatibility**

Collected: Philippines
Aquarium: Non-Reef
Survivability: Easy
Size: More than 8" (20 cm)

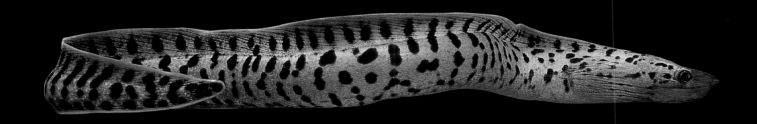

FAM: Muraenidae
*Gymnothorax gracilicaudus**
Spot & Line Moray Eel

**General
Aggression**

**Color
Maintenance**

**Dietary
Requirements**

**Con-Species
Compatibility**

Collected: Philippines
Aquarium: Non-Reef
Survivability: Easy
Size: More than 8" (20 cm)

FAM: Muraenidae
Gymnothorax rueppelliae
Yellowhead Moray Eel

General Aggression

Color Maintenance

Dietary Requirements

Con-Species Compatibility

Collected: Philippines
Aquarium: Non-Reef
Survivability: Easy
Size: More than 8" (20 cm)

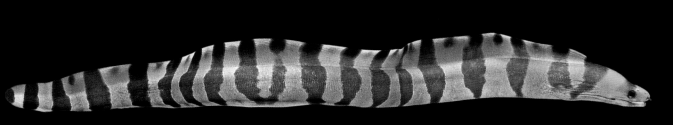

FAM: Muraenidae
Pseudechidna brummeri
Ghost Ribbon Eel

General Aggression

Color Maintenance

Dietary Requirements

Con-Species Compatibility

Collected: Indonesia
Aquarium: Non-Reef
Survivability: Difficult
Size: More than 8" (20 cm)

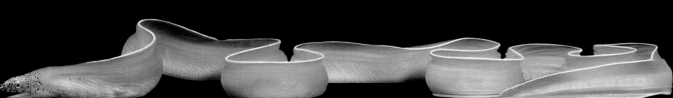

FAM: Muraenidae
Rhinomuraena quaesita (Black)
Black Ribbon Eel

General Aggression

Color Maintenance

Dietary Requirements

Con-Species Compatibility

Aquarium: Non-Reef
Survivability: Difficult
Size: More than 8" (20 cm)

FAM: Muraenidae
Rhinomuraena quaesita (Blue)
Blue Ribbon Eel

General Aggression

Color Maintenance

Dietary Requirements

Con-Species Compatibility

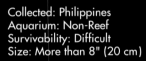

Collected: Philippines
Aquarium: Non-Reef
Survivability: Difficult
Size: More than 8" (20 cm)

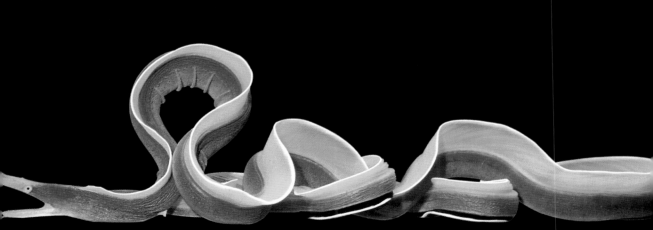

Family: Nemipteridae

(Breams) The Nemipteridae family are very uncommon in the marine aquarium trade. In my opinion, the reason for this is fairly obvious: a vast majority of these fishes are unattractive. They are overshadowed in beauty by even their cousins in the Lutjanidae family (who are not generally that spectacular). The fish we show in this book are among the more attractive of this family. And yet, even they are not that pretty. One notable exception shown in this book is the *pentapodus emeryii* (Double Whiptail Bream).

(Famille: Nemipteridae) On trouve très rarement la famille des Nemipteridae dans le commerce aquariophile, pour la raison évidente que la plus grande partie des poissons de cette famille ne sont p beaux. Même leurs cousins de la famille des Lutjanidae, pourtant rarement spectaculaires, les dépasse en beauté. Les poissons que nous montrons dans ce livre sont parmi les plus attirants de cette famille Mais, même dans ce cas, ils ne sont pas vraiment séduisants. L'exception à noter, illustrée dans ce livr est le *Pentapodus emeryii*.

(Pez Brema) Los miembros de la familia Nemipteridae (Pez Brema) no son muy comunes en el comerci de peceras. En mi opinión, esto se debe a una razón bastante obvia: la vasta mayoría de estos peces r son atractivos. En términos de belleza los sobrepasan hasta sus primos de la familia Lutjanidae (que generalmente no son muy espectaculares). Los ejemplares que se muestran en este libro se encuentran entre los más atractivos de esta familia y, sin embargo, no son tan hermosos que digamos. Una excepción notable que se muestra en este libro es el *Pentapodus emeryii* (Brema de Doble Cola).

(Bremas) A família Nemipteridae é muito incomum no comércio de aquários marinhos. Na minha opinião, o motivo para tal é bastante óbvio: a grande maioria desses peixes não é atraente. Perdem e beleza até mesmo para seus primos da família Lutjanidae (que em geral já não são tão espetaculares). Os peixes que mostramos neste livro encontram-se entre os mais atraentes dessa família. Entretanto mesmo estes não são lá tão belos. Uma notável exceção mostrada neste livro é a *pentapodus emeryil* ("Double Whiptail Bream").

(Famiglia: Nemipteridae) La famiglia Nemipteridae è molto rara sul mercato dei pesci d'acquario. Secondo la mia opinione, il motivo è piuttosto ovvio: la maggioranza di questi pesci è poco attraente. Vengono surclassati in bellezza persino dai loro cugini nella famiglia Lutjanidae (anche loro non tanto spettacolari). I pesci presentati in questo libro sono tra i più belli di questa famiglia, comunque non sono granché appariscenti. Un'eccezione notevole, messa in evidenza in questo libro, è *Pentapodus emeryii*.

FAM: Nemipteridae
Pentapodus emeryii
Double Whiptail

General Aggression

Color Maintenance

Dietary Requirements

Con-Species Compatibility

Collected: Philippines
Aquarium: Non-Reef
Survivability: Moderate
Size: 4" (10 cm) – 8" (20 cm)

FAM: Nemipteridae
Scolopsis bilineatus
Bridled Bream
FORM: Juvenile

General Aggression

Color Maintenance

Dietary Requirements

Con-Species Compatibility

Collected: Philippines
Aquarium: Non-Reef
Survivability: Moderate
Size: 4" (10 cm) – 8" (20 cm)

FAM: Nemipteridae
Scolopsis bilineatus
Bridled Bream
FORM: Subadult

General Aggression

Color Maintenance

Dietary Requirements

Con-Species Compatibility

Collected: Philippines
Aquarium: Non-Reef
Survivability: Moderate
Size: 4" (10 cm) – 8" (20 cm)

FAM: Nemipteridae
Scolopsis xenochrous
Pearl-streaked Bream

General Aggression

Color Maintenance

Dietary Requirements

Con-Species Compatibility

Collected: Philippines
Aquarium: Non-Reef
Survivability: Moderate
Size: 4" (10 cm) – 8" (20 cm)

Family: Ophidiidae

(Snake Eels) Members of this family have a particularly strong resemblance to snakes. While — to a certain extent — all eels resemble snakes, the fishes in the Ophichthidae family can actually be mistaken for snakes. Unlike the Muraenidae family, members of the Ophichthidae family have excellent eyesight. They tend to bury themselves tail-first. Their tails terminate in a hard point that helps them burrow. Like all eels, they are escape artists and can find a way out of an aquarium with even the smallest opening; so keep your tank sealed if you keep these fishes.

(Famille: Ophidiidae) Les membres de cette famille ressemblent fortement au serpent. Alors que toutes les murènes ressemblent, jusqu'à un certain point, à des serpents, les poissons de la famille des Ophichthidae peuvent littéralement *être pris* pour des serpents. Au contraire de la famille des Muraenidae, les membres de la familles des Ophichthidae ont une vue excellente. Ils ont tendance à s'enterrer la queue la première, cette queue se terminant en une pointe dure facilite l'opération. Comme toutes les anguilles, murènes et autres poissons serpentiformes, ce sont des experts de l'évasion qui peuvent s'échapper d'un aquarium par le plus petit des orifices. Alors, si vous voulez conserver ce poisson, soyez sûr de fermer hermétiquement votre aquarium.

(Serpientes de Mar) Los miembros de esta familia se asemejan fuertemente a las serpientes. Aunque todas las morenas se parecen a las serpientes hasta cierto punto, los miembros de la familia Ophchthidae se pueden efectivamente tomar por serpientes. A diferencia de los miembros de la familia Muraenidae, los miembros de la familia Ophichthidae tienen una vista excelente. Estos peces viven en el fondo marino y tienden a enterrarse con la cola primero. Las colas terminan en un punto duro que las ayuda a horadar. Al igual que todas las morenas, son expertos en el arte de escaparse y pueden encontrar como escaparse de una pecera que no tenga ni la más mínima apertura. Así que mantenga su tanque herméticamente cerrado si desea tener este tipo de pez.

(Família: Ophichthidae) Os membros dessa família são particularmente semelhantes às cobras. Embora em uma certa medida todas as enguias se assemelhem a cobras, os peixes da família Ophichthidae podem realmente ser confundidos com cobras. Ao contrário da família Muraenidae, os membros da família Ophichthidae têm excelente visão. Tendem a enterrar a cauda primeiro. As caudas terminam numa ponta dura, que os ajuda a escavar. Como todas as enguias, são astros da fuga e podem achar uma saída do aquário, mesmo com a mínima abertura. Portanto, mantenha seu tanque selado se quiser manter este peixe.

(Famiglia: Ophichthidae) I membri di questa famiglia somigliano molto ai serpenti. Se è vero che, fino a un certo punto, tutte le Murene sono simili a serpenti, i pesci della famiglia Ophichthidae possono essere veramente presi per serpenti. Diversamente dai Muraenid*ae*, gli Ophichthidae hanno una capacità visiva eccellente. Tendono a sotterrarsi con la coda rivolta in basso; infatti, la loro coda termina in un punto duro che consente loro di scavare. Come le Murene anche questi pesci sono esperti di evasione e possono trovare una via d'uscita attraverso la più piccola apertura, pertanto si dovrebbe tenere l'acquario perfettamente chiuso.

FAM: Ophichthidae
Myrichthys colubrinus (Band)
Banded Snake Eel

   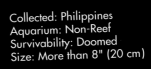

General Aggression **Color Maintenance** **Dietary Requirements** **Con-Species Compatibility**

Collected: Philippines
Aquarium: Non-Reef
Survivability: Doomed
Size: More than 8" (20 cm)

FAM: Ophichthidae
Myrichthys colubrinus (Band & Spot)
Band & Spot Snake Eel

General Aggression **Color Maintenance** **Dietary Requirements** **Con-Species Compatibility**

Collected: Philippines
Aquarium: Non-Reef
Survivability: Doomed
Size: More than 8" (20 cm)

FAM: Ostraciidae
Ostracion cubicus
Yellow Boxfish ·

**General
Aggression**

**Color
Maintenance**

**Dietary
Requirements**

**Con-Species
Compatibility**

Collected: Philippines
Aquarium: Non-Reef
Survivability: Difficult
Size: 4" (10 cm) – 8" (20 cm)

 FAM: Ostraciidae
Ostracion meleagris
Spotted Boxfish
FORM: Female

**General
Aggression**

**Color
Maintenance**

**Dietary
Requirements**

**Con-Species
Compatibility**

Collected: Philippines
Aquarium: Non-Reef
Survivability: Difficult
Size: 4" (10 cm) – 8" (20 cm)

FAM: Ostraciidae
Ostracion meleagris
Spotted Boxfish
FORM: Male

General Aggression

Color Maintenance

Dietary Requirements

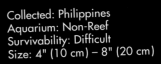
Con-Species Compatibility

Collected: Philippines
Aquarium: Non-Reef
Survivability: Difficult
Size: 4" (10 cm) – 8" (20 cm)

 FAM: Ostraciidae
Ostracion solorensis
Scribble Boxfish

General Aggression

Color Maintenance

Dietary Requirements

Con-Species Compatibility

Collected: Philippines
Aquarium: Non-Reef
Survivability: Difficult
Size: 4" (10 cm) – 8" (20 cm)

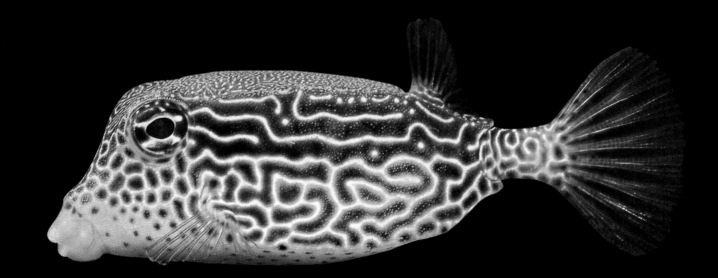

Family: Paralichthyidae

(Flounder) These crustacean eaters are bottom dwellers that often bury themselves in the sand when frightened. They lay on their side on the bottom and both eyes are on the same side of their body. People use them in aquariums to loosen the sand on the bottom of aquariums.

(Famille: Paralichthyidae) Ces mangeurs de crustacés vivent sur les fonds et s'enterrent souvent dans le sable lorsqu'ils sont effrayés. Ils s'allongent de côté sur le sol, les deux yeux étant du même côté de leur corps. On les utilise en aquarium pour aérer le sable.

(Lenguado) Estos comedores de crustáceos viven en los fondos marinos y a menudo se entierran en la arena cuando se ven asustados. Se acuestan de lado en el fondo y sus dos ojos se encuentran en el mismo lado de su cuerpo. Muchas personas los emplean en sus peceras para ablandar la arena del fondo.

(Linguado) Eles comem crustáceos, habitam o fundo do mar e, geralmente, enterram-se na areia quando se assustam. Repousam de lado e os dois olhos ficam no mesmo lado do corpo. As pessoas os usam em aquários para desprender a areia no fundo dos aquários.

(Famiglia: Paralichthyidae) Questi divoratori di crostacei vivono sul fondo dell'acquario e spesso si sotterrano nella sabbia se spaventati. Si posano sul fondo con gli occhi disposti sullo stesso lato del corpo. Sono utili nell'acquario per smuovere la sabbia del fondo.

FAM: Paralichthyidae
Pseudorhombus sp. "Sand"*
Sand Flounder

General Aggression

Color Maintenance

Dietary Requirements

Con-Species Compatibility

Collected: Philippines
Aquarium: Reef
Survivability: Difficult
Size: 4" (10 cm) – 8" (20 cm)

Family: Pholidichthydae

(Convict Blenny) As of 1996, this family consists of a single species. Juveniles are black and white with horizontal stripes like a Coral Catfish. As the fish matures, it becomes elongated like an Eel and its stripes change to spots. Adult Convict Blennies have a completely different appearance from juveniles.

(Famille: Pholidichthydae) Cette famille est constituée d'une seule espèce. Les jeunes sujets sont noirs et blancs et portent des bandes horizontales comme les membres de la famille Plotosidae. Au fur et à mesure de leur processus de maturation, ils s'allongent comme une anguille et leurs bandes se transforment en taches. L'espèce adulte a une apparence complètement différente de la forme juvénile.

(Blenios Rayados) Esta familia se compone de una sola especie. Los juveniles son blancos y negros con listas horizontales similares al bagre de coral. A medida que van madurando, se tornan como una anguila y sus listas se transforman en manchas. Los Blenios Rayados adultos tiene una apariencia completamente diferente a los juveniles.

(Família: Pholidichthydae) Esta família consiste de uma única espécie, os jovens são pretos e brancos com listras horizontais como um peixe-gato de coral. À medida que o peixe cresce, torna-se alongado como uma enguia e suas listras transformam-se em manchas. O amboré adulto tem uma aparência completamente diferente da do jovem.

(Famiglia: Pholidichthydae) Questa famiglia è composta di un'unica specie. I giovani sono bianchi e neri con strisce orizzontali. Non appena il pesce diviene adulto, si allunga come un'anguilla e le strisce si trasformano in macchie. I Pholidichthyidae adulti hanno caratteristiche fisiche completamente diverse dai giovani.

FAM: Pholidichthydae
Pholidichthys leucotaenia
Convict Blenny

General
Aggression

Color
Maintenance

Dietary
Requirements

Con-Species
Compatibility

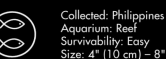

Collected: Philippines
Aquarium: Reef
Survivability: Easy
Size: 4" (10 cm) – 8" (20 cm)

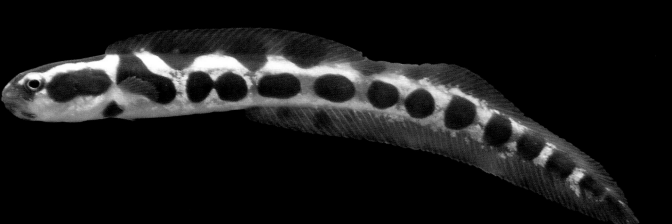

Family: Pinguipedidae

(Sandperches) Members of the Pinguipedidae family are elongated and prey on crustaceans and small fishes. They have behavior similar to the Cirrhitidae family, in that they are active and perch on their pelvic fin — always on the alert for passing prey. It is easy for a beginner to have success with these fishes.

This family is often confused with the family Synodontidae, which are commonly known as Lizardfishes. However, the fishes in this category (Pinquifedidae) are not in the same family as lizardfishes.

(Famille: Pinguipedidae) Les membres de la famille des Pinguipedidae ont un corps allongé et sont des prédateurs de crustacés et de petits poissons. Leur comportement ressemble à celui de la famille des Cirrhitidae, ils sont actifs et se perchent sur leur nageoire pelvienne, toujours à l'affût de nouvelles proies. Ce sont des poissons faciles, à conseiller aux débutants. Cette famille est souvent confondue par erreur avec celle des Synodontidae.

(Percas de Arena) Los miembros de la familia Pinguipedidae son elongados y cazan crustáceos y pequeños peces. Se comportan de forma similar a los miembros de la familia Cirrhitidae, en el sentido de que son activos y se mantienen nadando sobre su aleta pélvica, siempre en estado de alerta para posibles presas que puedan pasar. Resulta fácil para un principiante tener éxito con estos peces.

Esta familia se confunde a menudo con la familia Synodontidae, comúnmente conocidos como Pez Lagarto. Sin embargo, los peces en esta categoría (Pinguipedidae) no pertenecen a la misma familia que los Pez Lagarto.

(Percas-da-Areia) Os membros da família Pinguipedidae são alongados e caçam crustáceos e pequenos peixes. Têm comportamento semelhante ao da família Cirrhitidae, no sentido de que são ativos e pousam sobre a barbatana pélvica, sempre em alerta e à espera de uma possível presa. É fácil para um iniciante ter êxito com estes peixes.

Esta família é freqüentemente confundida com a família Synodontidae, que é comumente conhecida como peixe-lagarto. Entretanto, os peixes desta categoria (Pinguipedidae) não pertencem à mesma família que o peixe-lagarto.

(Famiglia: Pinguipedidae) I membri della famiglia Pinguipedidae hanno il corpo allungato e predano crostacei e piccoli pesci. Il loro comportamento è simile a quello dei Cirritidi perché sono attivi e si adagiano sulla pinna ventrale, sempre attenti alla preda che passa. E' facile per il principiante riuscire nell'allevamento di questi pesci. Spesso, questa famiglia viene confusa con la famiglia Synodontidae dalla quale si differenzia comunque per molti aspetti.

FAM: Pinguipedidae
Parapercis clathrata
Latticed Sandperch

General Aggression **Color Maintenance** **Dietary Requirements** **Con-Species Compatibility**

Collected: Philippines
Aquarium: Reef (Caution)
Survivability: Moderate
Size: 4" (10 cm) – 8" (20 cm)

FAM: Pinguipedidae
Parapercis cylindrica
Cylindrical Sandperch

General Aggression **Color Maintenance** **Dietary Requirements** **Con-Species Compatibility**

Collected: Philippines
Aquarium: Reef (Caution)
Survivability: Moderate
Size: 4" (10 cm) – 8" (20 cm)

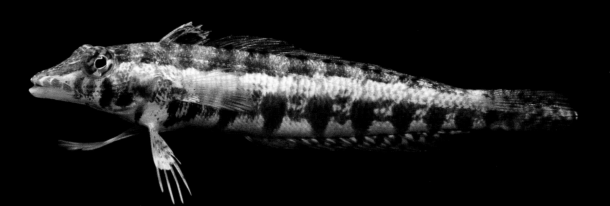

FAM: Pinguipedidae
Parapercis schauinslandi
Red-spotted Sandperch

General Aggression **Color Maintenance** **Dietary Requirements** **Con-Species Compatibility**

Collected: Indonesia
Aquarium: Reef (Caution)
Survivability: Moderate
Size: 4" (10 cm) – 8" (20 cm)

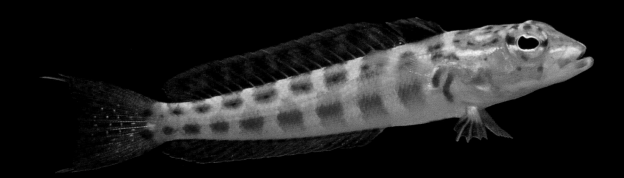

Family: Plesiopidae

(Bettas) This family consists of a relatively few number of genera. Overall, the species contained within this family are unspectacular. One notable exception to this rule is the Marine Betta. Its most spectacular feature is its large finnage which dominates its body. The entire fish is covered with jewel-like speckles. Of the entire family, the Marine Betta is also the most common in the marine aquarium trade. These fishes are excellent reef aquarium candidates. However, one potential problem when keeping these fishes is that when they are first introduced into your aquarium, they require live food (such as small shrimp or fishes) to induce them to begin feeding. Once this is accomplished, they will eat dead fishes or shrimp. They are slow moving and will not get enough food if they are mixed with aggressive, fast-moving fishes.

(Famille: Plesiopidae) Cette famille contient un nombre relativement restreint de genres qui, dans l'ensemble, ne sont pas spectaculaires. L'exception remarquable à cette règle est le *Calloplesiops altivelis* dont les magnifiqes nageoires sculptent tout le corps, lui même recouvert de petites taches blanches aux reflets bleutés ressemblant à des joyaux. De tous les membres de cette famille, le *Calloplesiops altivelis* est généralement le plus proposé dans le commerce de l'aquariophilie marine. Ce poisson est un excellent candidat pour les aquariums de type récifal. Il peut cependant poser un problème car il exige une nourriture vivante, telle que petites crevettes ou poissons, en phase d'acclimatation à l'aquarium. Une fois cette période passée, il se nourrit de crevettes ou de poissons morts. Souvent timide et se déplaçant lentement il peut souffrir d'une concurrence alimentaire préjudiciable, s'il est mis en présence de poissons agressifs ou trop rapides.

(Familia: Plesiopidae) Esta familia comprende un número relativamente pequeño de géneros. Por lo general, las especies contenidas dentro de esta familia no son espectaculares. Una excepción notable a esta regla es el *Calloplesiops altivelis* (Betta Marino). Sus grandes aletas que dominan su cuerpo constituyen su rasgo más espectacular. El pez está totalmente cubierto de manchitas que parecen joyas. De toda la familia, el *Calloplesiops altivelis* es también el ejemplar más común en el comercio de acuarios marinos. Estos peces son excelentes candidatos para peceras de arrecife. Sin embargo, un problema en potencial al mantener estos peces es que requieren alimentos vivos (como pequeños camarones o peces) al ser introducidos por primera vez en la pecera a fin de inducirlos a empezar a comer. Una vez que esto ha sido logrado, empezarán a comer pescados o camarones crudos. Se mueven lentamente y no conseguirán alimento suficiente si se mezclan con peces veloces y agresivos.

(Família: Plesiopidae) Esta família consiste de um número de gêneros relativamente pequeno. De modo geral, as espécies pertencentes a esta família não têm nada de espetacular. Uma notável exceção a esta regra é o *Calloplesiops altivelis* ("Marine Betta"). Sua característica mais espetacular é o grande conjunto de barbatanas que toma conta de seu corpo. O peixe inteiro é coberto por pontilhados semelhantes a jóias. Da família inteira, o *Calloplesiops altivelis* é também o peixe mais comum no comércio de aquário marinho. Estes peixes são excelentes candidatos para aquários de recifes. Entretanto, um problema potencial para a manutenção destes peixes é que, ao serem colocados inicialmente em seu aquário, vão requerer alimento vivo (tais como pequenos camarões ou peixes) para induzí-los a começar a comer. Depois deste período inicial, eles comerão peixe ou camarão mortos. Eles se locomovem devagar e não se alimentarão de forma adequada se forem misturados com peixes rápidos e agressivos.

(Famiglia: Plesiopidae) Questa famiglia è composta da un numero relativamente limitato di generi. Per di più le specie appartenenti a questa famiglia non sono molto belle. Un'eccezione notevole è *Calloplesiops altivelis*. La caratteristica più affascinante di questo pesce sono le pinne che ne dominano il corpo. Il pesce è interamente coperto di puntini che somigliano a gioielli. *Calloplesiops altivelis* è la specie di questa famiglia più diffusa sul mercato dell'acquariofilia. Si tratta di ottimi ospiti per l'acquario da barriera. Comunque, un certo problema costituisce l'alimentazione dei pesci appena introdotti in acquario: è necessario usare cibo vivo (come piccoli gamberetti o pesci) per indurli a mangiare. Quando si saranno acclimatati si nutriranno di polpa di pesce o di gamberetto. Si muovono lentamente e non riusciranno a cibarsi a sufficienza se dovranno condividere l'acquario con pesci veloci o aggressivi.

FAM: Plesiopidae
Calloplesiops altivelis
Marine Betta

General Aggression   Color Maintenance   Dietary Requirements   Con-Species Compatibility

Collected: Philippines
Aquarium: Reef
Survivability: Moderate
Size: 4" (10 cm) – 8" (20 cm)

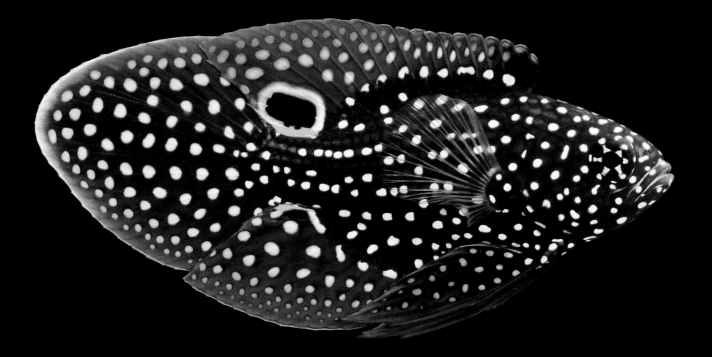

FAM: Plesiopidae
Plesiops corallicola
Poor Man's Betta

General Aggression   Color Maintenance   Dietary Requirements   Con-Species Compatibility

Collected: Philippines
Aquarium: Reef
Survivability: Moderate
Size: 4" (10 cm) – 8" (20 cm)

Family: Plotosidae

(Coral Catfish) This fish is essentially a scavenger, and is useful in a tank to clean the bottom and loosen the substrate. Members of the Plotosidae family have poisonous spines, so should not be handled with bare hands. In the ocean, the juveniles often travel in huge schools.

(Famille: Plotosidae) Les Plotosidae sont essentiellement des éboueurs. Gros mangeurs, ils trouvent leur utilité dans le fait qu'ils nettoient le fond de l'aquarium et aèrent le substrat. Les membres de la famille des Plotosidae portent des épines empoisonnées et ne doivent donc pas être manipulés à mains nues. Dans l'océan, les jeunes individus se déplacent souvent en bancs.

(Bagre de Coral) Estos peces se alimentan esencialmente de carroña y desechos y son útiles en una pecera para limpiar el fondo y aflojar el substrato. Los miembros de la familia Plotosidae poseen espinas venenosas, así que no deben ser manipulados con las manos descubiertas. En el océano, los juveniles a menudo viajan en cardúmenes inmensos.

(Peixe-Gato de coral) Estes peixes alimentam-se, essencialmente, de detritos orgânicos, úteis para limpar e desprender os resíduos do fundo do tanque. Os membros da família *Plotosidae* têm espinhos venenosos, portanto, não devem ser manipulados sem uma proteção para as mãos. No oceano, os peixes jovens geralmente se locomovem em cardumes enormes.

(Famiglia: Plotosidae) I membri di questa famiglia sono essenzialmente saprofagi e sono utili per pulire il fondo e per smuovere il substrato nell'acquario. I Plotosidae possiedono aculei velenosi e per questo motivo non devono essere toccati a mani nude. Nel mare i giovani spesso si spostano in grandi banchi.

 FAM: Plotosidae
Plotosus lineatus
Coral Catfish

 General Aggression

 Color Maintenance

 Dietary Requirements

 Con-Species Compatibility

Collected: Philippines
Aquarium: Reef (Caution)
Survivability: Moderate
Size: 4" (10 cm) – 8" (20 cm)

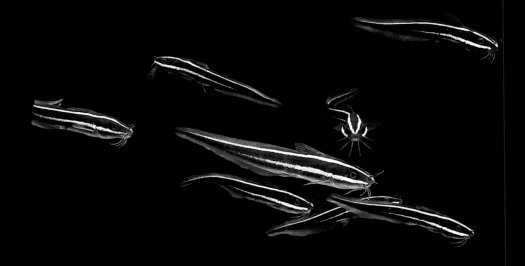

Family: Pomacanthidae

(Angelfishes) In general, this family is among the most attractive of the marine fishes. They are characterized by a large spike on the preopercular gill plate. Various members of this family range from simple to extremely difficult to maintain in an aquarium. When planning an aquarium that includes members of the Pomacanthidae family, keep in mind that they can be very aggressive toward other Pomacanthidae members with similar markings. Therefore, only one individual of the same species should be kept in the same tank.

Juveniles of many species in the Pomacanthus genus have a similar color scheme, but acquire very distinct color patterns as they mature. This is particularly true of the larger species. The pattern differences between juveniles and adults in the smaller Centropyge genus are less noticeable. Among most members of the Pomacanthidae family, there is no difference in color between the sexes (though males do tend to be larger than females). Members of the Genicanthus genus tend to be an exception to this rule. Other than protein-rich food, most of these fish also eat a lot of vegetable matter — which should be offered to them daily. The species which feed on coral and sponges are the most difficult to keep in captivity.

(Famille: Pomacanthidae) En général, cette famille est parmi les plus séduisantes de tous les poissons marins. Ils sont caractérisés par une large épine sur la partie préoperculaire des ouïes. Leur entretien et leur maintenance en aquarium peut aller du facile au très difficile. Selon l'espèce, ils peuvent être très agressifs envers d'autres Pomacanthidae ayant des similaires, il est donc important de ne garder qu'un individu de la même espèce dans un même aquarium.

Les formes juvéniles de nombreuses espèces de Pomacanthus possèdent des motifs et des couleurs très similaires, c'est lorsqu'ils arrivent à maturité qu'ils acquièrent leurs somptueuses robes d'adultes, totalement différentes les unes des autres. Ceci est particulièrement vrai pour les espèces plus grandes. Pour le le genre plus petit des Centropyges, les différences de motifs entre juvéniles et adultes sont moins remarquables. Bien que les mâles aient tendance à être plus gros que les femelles, pour la plupart des membres de cette famille, il n'existe pas de différence de couleur entre les sexes,. Les membres du genre Genicanthus sont une exception à cette règle. En plus d'une nourriture riche en protéines, la plupart de ces poissons se nourrissent d'une grande quantité de matière végétale qui doit leur être offerte tous les jours. Certaines espèces, qui se nourrissent de coraux et d'éponges, sont les plus difficiles à garder en captivité.

(Familia: Pomacanthidae) En general, esta familia se encuentra entre las más atractivas de los peces marinos. Se caracterizan por un espina grande sobre la placa preopercular de las agallas. Los diversos miembros de esta familia oscilan entre los peces extremadamente difíciles de mantener en acuarios y los más sencillos. Al planificar una pecera que incluye miembros de la familia Pomacanthidae, mantenga en mente que pueden ser muy agresivos hacia otros miembros de los Pomacanthidae con marcas similares. Por consiguiente, sólo debe mantenerse un individuo de la misma especie en el mismo tanque. Los juveniles de muchas especies de Pomacanthus poseen un esquema de color similar, pero adquieren configuraciones de color dramáticamente diferentes al ser adultos. Esto es particularmente cierto de las especies más grandes. Las diferencias en patrones de colores entre los juveniles y los adultos en el género más pequeño Centropyge son menos conspicuas.

Entre la mayoría de los miembros de la familia Pomacanthidae, no existen diferencia de color entre los sexos, aunque los machos tienden a ser más grandes que las hembras. Los miembros del género Genicanthus tienden a ser la excepción de esta regla. Además de alimentos ricos en proteína, la mayoría de estos peces también comen mucha materia orgánica, la cual se les debe ofrecer diariamente. Las especies que se alimentan de corales y esponjas son las más difíciles de mantener en cautiverio.

Family: Pomacanthidae

(Anjos-do-Mar) Em geral, esta família encontra-se entre as mais atraentes de peixes marinhos. Eles se caracterizam por um espigão na placa pré-opercular das guelras. A manutenção, no aquário, de vários membros desta família varia de simples até extremamente difícil. Ao planejar um aquário que inclua membros da família *Pomacanthidae,* tenha em mente que eles podem ser bastante agressivos com outros membros da *Pomacanthidae* com traços semelhantes; por esta razão, apenas um indivíduo da mesma espécie deve ser mantido no mesmo tanque.

Peixes jovens de muitas espécies da *Pomacanthus* têm combinação semelhante de cores, mas adquirem padrões de cores radicalmente diferentes, à medida que crescem. Este fato ocorre principalmente com espécies maiores. As diferenças de padrões entre jovens e adultos no gênero *Centropyge* são menos acentuadas.

Entre a maioria dos membros da família *Pomacanthidae,* não há diferença de cor entre os sexos, embora os machos tendam a ser maiores do que as fêmeas. Os membros do gênero *Genicanthus* tendem a ser uma exceção a esta regra. Além de alimentos ricos em proteínas, a maioria destes peixes também come muita matéria vegetal, que lhes deve ser oferecido diariamente. A espécie que se alimenta de corais e esponjas é a mais difícil de manter em cativeiro.

(Famiglia: Pomacanthidae) Questa famiglia è tra le più attraenti dei pesci marini; i suoi membri sono caratterizzati da un grande aculeo sulla placca preopercolare delle branchie. Il mantenimento di questi pesci in acquario varia da semplice a difficile. Durante la progettazione di un acquario che includa membri della famiglia Pomacanthidae, è necessario considerare che possono essere molto aggressivi verso altri Pomacanthidae con caratteristiche morfologiche simili. Per questo motivo dovrebbe essere allevato nello stesso acquario soltanto un individuo della stessa specie.

I giovani di molte specie di Pomacanthidae hanno una colorazione simile, ma acquistano livree di colori estremamente diversi con l'età adulta. Questo fatto è particolarmente pronunciato nelle specie più grandi, mentre le differenze di colorazione tra i giovani e gli adulti nel genere *Centropyge* sono meno spiccate.

Tra la maggior parte dei generi della famiglia Pomacanthidae, non esiste nessuna dimorfismo sessuale nella colorazione, ma i maschi tendono a essere più grandi delle femmine. I membri del genere *Genicanthus* tendono a essere un'eccezione a questa regola. Oltre a un'alimentazione ricca di proteine, la maggior parte di questi pesci si nutre di sostanze vegetali, che dovrebbero essere loro forniti ogni giorno. Le specie che si nutrono di coralli e spugne sono le più difficili da mantenere in acquario.

FAM: Pomacanthidae
Apolemichthys trimaculatus
Flagfin Angelfish
FORM: Adult

General Aggression · Color Maintenance · Dietary Requirements · Con-Species Compatibility

Collected: Philippines
Aquarium: Non-Reef
Survivability: Doomed
Size: 4" (10 cm) – 8" (20 cm)

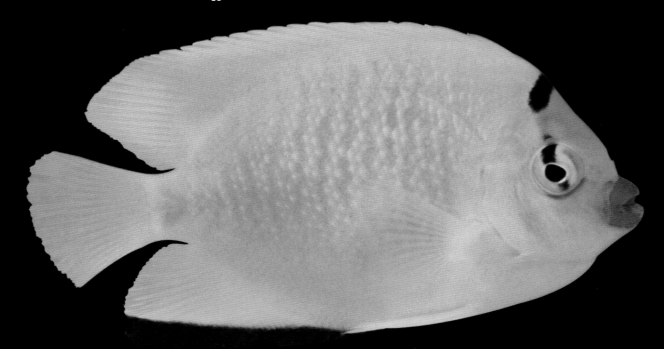

FAM: Pomacanthidae
Apolemichthys trimaculatus
Flagfin Angelfish
FORM: Juvenile

General Aggression · Color Maintenance · Dietary Requirements · Con-Species Compatibility

Collected: Philippines
Aquarium: Non-Reef
Survivability: Doomed
Size: 4" (10 cm) – 8" (20 cm)

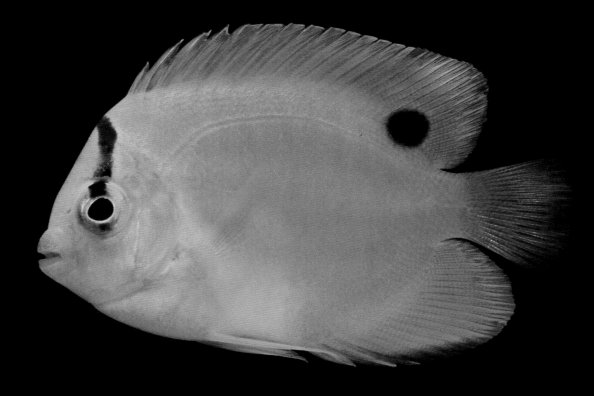

FAM: Pomacanthidae
Centropyge aurantius
Golden Angelfish

General
Aggression

Color
Maintenance

Dietary
Requirements

Con-Species
Compatibility

Collected: Indonesia
Aquarium: Non-Reef
Survivability: Moderate
Size: Less than 4" (10 cm)

FAM: Pomacanthidae
Centropyge bicolor
Bicolor Angelfish

General
Aggression

Color
Maintenance

Dietary
Requirements

Con-Species
Compatibility

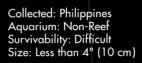
Collected: Philippines
Aquarium: Non-Reef
Survivability: Difficult
Size: Less than 4" (10 cm)

FAM: Pomacanthidae
Centropyge bispinosus
Coral Beauty Angelfish

General Aggression

Color Maintenance

Dietary Requirements

Con-Species Compatibility

Collected: Philippines
Aquarium: Reef (Caution)
Survivability: Moderate
Size: Less than 4" (10 cm)

FAM: Pomacanthidae
Centropyge colini
Colin's Angelfish

General Aggression

Color Maintenance

Dietary Requirements

Con-Species Compatibility

Collected: Philippines
Aquarium: Non-Reef
Survivability: Difficult
Size: Less than 4" (10 cm)

FAM: Pomacanthidae
Centropyge sp. "Dusky Gold"*
Dusky Gold Angelfish

General Aggression | Color Maintenance | Dietary Requirements | Con-Species Compatibility

Collected: Philippines
Aquarium: Non-Reef
Survivability: Moderate
Size: Less than 4" (10 cm)

FAM: Pomacanthidae
Centropyge eibli
Eibl's Angelfish

General Aggression | Color Maintenance | Dietary Requirements | Con-Species Compatibility

Collected: Indonesia
Aquarium: Reef (Caution)
Survivability: Moderate
Size: Less than 4" (10 cm)

233

FAM: Pomacanthidae
Centropyge ferrugatus
Rusty Angelfish

General Aggression

Color Maintenance

Dietary Requirements

Con-Species Compatibility

Collected: Indonesia
Aquarium: Reef (Caution)
Survivability: Easy
Size: Less than 4" (10 cm)

FAM: Pomacanthidae
Centropyge flavicauda
White-tail Angelfish

General Aggression

Color Maintenance

Dietary Requirements

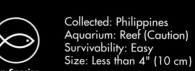
Con-Species Compatibility

Collected: Philippines
Aquarium: Reef (Caution)
Survivability: Easy
Size: Less than 4" (10 cm)

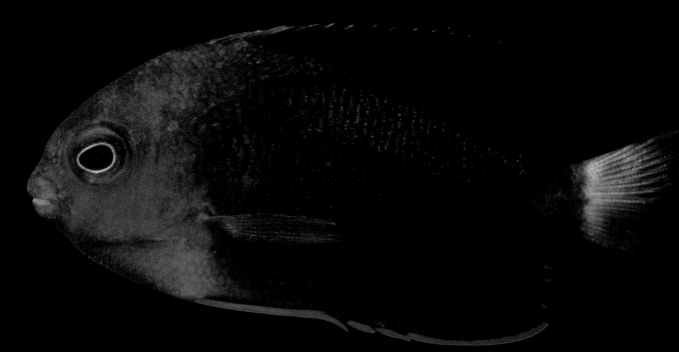

234

FAM: Pomacanthidae
Chaetodontoplus melanosoma
Grey Poma Angelfish
FORM: Adult

General Aggression

Color Maintenance

Dietary Requirements

Con-Species Compatibility

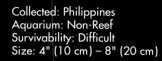
Collected: Philippines
Aquarium: Non-Reef
Survivability: Difficult
Size: 4" (10 cm) – 8" (20 cm)

FAM: Pomacanthidae
Chaetodontoplus melanosoma
Grey Poma Angelfish
FORM: Juvenile

General Aggression

Color Maintenance

Dietary Requirements

Con-Species Compatibility

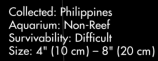
Collected: Philippines
Aquarium: Non-Reef
Survivability: Difficult
Size: 4" (10 cm) – 8" (20 cm)

239

General
Aggression

Color
Maintenance

Dietary
Requireme

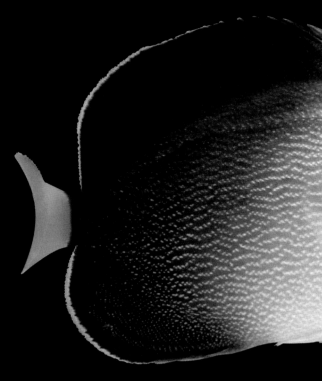

FAM: Pomacanthidae
Genicanthus bellus
Ornate Angelfish
FORM: Female

General
Aggression

Color
Maintenance

Dietary
Requirements

FAM: Pomacanthidae
Genicanthus bellus
Ornate Angelfish
FORM: Male

General Aggression

Color Maintenance

Dietary Requirements

Con-Species Compatibility

Collected: Philippines
Aquarium: Reef (Caution)
Survivability: Difficult
Size: 4" (10 cm) – 8" (20 cm)

FAM: Pomacanthidae
Genicanthus lamarck
Lamarck's Angelfish

General Aggression

Color Maintenance

Dietary Requirements

Con-Species Compatibility

Collected: Philippines
Aquarium: Reef (Caution)
Survivability: Moderate
Size: 4" (10 cm) – 8" (20 cm)

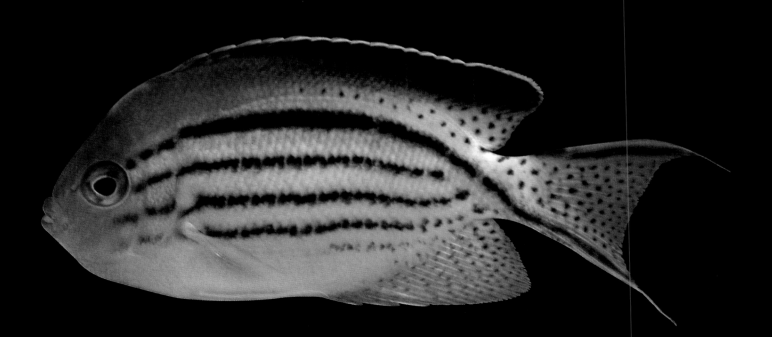

FAM: Pomacanthidae
Genicanthus melanospilos
Swallowtail Angelfish
FORM: Female

**General
Aggression**

**Color
Maintenance**

**Dietary
Requirements**

**Con-Species
Compatibility**

Collected: Philippines
Aquarium: Reef (Caution)
Survivability: Moderate
Size: 4" (10 cm) – 8" (20 cm)

FAM: Pomacanthidae
Genicanthus melanospilos
Swallowtail Angelfish
FORM: Male

**General
Aggression**

**Color
Maintenance**

**Dietary
Requirements**

**Con-Species
Compatibility**

Collected: Philippines
Aquarium: Reef (Caution)
Survivability: Difficult
Size: 4" (10 cm) – 8" (20 cm)

FAM: Pomacanthidae
Genicanthus watanabei
Watanabe's Angelfish
FORM: Female

General Aggression

Color Maintenance

Dietary Requirements

Con-Species Compatibility

Collected: Philippines
Aquarium: Reef (Caution)
Survivability: Moderate
Size: 4" (10 cm) – 8" (20 cm)

FAM: Pomacanthidae
Genicanthus watanabei
Watanabe's Angelfish
FORM: Male

General Aggression

Color Maintenance

Dietary Requirements

Con-Species Compatibility

Collected: Philippines
Aquarium: Reef (Caution)
Survivability: Difficult
Size: 4" (10 cm) – 8" (20 cm)

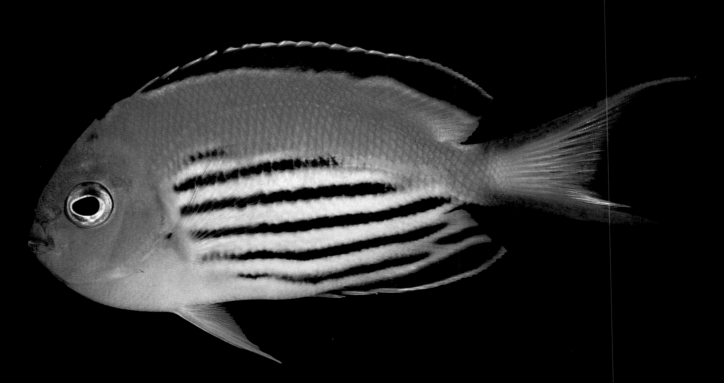

243

FAM: Pomacanthidae
Pomacanthus annularis
Blue-ring Angelfish
FORM: Adult

General Aggression **Color Maintenance** **Dietary Requirements** **Con-Species Compatibility**

Collected: Indonesia
Aquarium: Non-Reef
Survivability: Moderate
Size: More than 8" (20 cm)

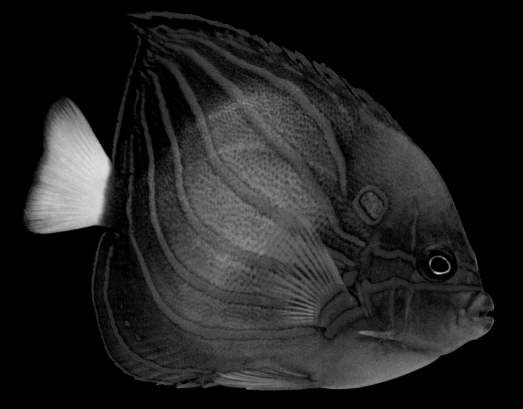

FAM: Pomacanthidae
Pomacanthus annularis
Blue-ring Angelfish
FORM: Juvenile

General Aggression **Color Maintenance** **Dietary Requirements** **Con-Species Compatibility**

Collected: Indonesia
Aquarium: Non-Reef
Survivability: Easy
Size: More than 8" (20 cm)

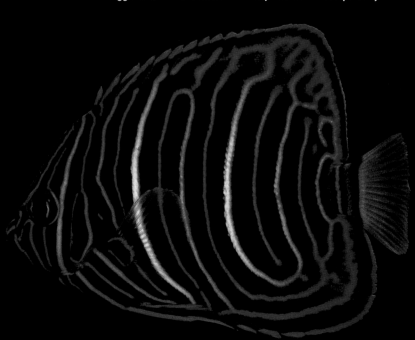

244

FAM: Pomacanthidae
Pomacanthus imperator
Emperor Angelfish
FORM: Adult

General
Aggression

Color
Maintenance

Dietary
Requirements

Con-Species
Compatibility

Collected: Philippines
Aquarium: Non-Reef
Survivability: Moderate
Size: More than 8" (20 cm)

FAM: Pomacanthidae
Pomacanthus imperator
Emperor Angelfish
FORM: Juvenile

General
Aggression

Color
Maintenance

Dietary
Requirements

Con-Species
Compatibility

Collected: Philippines
Aquarium: Non-Reef
Survivability: Moderate
Size: More than 8" (20 cm)

245

FAM: Pomacanthidae
Pomacanthus navarchus
Majestic Angelfish

General Aggression   Color Maintenance   Dietary Requirements   Con-Species Compatibility

Collected: Philippines
Aquarium: Non-Reef
Survivability: Difficult
Size: More than 8" (20 cm)

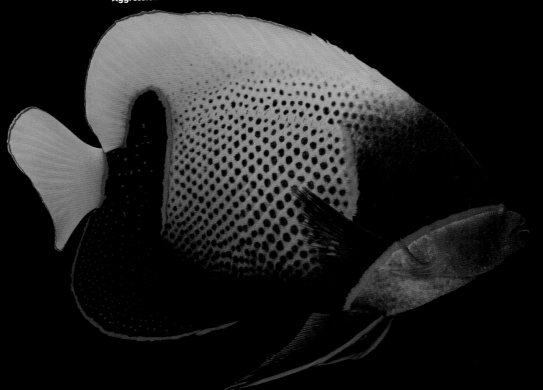

FAM: Pomacanthidae
Pomacanthus semicirculatus
Koran Angelfish
FORM: Juvenile

General Aggression   Color Maintenance   Dietary Requirements   Con-Species Compatibility

Collected: Philippines
Aquarium: Non-Reef
Survivability: Moderate
Size: More than 8" (20 cm)

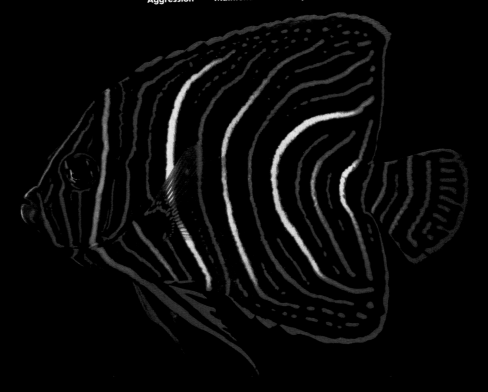

246

FAM: Pomacanthidae
Pomacanthus sextriatus
Six-banded Angelfish
FORM: Juvenile

 General Aggression

 Color Maintenance

 Dietary Requirements

 Con-Species Compatibility

Collected: Philippines
Aquarium: Non-Reef
Survivability: Moderate
Size: More than 8" (20 cm)

FAM: Pomacanthidae
Pomacanthus sextriatus
Six-banded Angelfish
FORM: Subadult

 General Aggression

 Color Maintenance

 Dietary Requirements

 Con-Species Compatibility

Collected: Philippines
Aquarium: Non-Reef
Survivability: Moderate
Size: More than 8" (20 cm)

247

FAM: Pomacanthidae
Pomacanthus xanthometapon
Blue-face Angelfish
FORM: Adult

General Aggression   Color Maintenance   Dietary Requirements   Con-Species Compatibility

Collected: Philippines
Aquarium: Non-Reef
Survivability: Moderate
Size: 4" (10 cm) – 8" (20 cm)

FAM: Pomacanthidae
Pomacanthus xanthometapon
Blue-face Angelfish
FORM: Juvenile

General Aggression   Color Maintenance   Dietary Requirements   Con-Species Compatibility

Collected: Philippines
Aquarium: Non-Reef
Survivability: Moderate
Size: 4" (10 cm) – 8" (20 cm)

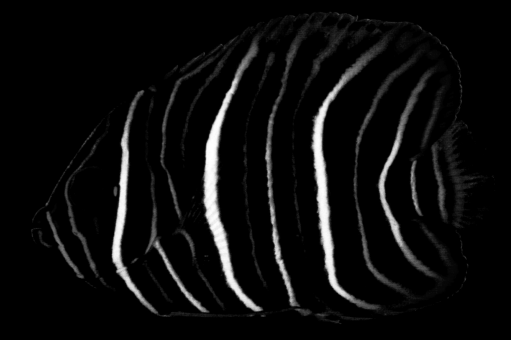

248

Pygoplites diacanthus
Regal Angelfish
FORM: Adult

 General Aggression

 Color Maintenance

 Dietary Requirements

Con-Species Compatibility

Aquarium: Non-Reef
Survivability: Doomed
Size: 4" (10 cm) – 8" (20 cm)

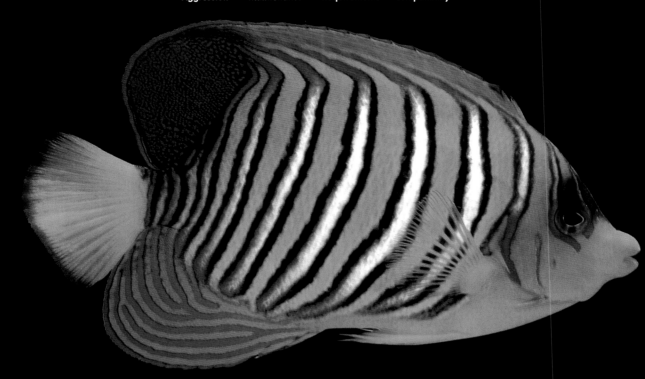

FAM: Pomacanthidae
Pygoplites diacanthus
Regal Angelfish
FORM: Subadult

 General Aggression

 Color Maintenance

 Dietary Requirements

 Con-Species Compatibility

Collected: Philippines
Aquarium: Non-Reef
Survivability: Doomed
Size: 4" (10 cm) – 8" (20 cm)

Family: Pomacentridae

(Anemonefishes & Damselfishes) members of the Amphiprioninae subfamily (Anemonefishes) have a classic symbio
elationship with anemones. Their surface slime is coated with anemone-like secretion, so that it is not recognized a
reign object by an anemone and does not get stung by the anemone's tentacles. These fishes likewise guard an anemor
om being picked at by members of the Chaetodontidae family. Amphiprioninae species have been observed taking
ftover food to an anemone. It is unclear whether this was intentional or accidental. Members of this family were
nong the first salt water fishes bred in captivity. Although Amphiprioninae species prefer to live with anemones,
ey can live without them and are suitable for a reef aquarium. They are hermaphroditic; when the female is remove
e largest and most aggressive individual changes to a functional female.
  Members of the Demoiselles and Chrominae subfamilies (Damsels and Chrominae) congregate around coral for protectior
ough some choose anemones. They are active fishes with a tendency to be aggressive toward their own kind. Juvenile
amsels are more colorful than adults. Many species have been bred in captivity and can be recommended to beginners
nce they are among the easiest marine fishes to maintain.

(Famille: Pomacentridae) Les membres de la sous-famille des Amphiprioninae ont une relation symbiotique très spécifiq
ec les anémones de mer. En se couvrant le corps de sécrétions naturelles d'anémones, ils ne sont pas perçus comr
η objet étranger et de ce fait ne se font pas piquer par ses tentacules. A leur tour, ces poissons protègent l'anémon
ontre certains prédateurs, dont les membres de la famille des Chaetodontidae. On a observé des espèces d'Amphiprionir
pportant des restes de nourriture à leur anémone, on ne sait pas si c'est de manière accidentelle ou intentionné
es Amphiprioninae sont parmi les premiers à s'être reproduits en captivité. Bien que les espèces Amphiprioninae préfèrer
vre parmi les anémones, elles peuvent vivre aussi sans elles et s'adapter, en aquarium, à un environnement récifal. Ce
ont des espèces hermaphrodites et lorsque la femelle fonctionnelle est enlevée, le spécimen le plus gros et le plus
gressif devient femelle à son tour.
  Bien que certains choisissent aussi les anémones, les membres des sous-familles des Demoiselles et des Chrominae
e regroupent plus volontiers autour de blocs coraux pour se protéger. Ce sont des poissons actifs, ayant une tendar
gressive envers leur propre espèce. Les Demoiselles, sous leur forme juvénile sont plus colorés que les adultes. [
ombreuses espèces ont été reproduites en captivité et on peut les recommander pour les débutants, ces poissor
e mer étant parmi les plus faciles à élever.

(Pez Payaso y Pez Damisela) Los miembros de la subfamilia Amphiprioninae (Pez Payaso) tienen una relación simbiótic
ásica con las anémonas. Su mucosa natural está cubierta de secreción de anémona, de modo que no son reconocid
omo un objeto extraño por una anémona y los tentáculos de la anémona no los pican. Del mismo modo, estos
eces impiden que una anémona sea mordida por los miembros de la familia Chaetodontidae. Las especies Amphiprioni
an sido observadas llevándole sobras de comida a una anémona, pero no está claro si ha sido intencional o accident
stos peces fueron entre los primeros peces de agua salada criados en cautiverio. Aunque los miembros de la
pecie Amphiprioninae prefieren vivir con anémonas, pueden vivir sin ellas y son apropiados para una pecera c
recife. Son hermatroditas, cuando la hembra se retira de la pecera, el individuo más grande y más agresivo se
ansforma en hembra funcional. Los miembros de las subfamilias Demoiselles y Chrominae (Pez Damisela y Crominios
e congregan alrededor de los corales para protección, aunque algunos escogen anémonas. Son peces activos cor
na tendencia agresiva hacia su propia especie. Los pez damisela juveniles tienen más colorido que los ejemplares
dultos. Muchas especies han sido criadas en cautiverio y se recomiendan para los principiantes puesto que estan
ntre los peces marinos más fáciles de mantener.
  Estos peces son mayormente pequeños, llenos de colorido, muy populares para peceras de arrecifes. La mayoría
e las especies dentro de la familia Pseudochromidae son extremadamente territoriales y quizás los peces más
gresivos de su tamaño, así que en una pequeña pecera deben mantenerse a solas. En una pecera más grande dor
uedan establecer su territorio, se pueden mantener varios ejemplares juntos. En el peor de los casos en un tanc
e ese tamaño habrán disputas territoriales, con espacio para retiradas. Miembros de la familia Pseudochromidae
ciles de alimentar y mantener así que resultan una excelente selección para aficionados principiantes.

Family: Pomacentridae

(Peixes-Palhaço e Donzelas) Os membros da subfamília Amphiprioninae (Peixes-Palhaço) têm uma clássica relação simbiótica com as anêmonas. Seu muco natural é coberto com a secreção da anêmona, de modo que não é reconhecido como um objeto estranho por uma anêmona e não é picado pelos tentáculos da anêmona. Estes peixes, além do mais, protegem a anêmona de ser atacada pelos membros da família Chaetodontidae. Já se observou uma espécie Amphiprioninae levando restos de alimento para uma anêmona. Não ficou claro se o ato foi intencional ou acidental. Estes peixes estão entre os primeiros peixes de água salgada a reproduzirem em cativeiro.

Embora a espécie Amphiprioninae prefira viver com as anêmonas, estes peixes podem viver sem elas, sendo adequados para uma aquário de recifes. Eles são hermafroditas e, quando a fêmea é afastada, o indivíduo maior e o mais agressivo transforma-se em fêmea funcional.

Os membros das subfamílias Demoiselles e Chrominae (Donzelas e Chrominae) concentram-se ao redor de corais para proteção, embora alguns escolham as anêmonas. São peixes ativos com uma tendência agressiva para com os de sua própria espécie. Os peixes donzelas jovens são mais coloridos do que os adultos. Muitas espécies já se reproduziram em cativeiro e podem ser recomendados a iniciantes, pois encontram-se entre os peixes marinhos de mais fácil manutenção.

(Famiglia: Pomacentridae) I membri del genere *Amphiprion* sono famosi per la loro simbiosi con gli anemoni di mare. Il loro umore viscoso è normalmente permeato da una secrezione dell'anemone ospite, per non essere riconosciuti come oggetti estranei dagli anemoni e per non essere punti dai loro tentacoli. Questi pesci proteggono l'anemone dai morsi dei pesci della famiglia Chaetodontidae. E' stato osservato che le specie di *Amphiprion* portano il cibo avanzato all'anemone simbionte, ma non è chiaro se fosse voluto o accidentale. Questi pesci furono tra i primi d'acqua marina a essere riprodotti in cattività. Benché le specie di *Amphiprion* preferiscano abitare con gli anemoni, possono vivere anche senza di loro e sono indicati per gli acquari da barriera. Sono ermafroditi: quando viene rimossa una femmina, l'individuo più grande e più aggressivo diventa una femmina attiva.

I membri delle sottofamiglie Demoiselles e Chrominae si congregano attorno alle madrepore per proteggersi, benché alcuni scelgano gli anemoni. Sono pesci con tendenze aggressive verso il loro stesso genere. Gli esemplari giovani di Chrominae hanno colori più vivaci degli adulti. Molte specie sono state riprodotte in cattività e possono essere raccomandate al principiante perché sono tra i pesci marini più facili da allevare.

General Aggression

Color Maintenance

Dietary Requirements

Con-Species Compatibility

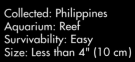
Collected: Philippines
Aquarium: Reef
Survivability: Easy
Size: Less than 4" (10 cm)

FAM: Pomacentridae
Amblyglyphidodon ternatensis
Ternate Damselfish

General Aggression

Color Maintenance

Dietary Requirements

Con-Species Compatibility

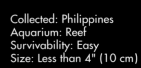
Collected: Philippines
Aquarium: Reef
Survivability: Easy
Size: Less than 4" (10 cm)

FAM: Pomacentridae
Amblypomacentrus breviceps
Tiger Damselfish

General Aggression

Color Maintenance

Dietary Requirements

Con-Species Compatibility

Collected: Philippines
Aquarium: Reef
Survivability: Easy
Size: Less than 4" (10 cm)

FAM: Pomacentridae
Amphiprion clarkii (Black Indo)
Clark's Anemonefish (Black Indo)

General Aggression

Color Maintenance

Dietary Requirements

Con-Species Compatibility

Collected: Indonesia
Aquarium: Reef
Survivability: Easy
Size: 4" (10 cm) – 8" (20 cm)

253

FAM: Pomacentridae
Amphiprion clarkii (Brown Indo)
Clark's Anemonefish (Brown Indo)

General Aggression **Color Maintenance** **Dietary Requirements** **Con-Species Compatibility**

Collected: Indonesia
Aquarium: Reef
Survivability: Easy
Size: 4" (10 cm) – 8" (20 cm)

FAM: Pomacentridae
Amphiprion clarkii (Dark Brown)
Clark's Anemonefish (Dark Brown)

General Aggression **Color Maintenance** **Dietary Requirements** **Con-Species Compatibility**

Collected: Indonesia
Aquarium: Reef
Survivability: Easy
Size: 4" (10 cm) – 8" (20 cm)

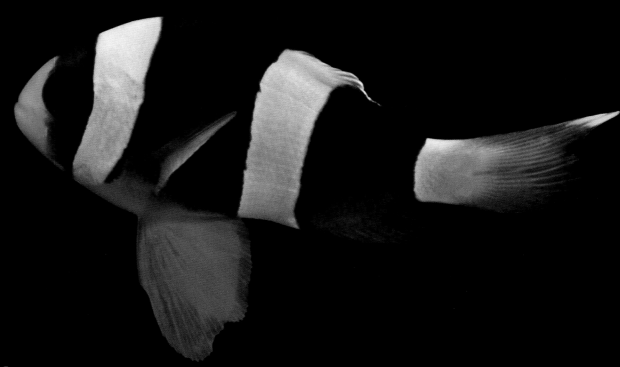

FAM: Pomacentridae
Amphiprion clarkii (Black)
Clark's Anemonefish (Black)

 General Aggression

 Color Maintenance

 Dietary Requirements

 Con-Species Compatibility

Collected: Philippines
Aquarium: Reef
Survivability: Moderate
Size: 4" (10 cm) – 8" (20 cm)

FAM: Pomacentridae
Amphiprion clarkii (Brown)
Clark's Anemonefish (Brown)

 General Aggression

 Color Maintenance

 Dietary Requirements

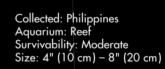 **Con-Species Compatibility**

Collected: Philippines
Aquarium: Reef
Survivability: Moderate
Size: 4" (10 cm) – 8" (20 cm)

255

FAM: Pomacentridae
Amphiprion ephippium
Red Saddleback Anemonefish

 General Aggression
 Color Maintenance
 Dietary Requirements
 Con-Species Compatibility

Collected: Philippines
Aquarium: Reef
Survivability: Moderate
Size: 4" (10 cm) – 8" (20 cm)

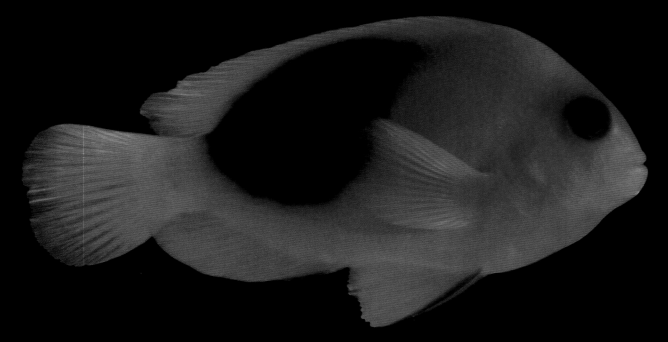

FAM: Pomacentridae
Amphiprion frenatus (Indo)
Tomato Anemonefish (Indo)

 General Aggression
 Color Maintenance
 Dietary Requirements
 Con-Species Compatibility

Collected: Indonesia
Aquarium: Reef
Survivability: Easy
Size: 4" (10 cm) – 8" (20 cm)

256

FAM: Pomacentridae
Amphiprion polymnus (Indonesia)
Saddleback Anemonefish (Indonesia)

General Aggression

Color Maintenance

Dietary Requirements

Con-Species Compatibility

Collected: Indonesia
Aquarium: Reef
Survivability: Easy
Size: 4" (10 cm) – 8" (20 cm

FAM: Pomacentridae
Amphiprion polymnus (Philippines)
Saddleback Anemonefish (Philippines)

General Aggression

Color Maintenance

Dietary Requirements

Con-Species Compatibility

Collected: Philippines
Aquarium: Reef
Survivability: Moderate
Size: 4" (10 cm) – 8" (20 cm

26

FAM: Pomacentridae
Amphiprion sandaracinos
Orange Skunk Anemonefish

General Aggression | Color Maintenance | Dietary Requirements | Con-Species Compatibility

Collected: Philippines
Aquarium: Reef
Survivability: Easy
Size: 4" (10 cm) – 8" (20 cm)

FAM: Pomacentridae
Chromis cyanea (Bluetail)
Blue Damselfish (Bluetail)

General Aggression | Color Maintenance | Dietary Requirements | Con-Species Compatibility

Collected: Indonesia
Aquarium: Reef
Survivability: Easy
Size: Less than 4" (10 cm)

FAM: Pomacentridae
Chromis cyanea (Orangetail)
Blue Damselfish (Orangetail)

General Aggression

Color Maintenance

Dietary Requirements

Con-Species Compatibility

Collected: Indonesia
Aquarium: Reef
Survivability: Easy
Size: Less than 4" (10 cm)

FAM: Pomacentridae
Chromis cyanea (Plain Tail)
Blue Damselfish (Plain Tail)

General Aggression

Color Maintenance

Dietary Requirements

Con-Species Compatibility

Collected: Philippines
Aquarium: Reef
Survivability: Easy
Size: Less than 4" (10 cm)

263

FAM: Pomacentridae
Chromis iomelas
Two-tone Chromis

General Aggression

Color Maintenance

Dietary Requirements

Con-Species Compatibility

Collected: Indonesia
Aquarium: Reef
Survivability: Easy
Size: Less than 4" (10 cm)

FAM: Pomacentridae
Chromis margaritifer
Bicolor Chromis

General Aggression

Color Maintenance

Dietary Requirements

Con-Species Compatibility

Collected: Indonesia
Aquarium: Reef
Survivability: Easy
Size: Less than 4" (10 cm)

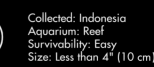

FAM: Pomacentridae
Chromis retrofasciata
Black-bar Chromis

General Aggression Color Maintenance Dietary Requirements Con-Species Compatibility

Collected: Indonesia
Aquarium: Reef
Survivability: Easy
Size: Less than 4" (10 cm)

FAM: Pomacentridae
Chromis viridis
Blue-green Chromis

General Aggression Color Maintenance Dietary Requirements Con-Species Compatibility

Collected: Philippines
Aquarium: Reef
Survivability: Moderate
Size: Less than 4" (10 cm)

265

FAM: Pomacentridae
Chrysiptera caeruleolineata
Blueback Damselfish

General Aggression

Color Maintenance

Dietary Requirements

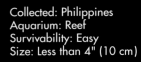

Con-Species Compatibility

Collected: Philippines
Aquarium: Reef
Survivability: Easy
Size: Less than 4" (10 cm)

FAM: Pomacentridae
Chrysiptera parasema
Yellowtail Damselfish

General Aggression

Color Maintenance

Dietary Requirements

Con-Species Compatibility

Collected: Philippines
Aquarium: Reef
Survivability: Easy
Size: Less than 4" (10 cm)

FAM: Pomacentridae
Dischistodus perspicillatus
White Damselfish

 General Aggression
 Color Maintenance
 Dietary Requirements
 Con-Species Compatibility

Collected: Philippines
Aquarium: Reef
Survivability: Easy
Size: Less than 4" (10 cm)

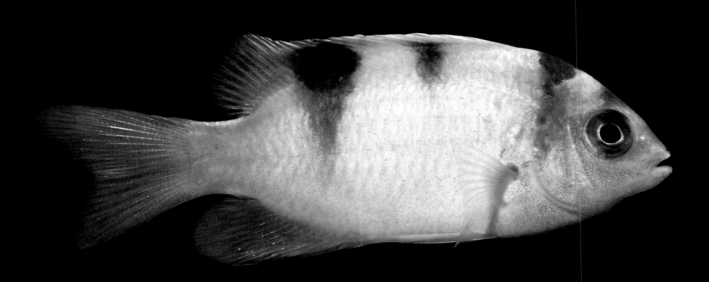

FAM: Pomacentridae
Dischistodus prosopotaenia
Honey-head Damselfish

 General Aggression
 Color Maintenance
 Dietary Requirements
 Con-Species Compatibility

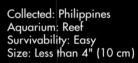

Collected: Philippines
Aquarium: Reef
Survivability: Easy
Size: Less than 4" (10 cm)

271

FAM: Pomacentridae
Neoglyphidodon crossi
Cross' Damselfish

 General Aggression

 Color Maintenance

 Dietary Requirements

Con-Species Compatibility

Collected: Philippines
Aquarium: Reef
Survivability: Easy
Size: Less than 4" (10 cm)

FAM: Pomacentridae
Neoglyphidodon melas
Blue-fin Damselfish

 General Aggression

 Color Maintenance

 Dietary Requirements

Con-Species Compatibility

Collected: Philippines
Aquarium: Reef
Survivability: Easy
Size: Less than 4" (10 cm)

FAM: Pomacentridae
Neoglyphidodon moluccensis
Lemon Damselfish

General
Aggression

Color
Maintenance

Dietary
Requirements

Con-Species
Compatibility

Collected: Philippines
Aquarium: Reef
Survivability: Easy
Size: Less than 4" (10 cm)

FAM: Pomacentridae
Neoglyphidodon nigroris
Black & Gold Damselfish

General
Aggression

Color
Maintenance

Dietary
Requirements

Con-Species
Compatibility

Collected: Philippines
Aquarium: Reef
Survivability: Easy
Size: Less than 4" (10 cm)

273

FAM: Pomacentridae
Neoglyphidodon oxyodon
Neon Velvet Damselfish

General
Aggression

Color
Maintenance

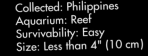
Dietary
Requirements

Con-Species
Compatibility

Collected: Philippines
Aquarium: Reef
Survivability: Easy
Size: Less than 4" (10 cm)

FAM: Pomacentridae
Neoglyphidodon thoracotaeniatus
Barhead Damselfish

General
Aggression

Color
Maintenance

Dietary
Requirements

Con-Species
Compatibility

Collected: Philippines
Aquarium: Reef
Survivability: Easy
Size: Less than 4" (10

FAM: Pomacentridae
Plectroglyphidodon lacrymatus
Pacific Jewel Damselfish

General Aggression

Color Maintenance

Dietary Requirements

Con-Species Compatibility

Collected: Philippines
Aquarium: Reef
Survivability: Easy
Size: Less than 4" (10 cm)

FAM: Pomacentridae
Pomacentrus alleni
Allen's Damselfish

General Aggression

Color Maintenance

Dietary Requirements

Con-Species Compatibility

Collected: Philippines
Aquarium: Reef
Survivability: Easy
Size: Less than 4" (10 cm)

275

FAM: Pomacentridae
Pomacentrus auriventrus
Yellow-bellied Damselfish

General Aggression

Color Maintenance

Dietary Requirements

Con-Species Compatibility

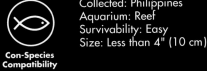

Collected: Philippines
Aquarium: Reef
Survivability: Easy
Size: Less than 4" (10 cm)

FAM: Pomacentridae
Pomacentrus sp. "Blotch"*
Blotch Damselfish

General Aggression

Color Maintenance

Dietary Requirements

Con-Species Compatibility

Collected: Philippines
Aquarium: Reef
Survivability: Easy
Size: Less than 4" (10 cm)

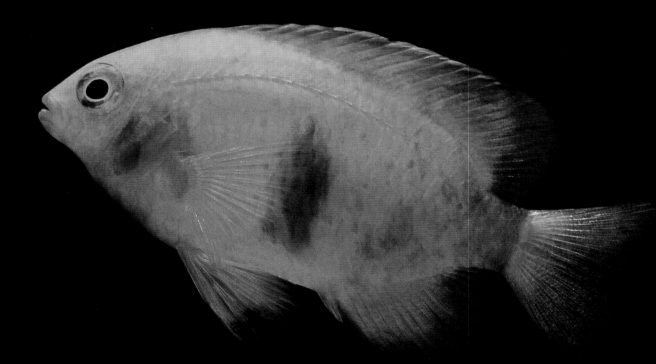

FAM: Pomacentridae
Pomacentrus philippinus
Philippines Damselfish

General Aggression

Color Maintenance

Dietary Requirements

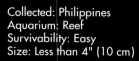
Con-Species Compatibility

Collected: Philippines
Aquarium: Reef
Survivability: Easy
Size: Less than 4" (10 cm)

FAM: Pomacentridae
Pomacentrus sp. "Red"*
Red Damselfish

General Aggression

Color Maintenance

Dietary Requirements

Con-Species Compatibility

Collected: Philippines
Aquarium: Reef
Survivability: Easy
Size: Less than 4" (10 cm)

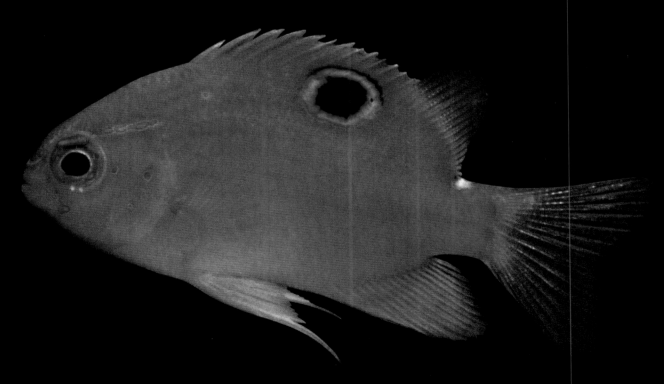

FAM: Pomacentridae
*Premnas biaculeatus**
Maroon Anemonefish

General Aggression   Color Maintenance   Dietary Requirements   Con-Species Compatibility

Collected: Philippines
Aquarium: Reef
Survivability: Difficult
Size: Less than 4" (10 cm)

FAM: Pomacentridae
Premnas biaculeatus (Domestic)
Maroon Anemonefish (Domestic)

General Aggression   Color Maintenance   Dietary Requirements   Con-Species Compatibility

Collected: Domestically Bred
Aquarium: Reef
Survivability: Easy
Size: Less than 4" (10 cm)

FAM: Pseudochromidae
Dampieria melanotaenia (Spot-fin)
Spot-fin Dottyback

General Aggression

Color Maintenance

Dietary Requirements

Con-Species Compatibility

Collected: Philippines
Aquarium: Non-Reef
Survivability: Easy
Size: 4" (10 cm) – 8" (20 cm)

FAM: Pseudochromidae
Labracinus lineatus
Lined Dottyback

General Aggression

Color Maintenance

Dietary Requirements

Con-Species Compatibility

Collected: Philippines
Aquarium: Non-Reef
Survivability: Easy
Size: 4" (10 cm) – 8" (20 cm)

FAM: Pseudochromidae
Pseudochromis cyanotaenia
Blue-stripe Dottyback

General
Aggression

Color
Maintenance

Dietary
Requirements

Con-Species
Compatibility

Collected: Philippines
Aquarium: Reef
Survivability: Easy
Size: Less than 4" (10 cm)

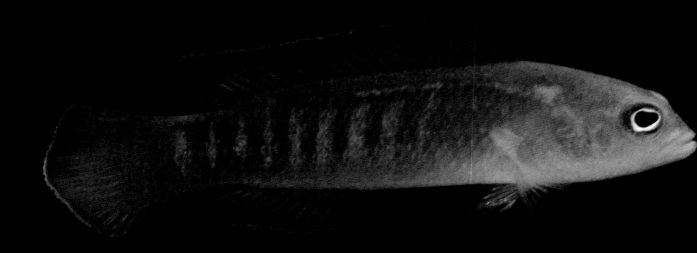

FAM: Pseudochromidae
Pseudochromis diadema
Diadem Dottyback

General
Aggression

Color
Maintenance

Dietary
Requirements

Con-Species
Compatibility

Collected: Philippines
Aquarium: Reef
Survivability: Easy
Size: Less than 4" (10 cm)

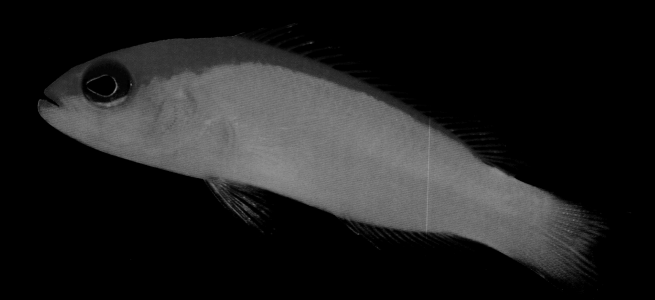

FAM: Pseudochromidae
Pseudochromis fuscus
Yellow Dottyback

**General
Aggression**

**Color
Maintenance**

**Dietary
Requirements**

**Con-Species
Compatibility**

Collected: Philippines
Aquarium: Reef
Survivability: Easy
Size: Less than 4" (10 cm)

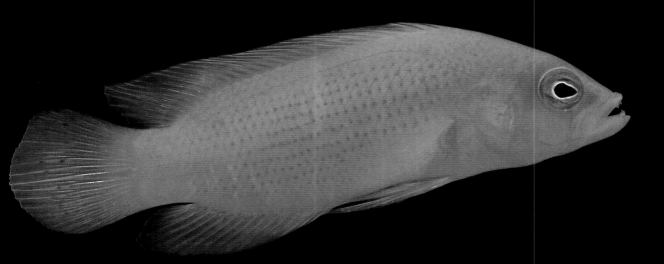

FAM: Pseudochromidae
Pseudochromis paccagnellae
Bicolor Dottyback

**General
Aggression**

**Color
Maintenance**

**Dietary
Requirements**

**Con-Species
Compatibility**

Collected: Philippines
Aquarium: Reef
Survivability: Easy
Size: Less than 4" (10 cm)

285

FAM: Pseudochromidae
Pseudochromis perspicillatus
Blackstripe Dottyback

General
Aggression

Color
Maintenance

Dietary
Requirements

Con-Species
Compatibility

Collected: Philippines
Aquarium: Reef
Survivability: Easy
Size: Less than 4" (10 cm)

FAM: Pseudochromidae
Pseudochromis porphyreus
Purple Dottyback

General
Aggression

Color
Maintenance

Dietary
Requirements

Con-Species
Compatibility

Collected: Philippines
Aquarium: Reef
Survivability: Easy
Size: Less than 4" (10 cm)

Family: Scaridae

(Parrotfishes) Fishes belonging to the Scaridae family (Parrotfishes) resemble parrots in more ways than one. Not only do they come in a range of vibrant colors (much like parrots), they have powerful, parrot-like beaks. Parrotfishes use these beaks to eat coral; and this feeding method grinds up coral skeletons and produces prodigious amounts of sand. Although they eat corals in the wild, members of the Scaridae family can adapt to a fairly typical aquarium diet, consisting of items such as frozen brine shrimp. Despite this, they are not very common in the aquarium trade. Part of the reason for this is that they do not stand up to the stresses of transport very well. Also, they become very large. An interesting trait of these fishes is their ability to build a mucus cocoon, in which they wrap themselves at night. This is probably to protect themselves while they rest.

(Famille: Scaridae) Les poissons appartenant à la famille des Scaridae ressemblent à bien des égards à des perroquets. Non seulement ils possèdent un bec puissant, mais ils affichent, comme les perroquets, une magnifiques diversité de couleurs vives. Ils utilisent leur bec pour se nourrir de corail. Leurs habitudes alimentaires leur font broyer des squelettes de coraux et produire ainsi des quantités prodigieuses de sable. Bien qu'ils se nourrissent de corail dans leur habitat naturel, les membres de la famille des Scaridae peuvent s'adapter à un régime d'aquarium plutôt classique composé d'artémias, de crevettes congelées ou de nourriture à croquer. Parce qu'ils supportent mal le stress du transport, on ne les voit pas très souvent dans les commerces de l'aquariophilie. De plus, ils deviennent rapidement très gros. Une particularité de cette famille est intéressante : ces poissons peuvent se fabriquer un cocon de mucus protecteur et s'en envelopper la nuit. C'est probablement à des fins de protection pendant leur sommeil.

(Pez Loro) Los peces pertenecientes a la familia Scaridae (Pez Loro) se parecen a loros en más formas que una. No solamente tienen poderosos picos como loros, sino que vienen en una gama de colores vibrantes (a semejanza de los loros). Usan sus picos como herramienta para comer coral. En su proceso de alimentarse trituran esqueletos de coral y producen cantidades prodigiosas de arena. Aunque comen corales en su ambiente natural, los miembros de la familia Scaridae pueden adaptarse a una dieta de acuario bastante normal que incluye artemia congeladas. Sin embargo, no son muy comunes en las tiendas de peces. Esto se debe en parte a que no soportan muy bien los estreses de transportación. También crecen hasta alcanzar un tamaño muy grande. Una característica interesante de esta familia es su habilidad de construir un capullo de mucosidad, en donde se enroscan de noche. Esto es probablemente para protegerse mientras descansan.

(Bodião ou Peixes-Papagaios) Os peixes que pertencem à família Scaridae (Bodião) parecem papagaios em muitas de suas características. Eles não somente têm bicos semelhantes aos dos papagaios, como têm uma variedade de cores vibrantes (bem semelhante aos papagaios). Eles usam os bicos para comer corais. Em seus hábitos de alimentação, eles trituram os esqueletos de corais e produzem incríveis quantidades de areia. Embora se alimentem de corais na vida selvagem, os membros da família Scaridae podem se adaptar a uma dieta bem típica de aquário, consistindo de itens como camarão em salmoura congelado. Entretanto, eles não são muito comuns no comércio de aquários. Isto ocorre em parte porque não agüentam muito as pressões que o transporte acarreta. Além disso, crescem muito. Uma característica interessante desta família é sua capacidade de formar um casulo de muco, no qual se enrolam, à noite, provavelmente para se protegerem enquanto descansam.

(Famiglia: Scaridae) I pesci che appartengono alla famiglia Scaridae assomigliano ai pappagalli. Non soltanto possiedono una bocca forte simile al becco di un pappagallo, ma sfoggiano pure livree con un'ampia gamma di colori vivaci (proprio come i pappagalli). Utilizzando i "becchi" per mangiare le madrepore, producono enormi quantità di sabbia corallina. Benché in natura si nutrano di madrepore, i membri della famiglia Scaridae possono adattarsi alla tipica dieta d'acquario, come per esempio Artemia congelati. Comunque, non sono molto diffusi in acquariofilia. In parte perché mal sopportano le difficoltà del trasporto e in parte perché diventano molto grandi. Una caratteristica interessante di questa pesci pappagallo è la capacità di costruire un bozzolo di muco nel quale si avvolgono durante la notte, probabilmente per proteggersi mentre riposano.

FAM: Scaridae
Cetoscarus bicolor
Bicolor Parrotfish
FORM: Juvenile

General Aggression

Color Maintenance

Dietary Requirements

Con-Species Compatibility

Collected: Indonesia
Aquarium: Non-Reef
Survivability: Moderate
Size: More than 8" (20 cm)

FAM: Scaridae
Chlorurus bowersi
Bower's Parrotfish

General Aggression

Color Maintenance

Dietary Requirements

Con-Species Compatibility

Collected: Philippines
Aquarium: Non-Reef
Survivability: Difficult
Size: More than 8" (20 cm)

FAM: Scaridae
Chlorurus sordidus
Bullethead Parrotfish

General Aggression

Color Maintenance

Dietary Requirements

Con-Species Compatibility

Collected: Indonesia
Aquarium: Non-Reef
Survivability: Difficult
Size: More than 8" (20 cm)

FAM: Scaridae
Scarus psittacus
Palenose Parrotfish

General Aggression

Color Maintenance

Dietary Requirements

Con-Species Compatibility

Collected: Indonesia
Aquarium: Non-Reef
Survivability: Difficult
Size: More than 8" (20 cm)

289

FAM: Scaridae
Scarus quoyi
Quoy's Parrotfish
FORM: Female

General
Aggression

Color
Maintenance

Dietary
Requirements

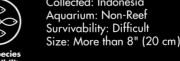
Con-Species
Compatibility

Collected: Indonesia
Aquarium: Non-Reef
Survivability: Difficult
Size: More than 8" (20 cm)

FAM: Scaridae
Scarus quoyi
Quoy's Parrotfish
FORM: Male

General
Aggression

Color
Maintenance

Dietary
Requirements

Con-Species
Compatibility

Collected: Indonesia
Aquarium: Non-Reef
Survivability: Difficult
Size: More than 8" (20 cm)

FAM: Scorpaenidae
Dendrochirus zebra
Dwarf Lionfish

**General
Aggression**

**Color
Maintenance**

**Dietary
Requirements**

**Con-Species
Compatibility**

Collected: Philippines
Aquarium: Non-Reef
Survivability: Moderate
Size: 4" (10 cm) – 8" (20 cm)

FAM: Scorpaenidae
Hypodytes sp. "High-fin"*
High-finned Scorpionfish

**General
Aggression**

**Color
Maintenance**

**Dietary
Requirements**

**Con-Species
Compatibility**

Collected: Philippines
Aquarium: Non-Reef
Survivability: Moderate
Size: 4" (10 cm) – 8" (20 cm)

295

FAM: Scorpaenidae
Inimicus filamentosus (Brown)
Popeye Scorpionfish (Brown)

General Aggression

Color Maintenance

Dietary Requirements

Con-Species Compatibility

Collected: Philippines
Aquarium: Non-Reef
Survivability: Moderate
Size: 4" (10 cm) – 8" (20 cm)

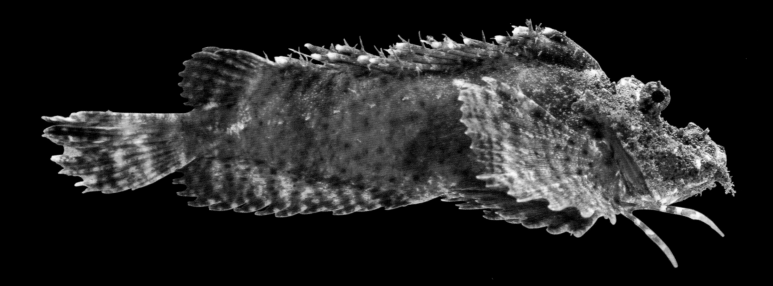

FAM: Scorpaenidae
Inimicus filamentosus (Rusty)
Popeye Scorpionfish (Rusty)

General Aggression

Color Maintenance

Dietary Requirements

Con-Species Compatibility

Collected: Philippines
Aquarium: Non-Reef
Survivability: Moderate
Size: 4" (10 cm) – 8" (20 cm)

FAM: Scorpaenidae
Pterois antennata
Spot-finned Lionfish

**General
Aggression**

**Color
Maintenance**

**Dietary
Requirements**

**Con-Species
Compatibility**

Collected: Indonesia
Aquarium: Non-Reef
Survivability: Moderate
Size: More than 8" (20 cm)

FAM: Scorpaenidae
Pterois radiata
Radiata Lionfish

General
Aggression

Color
Maintenance

Dietary
Requirements

Con-Species
Compatibility

Collected: Indonesia
Aquarium: Non-Reef
Survivability: Moderate
Size: More than 8" (20 cm)

FAM: Scorpaenidae
Scorpaenopsis neglecta*
Stripetail Scorpionfish

General
Aggression

Color
Maintenance

Dietary
Requirements

Con-Species
Compatibility

Collected: Indonesia
Aquarium: Non-Reef
Survivability: Moderate
Size: 4" (10 cm) – 8" (20 cm)

FAM: Scorpaenidae
Scorpaenopsis oxycephala
Tassled Scorpionfish

General
Aggression

Color
Maintenance

Dietary
Requirements

Con-Species
Compatibility

Collected: Philippines
Aquarium: Non-Reef
Survivability: Moderate
Size: 4" (10 cm) – 8" (20 cm)

FAM: Scorpaenidae
*Sebastapistes barbata**
Rusty Scorpionfish

**General
Aggression**

**Color
Maintenance**

**Dietary
Requirements**

**Con-Species
Compatibility**

Collected: Philippines
Aquarium: Non-Reef
Survivability: Moderate
Size: 4" (10 cm) – 8" (20 cm)

 FAM: Scorpaenidae
*Sebastapistes brevifrons**
Grey Scorpionfish

**General
Aggression**

**Color
Maintenance**

**Dietary
Requirements**

**Con-Species
Compatibility**

Collected: Indonesia
Aquarium: Non-Reef
Survivability: Moderate
Size: 4" (10 cm) – 8" (20 cm)

FAM: Scorpaenidae
*Sebastapistes cynostigma**
Dwarf Scorpionfish

General Aggression

Color Maintenance

Dietary Requirements

Con-Species Compatibility

Collected: Philippines
Aquarium: Non-Reef
Survivability: Moderate
Size: Less than 4" (10 cm)

FAM: Scorpaenidae
Synanceia verrucosa
Butterfly-fin Scorpionfish

General Aggression

Color Maintenance

Dietary Requirements

Con-Species Compatibility

Collected: Philippines
Aquarium: Non-Reef
Survivability: Moderate
Size: 4" (10 cm) – 8" (20 cm)

FAM: Scorpaenidae
Taenianotus triacanthus (Brown)
Brown Leaf Scorpionfish

General Aggression **Color Maintenance** **Dietary Requirements** **Con-Species Compatibility**

Collected: Philippines
Aquarium: Non-Reef
Survivability: Moderate
Size: Less than 4" (10 cm)

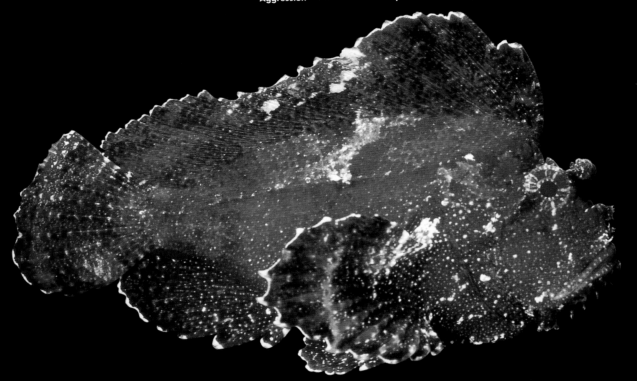

 FAM: Scorpaenidae
Taenianotus triacanthus (Marble)
Marble Leaf Scorpionfish

  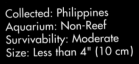

General Aggression **Color Maintenance** **Dietary Requirements** **Con-Species Compatibility**

Collected: Philippines
Aquarium: Non-Reef
Survivability: Moderate
Size: Less than 4" (10 cm)

FAM: Scorpaenidae
Taenianotus triacanthus (Red)
Red Leaf Scorpionfish

General Aggression

Color Maintenance

Dietary Requirements

Con-Species Compatibility

Collected: Philippines
Aquarium: Non-Reef
Survivability: Moderate
Size: Less than 4" (10 cm)

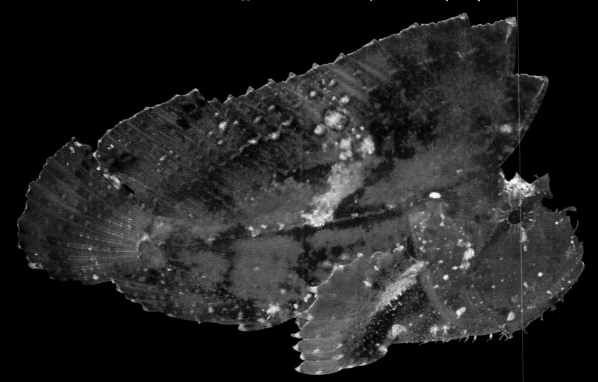

FAM: Scorpaenidae
Taenianotus triacanthus (Yellow)
Yellow Leaf Scorpionfish

General Aggression

Color Maintenance

Dietary Requirements

Con-Species Compatibility

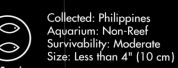

Collected: Philippines
Aquarium: Non-Reef
Survivability: Moderate
Size: Less than 4" (10 cm)

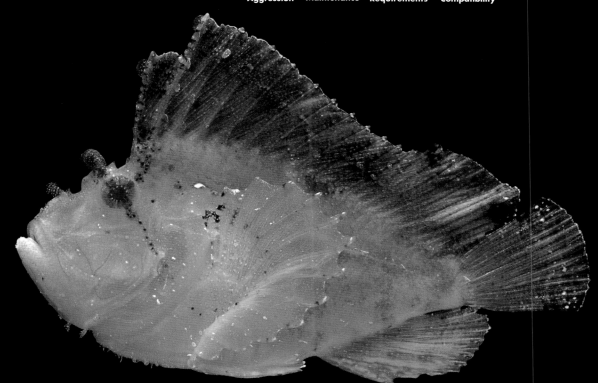

307

Family: Scyliorhinidae

(Cat Shark) This family is one of the more common sharks seen in the aquarium trade. People are fascinated by sharks. However, sharks often grow quite large and outgrow their aquarium.

(Famille: Scyliorhinidae) Cette famille représente la famille de requins les plus courants dans le commerce aquariophile. Le public est particulièrement fasciné par les requins mais ces requins deviennent souvent trop grands pour leur aquarium.

(Tiburón Gata) Esta es la familia de los tiburones más comunes en el comercio de acuarios. La mayoría de las personas se sienten fascinados con los tiburones. Sin embargo, los tiburones a menudo crecen hasta alcanzar un tamaño muy grande y no caben en su pecera.

(Família: Scyliorhinidae) Esta família de tubarões é uma das mais comuns vistas no comércio de aquário. As pessoas são fascinadas por tubarões. Entretanto, os tubarões geralmente crescem bastante e o aquário fica pequeno para eles.

(Famiglia: Scyliorhinidae) Questa famiglia è composta dai "pescicani" più comuni sul mercato dei pesci ornamentali. Moltissime persone sono affascinate dai pescicani. Comunque, i gattucci spesso raggiungono dimensioni troppo grandi per venire allevati in acquari domestici.

FAM: Scyliorhinidae
Atelomycterus marmoratus
Coral Catshark

General Aggression

Color Maintenance

Dietary Requirements

Con-Species Compatibility

Collected: Philippines
Aquarium: Non-Reef
Survivability: Moderate
Size: More than 8" (20 cm)

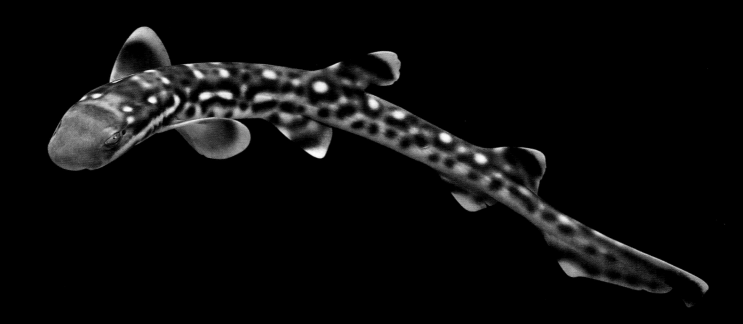

Family: Serranidae

(Groupers, Anthias & Soapfishes) Member species of this family range from among the easiest to the most difficult fishes to keep in captivity. Groupers are good fishes for beginners, for example, while the Anthias are a challenge to even an experienced hobbyist.

Grouper species are popular aquarium fishes because of their tameness and easy maintenance. Over the course of their lives these fishes usually change dramatically in color, with adult groupers less colorful than the juveniles. The wild, groupers can grow to be very large and are considered food fishes all over the world. Soapfishes can secrete toxins when frightened, which could poison other fishes and/or themselves in a tank, so they should be maintained in larger aquariums so that the toxin is diluted.

Anthias are naturally brightly colored fishes, but many fade dramatically in aquariums. They have the interesting trait of being hermaphroditic (which means that each fish is capable of changing sex). When a male is removed from the harem, for example, the largest female may change to a functional male. Anthias are challenging for hobbyists because many require live food and need to be fed more than once a day.

(Famille: Serranidae) Ce groupe de poissons comprend certaines des espèces les plus faciles et les plus difficile à garder en captivité. La sous-famille des Serranidae sont des poissons à conseiller même aux débutants, alors que la sous-famille des *Anthiinaei* représente un challenge même pour l'*afficionado* chevronné.

Les espèces de la sous-famille des Serranidae sont des poissons d'aquarium prisés parce qu'ils s'apprivoisent facilement et qu'ils sont faciles à entretenir. Ces poissons subissent des changements radicaux tout au long de leur vie, leur forme juvénile étant souvent beaucoup plus colorée que leur forme adulte. Dans leur habitat naturel ces poissons peuvent atteindre des tailles respectables et sont classés parmi les poissons de consommation courante dans le monde entier. Lorsqu'ils sont effrayés, les membres de la famille des Grammistinae peuvent secréter des toxines pouvant provoquer l'empoisonnement de tout l'aquarium, entraînant ainsi tous les poissons dans leur propre mort. Il est donc nécessaire de les garder dans un grand aquarium de manière à permettre, le cas échéant la dilution de ces toxines.

Les membres de la famille Anthiinae sont des poissons aux couleurs naturellement vives mais qui, très souvent, atténuent énormément en aquarium. Ils possèdent la caractéristique intéressante d'être hermaphrodites, ce qui veut dire que chaque poisson est capable de changer de sexe. Par exemple, lorsqu'un mâle est enlevé du harem, la femelle la plus grosse devient un mâle fonctionnel. Ces poissons représentent véritablement un défi pour l'aquariophile car beaucoup exigent une eau parfaite et une nourriture vivante plusieurs fois par jour.

(Meros, Antias y Pez Jabón) Este grupo de peces fluctúan entre los más fáciles y los más difíciles de mantener en cautiverio. La subfamilia Serraninae (Meros) son buenos peces para principiantes, por ejemplo, mientras que la subfamilia Anthiinaei (Antias) son un reto hasta para el acuarista aficionado más experimentado.

Las especies de la subfamilia Serraninae (Meros) son peces de acuario populares ya que son fuertes y fáciles de mantener. Durante el curso de sus vidas estos peces usualmente cambian dramáticamente de color y la mayoría de los meros adultos no tienen generalmente tanto colorido como los juveniles. En estado natural, los meros pueden crecer a un tamaño muy grande y son pescados de alimento en todas partes del mundo. El pez jabón puede segregar toxinas cuando se asusta, lo cual pudiera envenenar a otros peces o a ellos mismos en un tanque, así que deben mantenerse en peceras más grandes para que se diluyan las toxinas.

En estado natural, las Antias son peces de colorido brillante, pero muchas se descoloran dramáticamente en peceras. Tienen la característica interesante de ser hermafroditas, es decir, cada pez es capaz de cambiar sexo. Por ejemplo, cuando se retira el macho del harén, la hembra más grande se convierte en macho funcional. Las Antias representan un reto para los acuaristas aficionados ya que muchos ejemplares requieren alimentos vivos y deben alimentarse más de una vez al día.

Family: Serranidae

(Garoupas, Peixes-Sabão e "Soapfishes") Este grupo de peixes é distribuído entre os mais fáceis e os mais difíceis de serem mantidos em cativeiro. A subfamília Serraninae (garoupas) são bons peixes para iniciantes, por exemplo, enquanto a subfamília Anthiinaei ("Anthias") são um desafio até para os mais experientes na atividade.

As espécies da subfamília Serraninae (garoupas) são peixes de aquário populares por sua docilidade e fácil manutenção. No decorrer de suas vidas, estes peixes geralmente mudam radicalmente de cor, a maioria das garoupas adultas não são, em geral, tão coloridas quanto as jovens. Na vida selvagem, as garoupas podem crescer bastante e sua carne é bastante apreciada no mundo todo. Os peixes-sabão podem segregar toxinas quando assustados, o que pode envenenar outros peixes ou eles mesmos em um tanque, por isso devem ser mantidos em aquários maiores para que a toxina se dilua.

Os "Anthias" são peixes de cores naturalmente vivas, mas muitos perdem a cor radicalmente em aquários. Eles têm a interessante característica de serem hermafroditas, o que significa que todos os peixes têm a capacidade de mudar de sexo. Quando um macho é retirado do harém, por exemplo, a fêmea de maior tamanho se transformará em macho funcional. Os "Anthias" são um desafio para os praticantes da atividade, pois muitos requerem alimento vivo e devem ser alimentados mais do que uma vez ao dia.

(Famiglia: Serranidae) L'allevamento in acquario di questi pesci può rivelarsi facile o anche difficile. La sottofamiglia Serraninae è indicata per il principiante, mentre la sottofamiglia Anthiinae rappresenta una sfida anche per l'acquariofilo esperto. I Serranini sono popolari in acquariofilia grazie alla loro docilità e al loro facile allevamento. La colorazione di questi pesci varia molto durante i diversi stadi di crescita. Molte cernie adulte non presentano colori tanto vivaci quanto quelli dei giovani. In natura le cernie possono raggiungere grandi dimensioni e sono conosciute in tutto il mondo come pesci commestibili.

I pesci della sottofamiglia Grammistidae, quando si spaventano, possono emettere un veleno che danneggia sia gli altri pesci sia loro stessi; dovrebbero quindi essere allevati in grande vasche di modo che il veleno possa diluirsi in molta acqua.

Gli *Anthias* sono pesci dai vivaci colori, ma molti perdono quasi completamente la loro colorazione in acquario. Hanno l'interessante caratteristica di essere ermafroditi, cioè ogni pesce è in grado di mutare il proprio sesso. Quando un maschio viene rimosso dall'harem, per esempio, la femmina più grande diventerà un maschio funzionale. Gli *Anthias* rappresentano una sfida per l'acquariofilo, perché molti necessitano di cibo vivo più volte al giorno.

FAM: Serranidae
Belonoperca chabanaudi
Arrowhead Soapfish

General Aggression

Color Maintenance

Dietary Requirements

Con-Species Compatibility

Collected: Philippines
Aquarium: Non-Reef
Survivability: Easy
Size: 4" (10 cm) – 8" (20 cm)

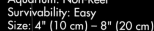

FAM: Serranidae
Cephalopholis argus
Argus Grouper
FORM: Juvenile

General Aggression

Color Maintenance

Dietary Requirements

Con-Species Compatibility

Collected: Philippines
Aquarium: Non-Reef
Survivability: Easy
Size: More than 8" (20 cm)

FAM: Serranidae
Cephalopholis cyanostigma
Blue-spotted Grouper
FORM: Juvenile

General Aggression

Color Maintenance

Dietary Requirements

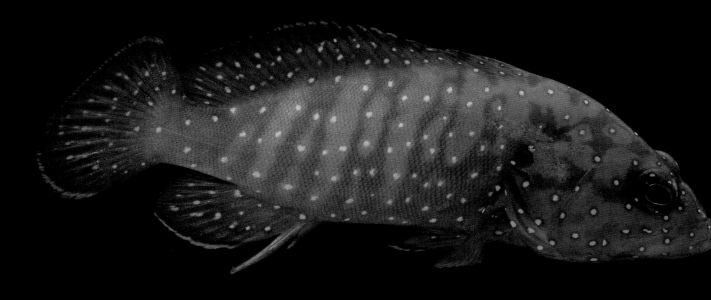
Con-Species Compatibility

Collected: Philippines
Aquarium: Non-Reef
Survivability: Easy
Size: More than 8" (20 cm)

FAM: Serranidae
Cephalopholis formosa
Blue-line Grouper
FORM: Juvenile

General Aggression

Color Maintenance

Dietary Requirements

Con-Species Compatibility

Collected: Philippines
Aquarium: Non-Reef
Survivability: Easy
Size: More than 8" (20 cm)

FAM: Serranidae
Cephalopholis leopardus
Leopard Grouper
FORM: Juvenile

General Aggression

Color Maintenance

Dietary Requirements

Con-Species Compatibility

Collected: Philippines
Aquarium: Non-Reef
Survivability: Easy
Size: More than 8" (20 cm)

FAM: Serranidae
Cephalopholis miniata (Dark)
Miniatus Grouper (Dark)
FORM: Juvenile

General Aggression

Color Maintenance

Dietary Requirements

Con-Species Compatibility

Collected: Philippines
Aquarium: Non-Reef
Survivability: Easy
Size: More than 8" (20 cm)

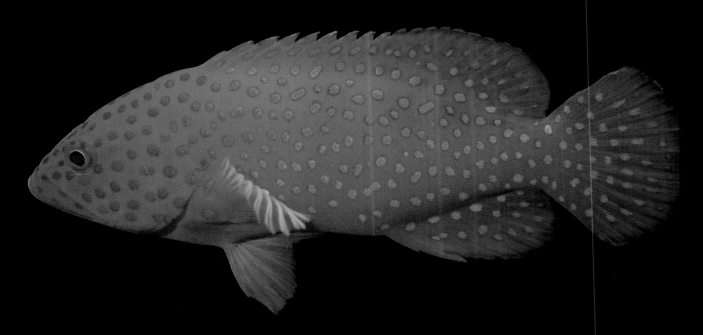

313

FAM: Serranidae
Cephalopholis miniata
Miniatus Grouper
FORM: Juvenile

General Aggression

Color Maintenance

Dietary Requirements

Con-Species Compatibility

Collected: Philippines
Aquarium: Non-Reef
Survivability: Easy
Size: More than 8" (20 cm)

FAM: Serranidae
Cephalopholis sexmaculata
Six-spot Grouper
FORM: Juvenile

   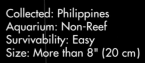

General Aggression Color Maintenance Dietary Requirements Con-Species Compatibility

Collected: Philippines
Aquarium: Non-Reef
Survivability: Easy
Size: More than 8" (20 cm)

FAM: Serranidae
Cephalopholis sonnerati
Strawberry Grouper
FORM: Juvenile

    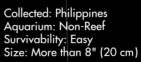

General Aggression Color Maintenance Dietary Requirements Con-Species Compatibility

Collected: Philippines
Aquarium: Non-Reef
Survivability: Easy
Size: More than 8" (20 cm)

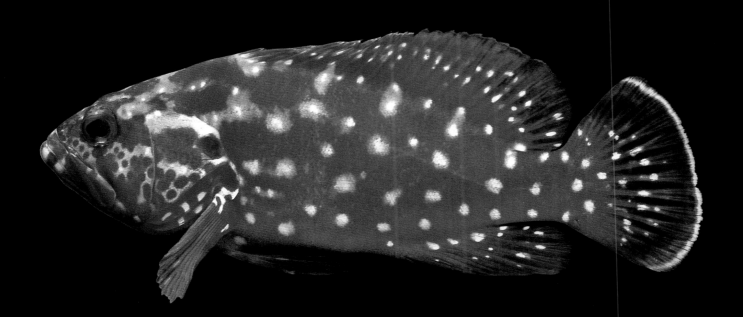

315

FAM: Serranidae
Cephalopholis urodeta
V-Tail Grouper
FORM: Juvenile

General
Aggression

Color
Maintenance

Dietary
Requirements

Con-Species
Compatibility

Collected: Philippines
Aquarium: Non-Reef
Survivability: Easy
Size: More than 8" (20 cm)

FAM: Serranidae
Cromileptes altivelis
Panther Grouper
FORM: Juvenile

General
Aggression

Color
Maintenance

Dietary
Requirements

Con-Species
Compatibility

Collected: Philippines
Aquarium: Non-Reef
Survivability: Easy
Size: More than 8" (20 cm)

FAM: Serranidae
Epinephelus corallicola
Coral Grouper
FORM: Juvenile

 General Aggression

 Color Maintenance

 Dietary Requirements

Con-Species Compatibility

Collected: Philippines
Aquarium: Non-Reef
Survivability: Easy
Size: More than 8" (20 cm)

FAM: Serranidae
Epinephelus fasciatus
Big-eyed Grouper
FORM: Juvenile

 General Aggression

 Color Maintenance

 Dietary Requirements

 Con-Species Compatibility

Collected: Philippines
Aquarium: Non-Reef
Survivability: Easy
Size: More than 8" (20 cm)

317

FAM: Serranidae
Epinephelus ongus
Specklefin Grouper
FORM: Juvenile

General
Aggression

Color
Maintenance

Dietary
Requirements

Con-Species
Compatibility

Collected: Philippines
Aquarium: Non-Reef
Survivability: Easy
Size: More than 8" (20 cm)

FAM: Serranidae
Epinephelus quoyanus
Longfinned Grouper
FORM: Juvenile

General
Aggression

Color
Maintenance

Dietary
Requirements

Con-Species
Compatibility

Collected: Philippines
Aquarium: Non-Reef
Survivability: Easy
Size: More than 8" (20 cm)

318

FAM: Serranidae
Pseudanthias dispar
Redhead Anthias
FORM: Male

General Aggression

Color Maintenance

Dietary Requirements

Con-Species Compatibility

Collected: Philippines
Aquarium: Reef
Survivability: Difficult
Size: 4" (10 cm) – 8" (20 cm)

FAM: Serranidae
Pseudanthias evansi
Evan's Anthias

General Aggression

Color Maintenance

Dietary Requirements

Con-Species Compatibility

Collected: Philippines
Aquarium: Reef
Survivability: Difficult
Size: 4" (10 cm) – 8" (20 cm)

FAM: Serranidae
Pseudanthias huchtii
Red-cheek Anthias

 General Aggression Color Maintenance Dietary Requirements  Con-Species Compatibility

Collected: Philippines
Aquarium: Reef
Survivability: Difficult
Size: 4" (10 cm) – 8" (20 cm)

FAM: Serranidae
Pseudanthias lori
Tiger Queen Anthias

 General Aggression Color Maintenance Dietary Requirements Con-Species Compatibility

Collected: Philippines
Aquarium: Reef
Survivability: Difficult
Size: 4" (10 cm) – 8" (20 cm)

324

FAM: Serranidae
Pseudanthias pleurotaenia
Square Block Anthias
FORM: Female

General Aggression

Color Maintenance

Dietary Requirements

Con-Species Compatibility

Collected: Philippines
Aquarium: Reef
Survivability: Difficult
Size: 4" (10 cm) – 8" (20 cm)

FAM: Serranidae
Pseudanthias pleurotaenia
Square Block Anthias
FORM: Male

General Aggression

Color Maintenance

Dietary Requirements

Con-Species Compatibility

Collected: Philippines
Aquarium: Reef
Survivability: Difficult
Size: 4" (10 cm) – 8" (20 cm)

325

FAM: Serranidae
Pseudanthias sp. "Purple"*
Purple Anthias

General
Aggression

Color
Maintenance

Dietary
Requirements

Con-Species
Compatibility

Collected: Philippines
Aquarium: Reef
Survivability: Difficult
Size: 4" (10 cm) – 8" (20 cm)

FAM: Serranidae
Pseudanthias rubrizonatus
Red Belted Anthias

General
Aggression

Color
Maintenance

Dietary
Requirements

Con-Species
Compatibility

Collected: Philippines
Aquarium: Reef
Survivability: Doomed
Size: 4" (10 cm) – 8" (20 cm)

FAM: Serranidae
Pseudanthias squamipinnis (Indo)
Lyretail Anthias (Indo)
FORM: Female

General Aggression

Color Maintenance

Dietary Requirements

Con-Species Compatibility

Collected: Indonesia
Aquarium: Reef
Survivability: Difficult
Size: 4" (10 cm) – 8" (20 cm)

FAM: Serranidae
Pseudanthias squamipinnis (Indo)
Lyretail Anthias (Indo)
FORM: Male

General Aggression

Color Maintenance

Dietary Requirements

Con-Species Compatibility

Collected: Indonesia
Aquarium: Reef
Survivability: Difficult
Size: 4" (10 cm) – 8" (20 cm)

FAM: Serranidae
Pseudanthias squamipinnis
Lyretail Anthias
FORM: Male

 General Aggression

 Color Maintenance

 Dietary Requirements

 Con-Species Compatibility

Collected: Philippines
Aquarium: Reef
Survivability: Difficult
Size: 4" (10 cm) – 8" (20 cm)

FAM: Serranidae
Pseudanthias tuka
Purple Queen Anthias
FORM: Female

 General Aggression

 Color Maintenance

 Dietary Requirements

Con-Species Compatibility

Collected: Philippines
Aquarium: Reef
Survivability: Doomed
Size: 4" (10 cm) – 8" (20 cm)

FAM: Serranidae
Pseudanthias tuka
Purple Queen Anthias
FORM: Male

General
Aggression

Color
Maintenance

Dietary
Requirements

Con-Species
Compatibility

Collected: Philippines
Aquarium: Reef
Survivability: Doomed
Size: 4" (10 cm) – 8" (20 cm)

FAM: Serranidae
Serranocirrhitus latus
Sunburst Anthias

General
Aggression

Color
Maintenance

Dietary
Requirements

Con-Species
Compatibility

Collected: Philippines
Aquarium: Reef
Survivability: Doomed
Size: 4" (10 cm) – 8" (20 cm)

329

FAM: Serranidae
Variola albimarginata
Lyretail Grouper

General
Aggression

Color
Maintenance

Dietary
Requirements

Con-Species
Compatibility

Collected: Philippines
Aquarium: Non-Reef
Survivability: Easy
Size: More than 8" (20 cm)

FAM: Serranidae
Variola louti
Skunk Grouper

General
Aggression

Color
Maintenance

Dietary
Requirements

Con-Species
Compatibility

Collected: Philippines
Aquarium: Non-Reef
Survivability: Easy
Size: More than 8" (20 cm)

Family: Siganidae

(Rabbitfishes) Rabbitfishes get their name from the appearance and shape of their mouth (not due to what they eat). Members of this family require protein in the form of crustaceans as well as vegetable matter. Rabbitfishes are continuous grazers that require large amounts of algae and vegetable matter in their diet. This can be supplied in the form of Romaine lettuce, spinach, watercress, or dried seaweed purchased in Oriental grocery stores. Overall, they are fairly hardy.

(Famille: Siganidae) La bouche des Siganidae ressemble à celle d'un lapin et dans certaines parties du monde, on les appelle communément « poissons-lapins ». Les membres de cette famille exigent des protéines sous forme de crustacés et sont de gros consommateurs d'algues. Ces poissons se nourrissent continuellement et leur régime exige de grosses quantités de matière végétale. Ces aliments peuvent être proposés sous forme de laitue romaine, d'épinards, de cresson et de varech sec acheté dans des épiceries orientales. Dans l'ensemble, ils sont assez robustes.

(Pez Liebre) El pez liebre recibe su nombre a partir de su apariencia y la forma de su boca y no a partir de lo que comen. Los miembros de esta familia requieren proteína en forma de crustáceos así como materia orgánica. Los peces liebre comen continuamente y requieren grandes cantidades de algas y materia orgánica en su dieta. Esto puede ser suministrado en la forma de lechuga romana, espinaca y berro o algas marinas secas compradas en mercados de comestibles orientales. En general son bastante fuertes.

(Peixes-Coelho) O peixe-coelho obtém seu nome pela aparência e forma da boca, não pelo que come. Os membros desta família necessitam proteínas na forma de crustáceos e de matéria vegetal. Os peixes-coelho comem continuamente, o que exige grandes quantidades de algas e matéria vegetal para sua dieta. Isto pode ser suprido na forma de alface romana, espinafre e agrião ou algas marinhas secas, que podem ser compradas em lojas de produtos orientais. Em termos gerais, são bastante resistentes.

(Famiglia: Siganidae) Gli Siganidi hanno ricevuto il loro nome comune in inglese e in tedesco, che tradotto in italiano significa "pesce coniglio," a causa dell'aspetto e della forma della bocca e non per ciò che mangiano. I membri di questa famiglia richiedono una nutrizione ricca di proteine, che soddisfano cibandosi di crostacei e di sostanze vegetali. I Siganidae mangiano continuamente e in natura la loro dieta comprende grandi quantità di alghe e di piante marine. In acquario il cibo vegetale può essere costituito da lattuga, spinaci e crescione o alghe marine liofilizzate acquistabili in negozi che vendano prodotti alimentari orientali. Al di là di ogni apparenza sono pesci molto robusti.

FAM: Siganidae
Siganus corallinus
Coral Rabbitfish

General
Aggression

Color
Maintenance

Dietary
Requirements

Con-Species
Compatibility

Collected: Philippines
Aquarium: Reef
Survivability: Moderate
Size: 4" (10 cm) – 8" (20 cm)

FAM: Siganidae
Siganus vulpinus
Foxface Rabbitfish

General
Aggression

Color
Maintenance

Dietary
Requirements

Con-Species
Compatibility

Collected: Philippines
Aquarium: Reef
Survivability: Easy
Size: 4" (10 cm) – 8" (20 cm)

332

Family: Syngnathidae

(Pipefishes & Seahorses) These fishes have some of the most interesting shapes of any fishes in the aquarium trade. They require live food, such as either adult or baby brine shrimp. Unfortunately, this requirement makes these fishes difficult to keep. With successful maintenance, members of this family can make excellent reef aquarium fishes. Unfortunately, the likelihood of success is slim.

Reproduction among members of the family Syngnathidae is interesting — the female deposits her eggs in the male's pouch. The male is then functionally "pregnant" and carries the eggs until they hatch. In some species without brood pouches, the eggs are simply attached to a male's abdomen.

(Famille: Syngnathidae) Ces poissons ont certaines des formes les plus insolites que l'on puisse trouver dans le commerce de l'aquariophilie. Ils exigent une nourriture vivante telle que artémias, crevettes adultes ou juvéniles et ceci les rend malheureusement difficiles à garder. Grâce à une maintenance suivie et méticuleuse, les membres de ce groupe peuvent devenir d'excellents poissons d'aquarium récifaux. Malheureusement, les chances de succès sont réservées.

Le plus populaire de ces poissons est le bien sympathique Hippocampe. La reproduction de la famille des Syngnathidae est particulièrement intéressante, la femelle déposant ses oeufs dans la poche du mâle qui devient alors «enceinte» et qui porte les oeufs jusqu'à l'éclosion. Chez certaines espèces sans poche de gestation, les oeufs sont simplement attachés à l'abdomen du mâle.

(Agujas de Mar y Caballitos de Mar) Estos peces poseen una de las formas más interesantes de cualquier pez en el comercio de acuarios. Requieren alimentos vivos tales como artemia o crustaceos pequeños. Lamentablemente, esto dificulta su mantenimiento. Con un mantenimiento exitoso, los miembros de este grupo se pueden convertir en excelentes ejemplares para una pecera de arrecife. Pero desafortunadamente, las probabilidades de éxito no son buenas.

La reproducción en la familia Syngnathidae resulta interesante ya que la hembra deposita sus huevos en el saquillo de cría del macho. El macho está entonces funcionalmente "embarazado" y lleva los huevos hasta que nacen. En algunas especies sin saquillos de cría, los huevos simplemente se adhieren al abdomen del macho.

(Peixes-Cachimbo e Cavalos-Marinhos) Estes peixes têm algumas das formas mais interessantes entre os peixes do comércio de aquário. Eles requerem alimento vivo, tal como camarão em salmoura, filhotes ou adultos. Infelizmente, isto torna sua manutenção difícil. Com uma boa manutenção, os membros deste grupo de peixes podem ser excelentes peixes para aquário de recifes. Infelizmente, a probabilidade de sucesso é limitada.

A reprodução da família Syngnathidae é interessante, pois a fêmea deposita os ovos na bolsa do macho. O macho está, assim, funcionalmente "grávido" e carrega os ovos até que eles choquem. Em algumas espécies sem as bolsas-chocadeiras, os ovos são simplesmente fixados ao abdômen do macho.

(Famiglia: Syngnathidae) Questi pesci hanno forme particolarmente interessanti. Richiedono cibo vivo come Artemia, giovane o adulta. Con adeguate attenzioni, i membri di questo gruppo possono diventare eccellenti ospiti per un acquario da barriera, ma purtroppo le probabilità di successo sono scarse.

La riproduzione della famiglia Syngnathidae è molto interessante, perché la femmina deposita le uova in una tasca del corpo del maschio. Il maschio incuba le uova fino alla schiusa. In alcune specie prive di questo "marsupio," le uova vengono attaccate all'addome del maschio.

FAM: Syngnathidae
Corythoichthys flavofasciatus*
Yellow-striped Pipefish

General
Aggression

Color
Maintenance

Dietary
Requirements

Con-Species
Compatibility

Collected: Philippines
Aquarium: Reef
Survivability: Doomed
Size: 4" (10 cm) – 8" (20 cm)

FAM: Syngnathidae
Doryrhamphus excisus
Red-tailed Pipefish

General
Aggression

Color
Maintenance

Dietary
Requirements

Con-Species
Compatibility

Collected: Philippines
Aquarium: Reef
Survivability: Doomed
Size: 4" (10 cm) – 8" (20 cm)

FAM: Syngnathidae
Dunckerocampus dactyliophorus
Banded Pipefish

General
Aggression

Color
Maintenance

Dietary
Requirements

Con-Species
Compatibility

Collected: Philippines
Aquarium: Reef
Survivability: Doomed
Size: 4" (10 cm) – 8" (20 cm)

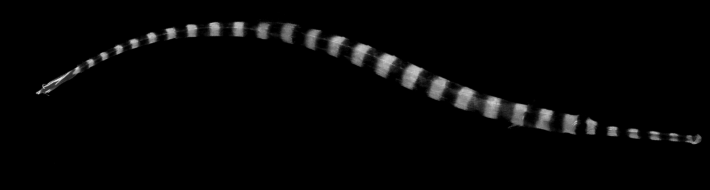

FAM: Syngnathidae
Dunckerocampus pessuliferus
Multi-banded Pipefish

General Aggression   Color Maintenance   Dietary Requirements   Con-Species Compatibility

Collected: Philippines
Aquarium: Reef
Survivability: Doomed
Size: 4" (10 cm) – 8" (20 cm)

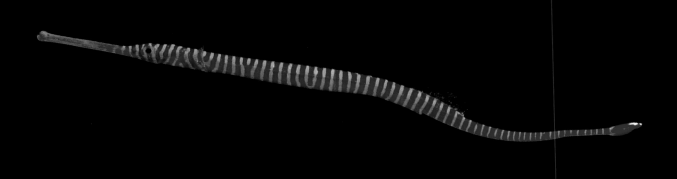

FAM: Syngnathidae
Hippocampus sp. "Histrix"
Seahorse (Histrix)

General Aggression   Color Maintenance

Dietary Requirements   Con-Species Compatibility

Collected: Philippines
Aquarium: Reef
Survivability: Doomed
Size: 4" (10 cm) – 8" (20 cm)

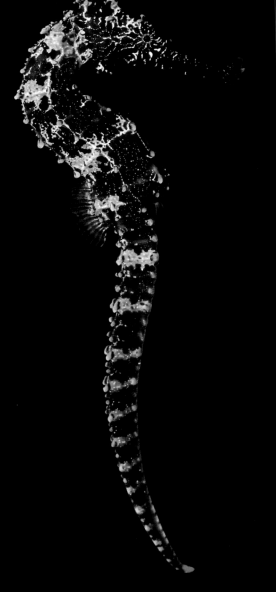

335

FAM: Syngnathidae
Hippocampus **sp. "Kuda"***
Seahorse (Kuda)

General Aggression

Color Maintenance

Dietary Requirements

Con-Species Compatibility

Collected: Philippines
Aquarium: Reef
Survivability: Doomed
Size: 4" (10 cm) – 8" (20 cm)

FAM: Syngnathidae
*Syngnathoides biaculeatus***
Alligator Pipefish

General Aggression

Color Maintenance

Dietary Requirements

Con-Species Compatibility

Collected: Philippines
Aquarium: Reef
Survivability: Doomed
Size: 4" (10 cm) – 8" (20 cm)

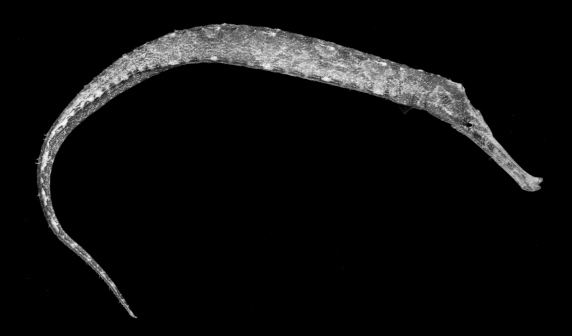

336

Family: Tetraodontidae

(Pufferfishes) Pufferfishes have two lines of defense: toxins in their internal organs that is lethal when eaten, and the ability to inflate themselves so they are not eaten in the first place. The members of this family lack a pelvic fin, so they use the dorsal, anal and pectoral fins for propulsion. The tail fin is closed most of the time, since it plays little part in locomotion. This family is among the most hardy of the marine fishes to keep, but should be handled carefully as they bite. In addition, these fishes are equipped with four fused teeth (two on top and two on the bottom) which they use to crack mollusks or crustaceans.

(Famille: Tetraodontidae) Les organes internes des espèces de la famille des Tetraodontidae contiennent des toxines fatales lorsqu'on les consomme. Ils ont également le pouvoir de se gonfler démesurément pour ne pas être dévorés. Les membres de cette famille ne possèdent pas de nageoire pelvienne et utilisent leurs nageoires dorsales, anales et pectorales pour se propulser. Ne jouant pas grand rôle dans la locomotion, la nageoire caudale est la plupart du temps repliée. Ils sont parmi les poissons marins les plus robustes mais doivent être manipulés avec précaution car ils mordent. En effet, ils sont dotés de 4 dents réunies, 2 sur la mâchoire supérieure et 2 sur la mâchoire inférieure qu'ils utilisent pour broyer mollusques ou crustacés.

(Pez Globo) Las especies de la familia Tetraodontidae tienen toxinas en sus órganos internos que son letales cuando consumidos, y también poseen la habilidad de inflarse para evitar ser comidos. Los miembros de esta familia carecen de aleta pélvica, y usan las aletas dorsales, anales y pectorales para propulsarse. La aleta de cola se mantiene cerrada la mayor parte del tiempo ya que apenas desempeña un papel en la locomoción. Se encuentran entre los peces marinos más fuertes a la hora de mantenerlos, pero deben manipularse con cuidado ya que muerden. Además, estos peces están equipados con cuatro dientes fusionados, dos arriba y dos abajo, que utilizan para quebrar moluscos o crustáceos.

(Peixes Baiacus) As espécies na família Tetraodontidae têm toxinas em seus órgãos internos que são letais quando ingeridas, tendo também a capacidade de inflarem para que não sejam comidas por nenhuma outra espécie. Os membros desta família não têm a barbatana pélvica e usam as barbatanas dorsal, anal e peitoral para propulsão. A barbatana caudal fica fechada a maior parte do tempo, pois tem um papel pequeno na locomoção. Eles estão entre os peixes marinhos mais resistentes que existem, mas devem ser manipulados com cuidado, pois mordem. Além disso, estes peixes estão equipados com 4 dentes amalgamados - 2 em cima e 2 em baixo, que usam para quebrar moluscos e crustáceos.

(Famiglia: Tetraodontidae) I Tetraodontidi possiedono negli organi interni un veleno micidiale per chiunque li mangia. Questi pesci hanno anche la capacità di gonfiarsi per evitare di essere divorati. I membri di questa famiglia sono privi di pinne ventrali e utilizzano le pinne dorsale, anale e pettorali per spostarsi. La pinna caudale è quasi sempre chiusa perché non ha un ruolo importante nella propulsione. Sono tra i pesci marini più robusti, ma devono essere maneggiati con cautela perché mordono. Inoltre, questi pesci hanno quattro denti a mo' di placca, due nella mascella superiore e due nella parte inferiore, che utilizzano per rompere molluschi o crostacei.

FAM: Tetraodontidae
Arothron hispidus **(Stripe & Dot)**
Stripe & Dot Pufferfish

General
Aggression

Color
Maintenance

Dietary
Requirements

Con-Species
Compatibility

Collected: Indonesia
Aquarium: Non-Reef
Survivability: Easy
Size: 4" (10 cm) – 8" (20 cm)

FAM: Tetraodontidae
Arothron hispidus **(Whitespot)**
Whitespotted Pufferfish

General
Aggression

Color
Maintenance

Dietary
Requirements

Con-Species
Compatibility

Collected: Philippines
Aquarium: Non-Reef
Survivability: Easy
Size: 4" (10 cm) – 8" (20 cm)

FAM: Tetraodontidae
Arothron manilensis
Pinstriped Pufferfish

General Aggression

Color Maintenance

Dietary Requirements

Con-Species Compatibility

Collected: Philippines
Aquarium: Non-Reef
Survivability: Easy
Size: 4" (10 cm) – 8" (20 cm)

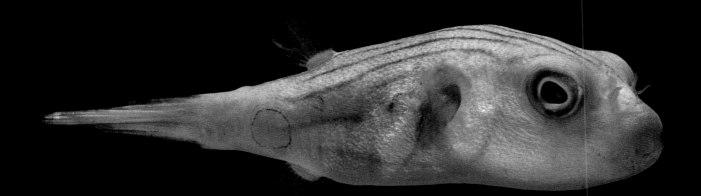

FAM: Tetraodontidae
Arothron meleagris
Guinae Fowl Pufferfish

General Aggression

Color Maintenance

Dietary Requirements

Con-Species Compatibility

Collected: Philippines
Aquarium: Non-Reef
Survivability: Easy
Size: 4" (10 cm) – 8" (20 cm)

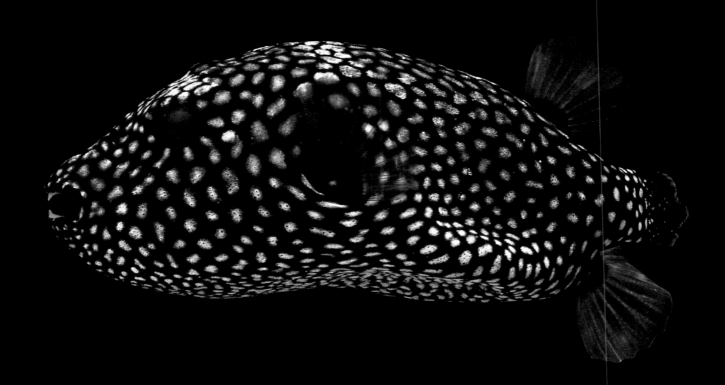

FAM: Tetraodontidae
Arothron nigropunctatus
Black-spotted Pufferfish

General Aggression

Color Maintenance

Dietary Requirements

Con-Species Compatibility

Collected: Philippines
Aquarium: Non-Reef
Survivability: Easy
Size: 4" (10 cm) – 8" (20 cm)

 FAM: Tetraodontidae
Canthigaster coronota
Crown Pufferfish

General Aggression

Color Maintenance

Dietary Requirements

Con-Species Compatibility

Collected: Philippines
Aquarium: Non-Reef
Survivability: Easy
Size: Less than 4" (10 cm)

FAM: Tetraodontidae
Canthigaster valentini
Valentini Pufferfish

**General
Aggression**

**Color
Maintenance**

**Dietary
Requirements**

**Con-Species
Compatibility**

Aquarium: Non-Reef
Survivability: Easy
Size: Less than 4" (10 cm)

Family: Zanclidae

(Moorish Idol) The *Zanclus cornutus* (Moorish Idol) is the only fish in the family Zanclidae. The diet of the individuals collected from Southeast Asia is coral, and because of this it is difficult to maintain. There are reports that the Costa Rican Moorish Idol can be kept successfully in an aquarium because it has a different diet in its natural habitat (there is no coral reef in Costa Rica). Unfortunately, they are not collected in large quantities from that region of the world.

This beautiful fish is what many people think of when they think of marine aquarium fish. Ironically, this fish has a very poor life expentancy in an aquarium; yet this fish has been shipped in by the ton since *at least* the 1970's. More than any other fish, the Moorish Idol Illustrates why I wrote this book. I wish to point out when a fish is fragile and a "bad bet" for marine aquariums.

(Famille: Zanclidae) *Zanclus cornutus* est le seul poisson dans la famille des Zanclidae. Le régime alimentaire principal des spécimens capturés en Asie du Sud-est est le corail, il est pour cela difficile à garder. Certains rapports indiquent que l'on peut réussir à acclimater en aquarium le *Zanclus cornutus* de Costa Rica, parce qu'il a un régime différent dans son habitat naturel (il n'y a pas de récifs de corail en Costa Rica), malheureusement, on ne le trouve pas en abondance dans cette partie du monde.

Par sa forme, ce ravissant poisson est représentatif de l'idée que se fait le public des espèces d'aquarium marin. Dire que sa durée de vie en aquarium est très limitée est un euphémisme, tant les cas de survie sont rares .On en expédie cependant toujours en grande quantité et ce, depuis les années 70 ! Bien plus que tout autre poisson, le *Z. cornutus* illustre la raison pour laquelle j'ai écrit ce livre, le souci de mettre en évidence les espèces dont l'acclimatation est bien trop délicate pour être conseillée dans un aquarium marin.

(Ídolo Moruno) El *Zanclus cornutus* (Ídolo Moruno) es el único pez de la familia Zanclidae. La dieta de los ejemplares capturados en el Sudeste Asiático consiste de coral y resulta difícil mantener en cautiverio. Existen informaciones que el Ídolo Moruno de Costa Rica puede mantenerse con éxito en un acuario ya que mantiene una dieta diferente en su ambiente natural, (no hay arrecifes de coral en el pacifico de Costa Rica). Lamentablemente, no son capturados en grandes cantidades de esa región del mundo.

Muchas personas piensan en este bello pez cuando piensan en peces de acuario marino. Irónicamente, este pez tiene una expectativa de vida en una pecera muy pobre. Sin embargo, este pez ha sido embarcado por miles desde los años 1970. Más que ningún otro pez, el *Zanclus cornutus* ilustra la razónes por la cuales escribí este libro. Quiero demostrar cuando un pez es frágil y no adecuado para acuarios marinos.

(Família: Zanclidae) O *Zanclus cornutus* ("Moorish Idol") é o único peixe da família Zanclidae. A dieta dos exemplares recolhidos no sudoeste da Ásia é à base de corais, o que torna sua manutenção difícil. Há relatórios que dizem que o "Moorish Idol" da Costa Rica pode ser mantido, com sucesso, em um aquário, pois tem uma dieta diferente em seu hábitat natural (não há recifes de coral na Costa Rica). Infelizmente, eles não são recolhidos em grandes quantidades naquela região do mundo.

Este lindo peixe é o que muitas pessoas imaginam quando pensam em peixe de aquário marinho. Ironicamente, este peixe tem uma expectativa de vida bastante curta em um aquário. Mesmo assim, este peixe tem sido enviado, em toneladas, desde, pelo menos, a década de 70. Mais do que qualquer outro peixe, o Zanclus cornutus é uma demonstração do motivo pelo qual escrevi este livro. Quero com isto ressaltar quando um peixe é frágil e uma "aposta errada" para os aquários marinhos.

(Famiglia: Zanclidae) *Zanclus cornutus* è l'unico pesce nella famiglia. La dieta di questo pesce proveniente dal Sudest asiatico è a base di polipi di corallo. Si tratta quindi di una specie difficile da allevare. E' stato riscontrato che gli esemplari di *Zanclus cornutus* provenienti dal Costa Rica possono essere allevati con successo in acquario perché in natura la loro dieta è diversa (in Costa Rica non esistono barriere coralline). Purtroppo da quell'area non vengono esportati molti esemplari.

Questo bellissimo pesce è quello cui spesso si riferiscono le persone quando pensano ai pesci marini d'acquario, ma proprio questo pesce ha una vita estremamente breve in un acquario. Disgraziatamente fino alla fine dagli anni '70 questi pesci venivano importati a tonnellate. Più di qualsiasi altro pesce, Zanclus cornutus costituisce uno dei motivi principali per cui ho scritto questo libro: desidero puntualizzare quando un pesce è da considerare "difficile" e quindi costituisce una "cattiva scelta" per l'acquario.

INDEX

INDEX

INDEX

INDEX

INDEX

INDEX

INDEX

INDEX

INDEX

LITERATURE

ALLEN, Dr. G. R. (1985) *Buttefly
& Angelfishes of the World.* 3rd English Ed.
MERGUS Publishers Hans A. Baensch/
Aquarium Systems. Melle, Germany.

ALLEN, Dr. G. R. (1991) *Damselfishes*
of the World. MERGUS Publishers
Hans A. Baensch/ Aquarium Systems.
Melle, Germany.

BURGESS, Dr. W.E., Axelrod, Dr. H.R. and
Hunziker III, R.E. (1990) *Dr. Burgess's Atlas
of Marine Aquarium Fishes.* 2nd English Ed.
T.F.H Publications. Neptune, N.J., U.S.A.

DAKIN, N. (1992) *The Book of the Marine
Aquarium.* Salamander Books Ltd./Tetra Press
Blacksburg, Virginia U.S.A.

FOSSÅ, S. A. and **Nilsen, A. J.** (1995)
Korallenriff-Aquarium. 2nd German Ed.
Birgit Schmettkamp Verlag GmbH. Germany.

KUITER, R. H. and **Debelius, H.** (1994)
Southeast Asia Tropical Fish Guide.
Tetra Press (Division of Warner-Lambert).
Blacksburg, Virginia U.S.A.